We Mean to Be Counted

WHITE WOMEN & POLITICS

IN ANTEBELLUM VIRGINIA

Elizabeth R. Varon

THE UNIVERSITY OF NORTH CAROLINA PRESS

CHAPEL HILL AND LONDON

The paper in this book meets the guidelines for
permanence and durability of the Committee on
Production Guidelines for Book Longevity of the
Council on Library Resources.

Library of Congress Cataloging-in-Publication Data
Varon, Elizabeth, 1963–
We mean to be counted: white women and politics
in antebellum Virginia / Elizabeth Varon.
    p.   cm. — (Gender & American culture)
Includes bibliographical references and index.
ISBN 0-8078-2390-2 (cloth: alk. paper). —
ISBN 0-8078-4696-1 (pbk.: alk. paper)
1. Women in politics — Virginia — History —
19th century.   2. Women social reformers — Virginia —
History — 19th century.   3. White women — Virginia —
Societies and clubs — History — 19th century.
4. Elite (Social sciences) — Virginia — History —
19th century.   5. Virginia — Politics and government —
1775–1865.   6. Whig Party (Va.) — History.   I. Title.   II. Series.
HQ1236.5.U6V37   1998
306.2'082 — dc21   97-21587
                    CIP

02 01 00 99 98   5 4 3 2 1

An earlier version of Chapter 3 appeared as "Tippecanoe
and the Ladies, Too: White Women and Party Politics in
Antebellum Virginia," *Journal of American History* 82
(September 1995): 494–521.

We Mean to Be Counted

GENDER & AMERICAN CULTURE

This book is dedicated to my mother, Barbara

Contents

Acknowledgments

Since this project began, I have relied on the generous assistance of teachers, colleagues, friends, and family. My greatest debt of gratitude is to my thesis adviser, Nancy F. Cott. She has been in every way the ideal mentor. Her own writing and teaching have represented a benchmark (albeit an impossibly high one) for me. Her comments on my work have been breathtakingly insightful, often sending me back to the drawing board but always with renewed enthusiasm. Melvin Patrick Ely, who trained me in the field of Southern history and pushed me to confront its complexities, has also been an indispensable guide and cherished friend. He has given this manuscript its most thorough line editing and has clarified its logic and language in innumerable ways. David Brion Davis, with whom I studied intellectual and cultural history, has represented professional achievement and personal grace; his comments on my dissertation were an invaluable blueprint for my revisions.

In Richmond, Virginia, the site of most of my research, I relied on the skilled staffs of the Library of Virginia and the Virginia Historical Society. Three women in particular facilitated my work. Sandra Gioia Treadway of the Library of Virginia shared with me her extensive knowledge of women's history and gently pushed me in the direction of useful sources and promising themes. Frances Pollard of the Virginia Historical Society also gave me the benefit of her wisdom and time. Elizabeth M. Gushee of the VHS kindly helped me double-check my citations and extended me her hospitality on my many trips to Richmond. The staffs of the Ann Pamela Cunningham Library at Mount Vernon; Library of Congress; Alderman Library at the University of Virginia; Southern Historical Collection at the University of North Carolina, Chapel Hill; Swem Library at the College of William and Mary; and Sterling Library at Yale were unfailingly expert and kind.

I would also like to thank the following persons for taking the time to assist my research and comment on chapter drafts, conference papers, and article manuscripts: Edward D. C. Campbell, Jane Turner Censer, Janet Coryell, Jane Sherron De Hart, Drew Gilpin Faust, Ronald Formisano, Michael Holt, Jacqueline Jones, Suzanne Lebsock, Anne Firor Scott, William Shade, Mitchell Snay, Brent Tarter, Marie Tyler-McGraw, and Harry Watson. There is no way of overemphasizing what their encouragement has meant to me. Nor can I overstate my gratitude to those who have helped to fund my research—Robert Leylan, the American Historical Association, and the Virginia Historical Society.

An abbreviated version of my third chapter was published in the *Journal of American History*; I am grateful to the staff of the *JAH* for their editorial input and their permission to reprint this work here. The staff of the University of North Carolina Press has in every way lived up to its sterling reputation. I am especially indebted to Lewis Bateman for his invaluable suggestions on how to turn a dissertation into a book.

The Wellesley College community deserves my thanks. My colleagues have shown me how to balance the demands of teaching and research; my students have energized me with their passion for learning; the administration has generously extended to me the research support and leave time I needed to see the process through.

My parents, Barbara and Bension, and my brother, Jeremy, have inspired me with their commitment to a life of the mind. My husband, Will Hitchcock, a fellow historian, has been my mainstay, my partner in work and in escaping from work. Thanks to him, I look back on the years I spent writing this book not as a time of struggle but as a time of joy. Our son, Benjamin, who was born a few weeks after I finished my revisions, has opened for us a glorious new chapter. We already look forward to watching him fall under the spell of books.

We Mean to Be Counted

Introduction

Few fields in American history can claim to be as vital and contentious as the study of white women in the Old South. Recent years have seen the publication of a wealth of pathbreaking books on the experiences of plantation mistresses, urban women, the female yeomanry, and the rural poor. The authors of these works have engaged in lively debates over white women's attitudes toward slavery; the distinctiveness of Southern gender conventions from those in the North; the nature and significance of Southern women's voluntary associations; the extent to which elite plantation mistresses set the cultural standards to which nonelites aspired; and the impact of the Civil War on antebellum gender norms.[1]

Through all of these debates, a consensus has prevailed that white Southern women were excluded from participation in the male arena of politics. The circumstances most often invoked in support of this thesis are a kind of negative evidence — the absence in the South of abolitionist and woman's rights movements. Unlike Northern abolitionists/feminists, Southern women did not — so the argument goes — embrace reform causes; indeed, they did not, by and large, express political opinions in public. This negative case is buttressed by positive evidence in the form of pronouncements by antebellum Southerners who seem to have championed a particularly rigid interpretation of the influential notion of separate spheres. (That doctrine declared the private, domestic sphere to be women's realm and the public sphere of business and politics to be the arena of men.) The most frequently quoted spokesman for the South is proslavery ideologue George Fitzhugh. Taking aim at the North and at the woman's rights movement, Fitzhugh wrote in his *Sociology for the South* (1854) that a true woman "naturally shrinks from the public gaze, and from the struggle and competition of life"; she gladly accepts her subordination to man in return for his protection. Southern women's exclusion from politics, modern-day scholars contend, was a hallmark of the region's conservative social system.[2]

This book challenges the received wisdom. A case study of Virginia, it argues that elite and middle-class women played an active, distinct, and evolving role in the political life of the Old South. To be sure, they did not lay claim to the male prerogatives of voting, office-holding, and public speaking. But they did use legislative petitions, voluntary associations, political campaigns, and published reports, appeals, essays, and novels to register their political views. Over the course of the antebellum period, the doctrine of separate spheres came to coexist with a countervailing conception of female civic duty. Virginians of both sexes argued that women were vital partners to men in the forging of political consensus; that they were naturally more "disinterested" and patriotic than men and therefore better able to perceive the commonweal; and that they had political duties not only in the private but also in the public sphere.

Rather than define politics narrowly, as the business of running the government, or broadly, as a signifier for all power contests and relations, I have sought to recover the antebellum meanings of the term. The people I have studied equated politics, first and foremost, with electoral activity—campaigning, voting, office-holding, legislating. By this core definition, politics was the preserve of white men who owned specified amounts of property. (All black men, the free included, were denied the franchise. So, too, were many whites, as Virginia did not repeal its property qualifications for voting until the Constitutional Convention of 1850/51.)[3] Since elected officials were armed with the power to make and enforce laws, the practice of politics was by definition coercive; since men expressed their electoral preferences through political parties, which worked relentlessly to stoke voters' passions, politics was by definition divisive. And because it was carried out in the streets, legislative halls, and partisan press, politics was inherently public.

The public, an often-invoked term with many layers of meaning, was understood as a set of physical spaces—literally the world outside the home—such as courthouses, churches, and businesses. It was also a figurative space—the world of letters—constituted by newspapers, novels, journals, and other publications. And finally, the public was a social entity, a grouping of citizens who, literally and figuratively, embodied "public opinion." While the public sphere was the stage for a wide array of activities, the most important, antebellum Americans would have agreed, were those marked as political.[4]

Southern women, like their Northern counterparts, first elaborated for themselves a political role through their benevolent activities. In the theory of the time, a sharp line of demarcation separated the terrain of politics from that of benevolence: the latter was carried out in the spirit of voluntarism and harmony, and thus was admirably suited to the nature of women. In practice, in the South no less than in the North, the rhetorical distinction between politics and benevolence proved very difficult to maintain. Virginia women's benevolent activity, as Chapters

1 and 2 demonstrate, covered a broad spectrum, from work on behalf of local charities to participation in national moral-reform societies. Local charities maintained a status above politics throughout the antebellum period, and fostered an image of elite women as moral paragons and as efficient managers and fund-raisers. In the 1820s, male advocates of national reform causes such as temperance eagerly enlisted female support, hoping that women could legitimize their organizations' claims to moral rectitude and benevolence. By the mid-1830s, however, reformist men and women in Virginia were embroiled in debates with critics who argued that Southern reformers, like Northern abolitionists, were using political means to coerce and divide the public.

Most controversial of all benevolent causes was the American Colonization Society. In its heyday, it served as an outlet for hundreds of Virginia women who considered themselves opponents of slavery and thought that the colonization of blacks in Liberia would pave the way for the gradual demise of the "peculiar institution." Self-styled defenders of the "middle ground" in the national debate over slavery, antislavery colonizationists were unable to withstand attacks from abolitionists, who saw them as cowardly hypocrites, and from proslavery Southerners, who considered them dangerous radicals. Female colonizationists, nonetheless, had a profound effect on the political culture of Virginia: they publicly advanced the notion that slavery was both a domestic and a political problem, and they aroused anxieties in the Old Dominion about the loyalty of white Southern women to the slave system.

While their causes entered a phase of decline in the mid-1830s, many reform-minded men and women found a new vehicle for their views in the Whig Party. During the presidential campaign of 1840, Chapter 3 shows, the Whigs initiated a revolution in campaign tactics by encouraging women to attend Whig rallies and other party events. Whig womanhood, as I have dubbed the party's innovative gender ideology, held that women could serve both as partisans and mediators in the public sphere — partisans who expressed their allegiance to the Whig Party, and mediators whose "disinterestedness" enabled them to promote civic virtue, temper political passions, and focus public affairs on the common good. Virginia Democrats, at first unwilling to encourage female partisanship, eventually assimilated the idea of Whig womanhood; so did the new American and Republican Parties. By the 1850s, Virginians across the political spectrum agreed that women could play a role in electoral politics complementary to that of men.

Chapter 4 argues that women's political roles were further transformed during the "age of sectionalism." In the 1850s, as the issue of slavery came increasingly to dominate electoral politics, some women tried to adapt their paradoxical mandate—to be partisans *and* mediators—to the volatile political climate. Galvanized by the publication of *Uncle Tom's Cabin* in 1852, a new breed of Virginia writers rallied to the defense of the South and slavery; they aspired, so they claimed, to restore sectional harmony by describing Southern life "the way it really was." The image of women as sectional mediators was also advanced by the Mount Vernon Association (MVA), a Virginia-based group that launched a national campaign at mid-decade to save George Washington's estate from speculators. However, women writers and civic leaders like those of the MVA found that the twin goals of promoting Southern values and fostering sectional harmony grew increasingly incompatible during the 1850s; by the eve of John Brown's raid, the image of women as sectional mediators was attracting growing criticism from advocates of Southern rights.

The secession crisis is the subject of Chapter 5. In the years 1859 to 1861, a new ideal of female civic duty gradually emerged as a reflection of the rise of Southern nationalism. That new ideal, which by 1861 can be called "Confederate womanhood," grew directly out of the antebellum discourse on women's political roles. Male and female advocates of secession appropriated the notion that women were public partisans even as they rejected the antebellum vision of women as mediators. On the eve of Virginia's secession, Confederate propaganda celebrated those women who declared themselves Southern partisans—women who thronged the legislative halls during the secession convention, hung Confederate flags from their residences, wrote pro-secession appeals to the newspapers. Women, Confederate propagandists of both sexes asserted, were purer patriots than men. Not only was it their duty but also their desire to assume the role of "Spartan mothers," accepting the loss of their men in defense of states' rights.

In short, the rise of sectionalism in the 1850s and the determination to prevail in the contest with the North produced conflicting impulses in Virginia. On the one hand, Virginians such as George Fitzhugh upheld a vision of their society as a stable hierarchy: Southern women, unlike their Northern counterparts, were supposedly content to leave politics to men. Other Virginians, however, recognized that women's ascribed moral virtue and domestic influence made them politically potent; these Virginians energetically enlisted women in the defense of the South. The latter view of women's role prevailed in the end. Defining politics exclusively as the realm of men proved impractical in the high-stakes conflicts of the antebellum period; women were indispensable as allies.

I have used the term "women" in this overview of my argument, but it might have been more descriptive of reality to use the word "ladies," for that is how antebellum sources most often designated those women who wielded political influence. In Southern society, the term "lady" was a marker both of race and class status, of whiteness and wealth. Historian Anne Firor Scott has offered the most nuanced elucidation to date of the gap between the mythology and the reality of the Southern lady. The archetypal lady was a "paragon of virtue" — pampered, submissive, pious, genteel, compassionate. In reality, Scott explains, ladies were hard workers and often resentful of their men for the power they exercised; white men, for their part, were anxious at the prospect that "the women to whom they had granted the custody of conscience and morality might apply that conscience to male behavior."[5] This book seconds Scott's notion that profound tensions lay beneath the placid surface of the cult of the lady. The term itself, I argue, became politically contested: male adherents to a variety of causes routinely claimed that "the ladies" were all on their side and that female supporters of the other side were not "ladies."

The flesh-and-blood "ladies" who figure prominently in this study share certain important characteristics, the most salient of which is that they or their families owned slaves. They represent the ranks of both the planter class and the middle class in each of the four sections — the Tidewater, Piedmont, Mountain-and-Valley, and trans-Allegheny regions — of the Commonwealth. Following the standard practice, I have used the term "plantation mistress" to refer to women, such as Whig Party activist Lucy Barbour or proslavery essayist Julia Gardiner Tyler, who belonged to families owning twenty or more slaves. Middle-class masters, according to historian James Oakes's typology, were city- or town-dwelling businessmen and professionals who owned fewer than twenty bondsmen; my sources include scores of women, such as colonizationist Mary Blackford of Fredericksburg and journalist Rebecca Hicks of Petersburg, whose menfolk fit that category.[6]

The second salient characteristic of the "ladies" is that they were the wives, daughters, mothers, and sisters of voters. According to Whig womanhood and its variants, women's political role was fundamentally to influence the behavior of enfranchised men. Women who assumed the mantle of civic leadership were often, although not always, connected to men who were themselves politically prominent. To give two examples: Judith Rives of Albemarle County, a manager of the Mount

Vernon Association, was the wife of U.S. senator William Cabell Rives; proslavery writer Martha Fenton Hunter of Essex County was the sister of Senator Robert Mercer Taliaferro Hunter.[7]

The third salient characteristic of my subjects is their literacy. Whether, like Judith Rives, they were educated at home or, like Rebecca Hicks, attended female seminaries, the women in this book left private and public records of their thoughts and activities. The political culture of antebellum Virginia was in some respects an oral one: speeches and debates were the centerpieces of political campaigns, and women influenced "their" men through conversation in the home and elsewhere. Nevertheless, I posit that literacy was a prerequisite for an active role in politics. Barred by social convention from practicing the art of oratory and by law from registering their opinions at the ballot box, women often relied on the written word and the public press to make their views known. Newspapers, secular and religious, did more than any other institutions to carve out a political niche for women. They reported on the proceedings of voluntary associations, described women's deportment at campaign events, and published their letters and appeals on the subjects of temperance, slavery, party politics, and secession. Literary journals such as the *Southern Literary Messenger*; reform publications such as the American Colonization Society's *African Repository*; and the publishing houses that brought out domestic fiction all counted women among their avid readers and contributors.[8]

While it is possible to describe the social milieu of those women who have left written records, one is left to speculate about the many women—the thousands who signed petitions, joined voluntary associations, and attended political rallies—who appear only fleetingly in the sources. The extent to which they included in their ranks farm women, the numerical majority of women in Virginia, is unclear. While the yeoman class was diverse, composed of both small slaveholders and nonslaveholders, farm women shared with each other the experience of providing agricultural labor that was essential to the subsistence of their families. Of the many political causes described below, only the agricultural reform movement of the mid-1850s and the 1859 homespun movement, which aimed to boycott Northern goods, incorporated the female yeomanry into their public rhetoric. I sense that while some yeomen's wives number among the signatories of petitions and auditors at political rallies, those struggling to eke out a subsistence remained on the periphery of the political arena.[9]

African-American women in antebellum Virginia, slave and free, were unequivocally barred from the political arena, as whites defined it.

Just as the Commonwealth's racist legal system denied to black men the rights of voters, so too did its racist culture deny to black women the status of "ladies." Blacks were not accepted in white reform societies or political parties, and the law code of the Commonwealth severely restricted the formation of black benevolent organizations. In 1831, the General Assembly passed a statute prohibiting blacks from meeting for the purpose of learning to read or write; the following year, the legislature forbade blacks to hold their own religious meetings (only white ministers could preach to them) and levied harsh penalties on slaves or free blacks who participated in "unlawful assembl[ies]." [10]

Despite this repressive climate, Afro-Virginian men and women formed a variety of mutual aid societies. Some of these operated openly, with white endorsement: for example, deacons of the First African Baptist Church of Richmond, under the authority of white minister Robert Ryland, formed a "Poor Saints Committee" to dispense charity to indigent blacks. More numerous and, for historians, more elusive were extralegal secret societies, such as the Grand United Order of Tents, established by two Norfolk slaves, Annetta Lane and Harriet Taylor, to aid fugitive bondspeople. Because of the restrictions on black literacy and the fact that unauthorized societies were compelled to operate clandestinely, very little documentary evidence on antebellum black benevolence in Virginia exists. [11]

Studies of black women in the Old South have, of necessity, employed a different conceptual framework than the one that governs this book. Rather than focus on expressly political organizing and writing, they have explored women's implicitly political efforts to sustain, as historian Elsa Barkley Brown has put it, "alternative visions of the world" in the face of white oppression. Pioneering works by Deborah White and Jacqueline Jones, among others, demonstrate that women's commitments to their families and to a communal ethos represented potent forms of resistance to slavery. After emancipation, when mutual aid societies could operate openly and freedmen entered the electoral arena, black women in Virginia established an extensive network of benevolent organizations and assumed a role in partisan politics; I return to the subject of black women's postwar activism in my epilogue. [12]

The question of Virginia's "representativeness" is addressed periodically in this book, but it may be helpful here to offer a word on the subject. Virginia, it should be noted, was in many ways a peculiar state. The birthplace of American representative government, it possessed an unabashedly patrician political culture. The largest slaveholding state in the nation, Virginia also had, arguably, the strongest antislavery tradition of the states that would make up the Confederacy. The seedbed of the plantation system and home to many of its most famous defenders, Virginia also boasted more cities than any other state in the South and was the industrial hub of the region. Site of the Confederate capital, Virginia also was the only Southern state to split literally in two over secession.[13]

All of these peculiarities, rather than rendering Virginia anomalous, make it an excellent window into both national and sectional transformations in white women's roles. On the one hand, the kind of female political participation I observe in Virginia can be found in abundance elsewhere in the country. The moral-reform societies (Bible, tract, Sunday school, temperance, and colonization) that are the focus of Chapters 1 and 2 were part of a national evangelical crusade with female devotees in every state; the colonization movement, which has yet to receive its due from women's historians, boasted such influential Northern supporters as Catharine Beecher and Harriet Beecher Stowe. The emergence of Whig womanhood was likewise a national phenomenon. Virginia Whigs joined together with Whigs from around the country, including such figures as Daniel Webster of Massachusetts and Henry Clay of Kentucky, to articulate their new ideal of women's civic duty. The Mount Vernon Association, committed to promoting nationalism, counted among its strongest advocates Northerner Sarah Hale, editor of *Godey's Lady's Book*, the country's most popular journal.

On the other hand, the principal story I tell is one in which Virginia women gradually withdraw their support from national political causes and embrace sectional ones. Such a transformation, I contend, took place in every Southern state. The closest parallels to the Virginia case are most likely to be found in the upper South. Women in states such as Maryland, Kentucky, Tennessee, and North Carolina, where the causes of moral reform, of the Whig Party, and of Unionism proved more resilient than in the lower South, had much in common with their Virginia counterparts. Women in the lower South, where the political balance of power favored Southern nationalists much sooner than it did in the upper South, may have begun to contribute to the literary defense of slavery and to the construction of Confederate womanhood before women in the upper South did.[14]

Finally, while this is a book about the antebellum period, it can be seen as part of a broader project in women's history: that of confronting and chronicling the political divisions among women. When the field of women's history was first being established, its practitioners naturally focused on progressive causes, such as the abolitionist and settlement house movements, that furnished examples of female empowerment and contributed to the development of feminism. More recently, as the field has matured, women's historians have not only mapped out the divisions within the progressive ranks, but also brought to light the activism of those women, such as the turn-of-the-century antisuffragists, who opposed reform.[15]

This book explores the theme of political conflict on two levels. It finds women on the battle lines both of the intrasectional debates that gripped the South and of the intersectional conflict that culminated in the dissolution of the Union. It brings to light instances of women's dissent from regional orthodoxies, but speaks more forcefully still to their complicity in a political system founded on inequality. The women who populate my study, as a group, rejected abolitionism and feminism; they did not seek to topple the racial and gender hierarchies that undergirded Southern society.

We should not equate these women's conservatism with uniformity of opinion or passivity, however. For they sought, each in her own way, to resolve an enduring paradox — to reconcile a commitment to the traditional gender order, in which women deferred to the leadership of men, with a passion for politics and a desire to be heard.

CHAPTER 1 *The Representatives of Virtue*

FEMALE BENEVOLENCE AND MORAL REFORM

Each of the sexes, wrote Mary Early, a student at Virginia's Buckingham Female Collegiate Institute in her 1842 commencement address, "has a separate and distinct sphere." Because woman was superior to man in "matters of the heart," her mission was to "promote peace, love and happiness in the social circle." That circle extended beyond the boundaries of the household. Woman's special calling was "to seek out and to succor the unfortunate and distressed . . . [and] to regulate the corruptions of the age in which she lives." A few years after her graduation, Mary Early married Lynchburg merchant James Leftwich Brown and embarked on a career of benevolent activism. In 1846, she helped found the Orphan Asylum Society of Lynchburg, an institution which furnished shelter and education to indigent girls. Later still, she became secretary of a second benevolent association in her hometown, the Lynchburg Dorcas Society, which ran a Sabbath school and provided food, clothes, and shelter to poor whites during the winter months. Mary (Early) Brown supplemented her charitable activities by attending meetings of the local temperance society.[1]

Early belonged to the second generation of benevolent women in Virginia, and she owed much to the first. By the time she assumed a leading role in Lynchburg's civic life in 1846, white women in Virginia had been active in organized benevolence for more than four decades. Women served as managers and members of a wide array of voluntary associations, including female charities, evangelical societies, and temperance organizations. Such associations and their allies worked hard to uphold the rhetorical distinction between benevolence and politics. This distinction hinged on the argument that women, paragons of virtue, were as well suited to benevolence as they were ill suited to politics; women's support for a given cause constituted proof that it was benevolent and therefore beyond the pale of controversy and reproach. Even as they sought to cloak women in the mantle of benevolence, however, voluntary associations initiated a profound transformation in women's public images and roles. Through their alliances with politicians, editors, ministers, and other influential men, benevolent women established a reputation as opinion-makers and even as architects of public policy. As the tide of sectionalism rose and the very concept of reform became politicized in the South, white women were implicated in highly charged debates over the propriety of educating blacks, the nature of the abolitionist threat, and the viability of legislating moral reform. In short, their claims to the contrary notwithstanding, poor relief, evangelistic, and anti-liquor societies drew women — inextricably — into the web of politics.[2]

Virginia's first female charities were founded early in the nineteenth century. Women in the city of Fredericksburg established a boarding school for poor white girls in 1803. Within the decade, Norfolk, Richmond, Petersburg, and Alexandria boasted similar institutions. Each was governed by an elaborate constitution which provided for regular meetings and the election of officers. Female "visitors" were chosen from among each institution's members to seek out "proper" objects for charity and decide who among the applicants for admission should be selected; once old enough, orphan girls were generally hired out to suitable employers.[3]

The officers and members of female charities were generally married women from socially and politically prominent families. The original subscribers to the Fredericksburg enterprise included Lucy Minor, daughter of planter/aristocrat Landon Carter and wife of state legislator John Minor; Petersburg's orphan asylum boasted the leadership of Jane Taylor, sister of Chief Justice John Marshall. Richmond's Female Humane Association included among its founders Jean Moncure Wood, the wife of former state governor General James Wood.[4]

The pioneers of charity wasted no time in reaching out to the Virginia General Assembly for assistance in their endeavors. The earliest appeal to the legislature is an 1803 petition by the subscribers to the Fredericksburg charity school. It began by informing the legislature that many young and indigent females in the town "were exposed to ignorance, Vice and Infamy." The petitioners had established a boarding school in the hopes of teaching these girls to "pursue the Paths of Virtue." Finding themselves short of funds, they asked the legislature to authorize them to hold a lottery.[5]

The 1803 petition gives a new twist to the Revolutionary-era doctrine of republican motherhood — the idea that for free government to survive, the mothers of the Republic must train up their sons in civic virtue. Having observed the "Sedulous and Commendable Care" the legislature devoted to the education of young men, and having heard its members intone that knowledge was the "life of Free Government," the petitioners felt compelled to remind the assembly of its responsibilities to the poor females of the Commonwealth. Even the poor might someday be "the Mothers of free men, from whom the Infant mind receives its first and most lasting impressions." The memorial is as interesting for what it does not say as for what it does. The appeal is short on the deference which characterized many antebellum memorials. Rather than adopting an apologetic tone, the women presented their case to the legislature as social equals, who were familiar with the lofty republican rhetoric of male politicians and who expected men to extend the benefits of that ideology to females. The legislature was moved enough by the argument to grant the charity school permission to hold its lottery.[6]

A similarly matter-of-fact tone characterizes petitions in which women requested corporate charters for their institutions. In an 1810 memorial to the General Assembly, the managers of the Female Humane Association noted that their efforts to help destitute girls had been quite successful. But the managers also confessed to having "experienced great inconvenience, from want of a legal sanction to their proceedings." "Their incapacity to hold property," they concluded, could "only be remedied by their incorporation." Upon marriage, the petitioners were reminding the legislature, a woman suffered "civil death" — legally subordinate to her husband, she could not own property or transact business on her own account. A corporate charter granted a collective of married women such as those who ran the Humane Association the legal status of a single — male — person, fully empowered to control property. Despite the fact that incorporation effected a dramatic change in women's legal status, the Virginia General Assembly readily granted charters to the Female Humane Association and to similar concerns in Fredericksburg, Petersburg, and Norfolk.[7]

While the legislature could give female charities legal sanction, only the general public could fund their operations. Female asylums relied primarily on private sources for their support — dues from members and contributions from churches and prominent citizens. Specially elected female "solicitors" sallied forth on behalf of each institution to raise funds. Associations also raised money at fairs, at which they sold goods made by the orphans. Such efforts received extensive coverage in newspapers and journals. A correspondent to the Fredericksburg *Political Arena* concluded his 1831 report on the local charity fair with this observation: "We know of not one [voluntary association] which addresses itself to the Fredericksburg public, in language more palpably rational and eloquently persuasive than the Female Charity School." No one did more to publicize female charities than Presbyterian clergyman John Holt Rice of Prince Edward County and Richmond, editor of the *Virginia Evangelical and Literary Magazine*. His publication took frequent note of female charities and exhorted women to be "zealous and active in their support." Among the enterprises singled out for praise by the magazine was Richmond's Female Humane Association. Its work "must commend itself to the heart of every one who has the ordinary human feelings," he averred. Its managers he described as "generous hearted missionaries." [8]

By the mid-1830s, Virginians were lending their hands to the creation of a popular new literary genre — prescriptive literature aimed at women. Though it spoke in the abstract about the duties of "woman" rather than praising the works of actual women, this literature was, no less than the notices quoted above, a form of homage to Virginia's benevolent women. It sketched out a distinct ideology of female civic duty, dubbed "benevolent femininity" by one modern-day historian. Virginia authors made the following case: that women were more pious and moral than men; that women should lead lives of "usefulness" and not "idleness"; and that women's domestic and religious duties included charitable activities, provided these were performed in an "unostentatious manner" and directed at the "virtuous" poor. The expositors of benevolent femininity also implied that solutions to poverty and irreligion could best be effected by "benevolent" rather than "political" means. Instead of explicitly defining the benevolent and political, writers in Virginia, like those in the North, associated each sphere of activity with certain qualities. Benevolence was "disinterested" in nature, while politics involved ambition and self-aggrandizement. Benevolent reformers relied on "influence" and "suasion," while politicians, vested with the power to make laws, could practice "coercion." Benevolence involved the exercise of compassion, while politics unleashed passion and even fanaticism; benevolence created social harmony, while politics could produce controversy, conflict, and strife. Benevolence was suited to the nature and sphere of women; politics was not. [9]

Among Virginia's leading authors of prescriptive literature was James M. Garnett, a legislator and educator from one of the Tidewater's most prominent families. Garnett's collected *Lectures on Female Education* (1824) was highly acclaimed. Delivered before the pupils at a primary school taught by his wife, Mary, Garnett's lectures asserted that the "lives of Virginia Ladies are essentially domestick." The world outside the domestic sphere was one of "empty pageantries," of "fantastic and frivolous men," of "impudence and licentiousness." But even as Garnett

cautioned women to shun that world, he also urged them to reform it —
to "continually practice that heavenly grace of truly christian beneficence, which is summed up in the comprehensive term — charity." [10]

Thomas R. Dew, a professor at the College of William and Mary
most famous for his 1832 defense of slavery, offered up his own version
of benevolent femininity in his "Dissertation on the Characteristic Differences between the Sexes" (1835). According to Dew, women and men
occupied two separate, distinct spheres. The world of politics was one of
ambition, conflict, and danger and therefore "unfitted" for women. But
Dew also argued that because of their superior piety, women were more
apt than men to practice "disinterested benevolence." "Woman is most
deeply interested in the success of every scheme which curbs the passions and enforces a true morality," Dew claimed, stressing that women
should teach by a mild, meek, quiet demeanor.[11]

Perhaps the most influential articulation of the ideology of benevolent femininity by a Virginian was Virginia Cary's *Letters on
Female Character* (1828). Born in 1786 into an elite planter family from
Goochland County, Cary married a lawyer from neighboring Fluvanna
County, Wilson Jefferson Cary, in 1805. After her husband's death, Cary
took up writing. Her *Letters on Female Character* was widely praised and
is considered by scholars one of the defining texts of domestic ideology. Organized as a series of advice-giving lectures to her niece, Cary's
book was designed to "train women for usefulness." She advocated that
women remain content with their subordination to male authority, but
she also made the case that because of their very physical inferiority and
vulnerability, women were superior to men in religiosity.[12]

The world of politics Cary associated with "fierce turmoil" and
"withering excitement"; she condemned women who forsook the domestic sphere for the "intrigues of state." Benevolent work, by contrast,
was specially suited to woman's nature and her sphere. Cary argued that
woman's religious temperament, her "natural tenderness," fitted her "to
practice without difficulty, the duties of charity." She saw acts of charity
as essential to spiritual salvation. "Remember that good works are the
only test of a true faith," she told her readers, "and let your works,
therefore be manifest." Cary was quite specific in defining the spirit of
charity — charity was by nature humble, unostentatious, unambitious.
She cautioned her readers that some charitable associations were undermined by rivalries and jealousies, and warned them to seek virtue, not
notoriety.[13]

The idealized and one-dimensional image of "woman" offered up in
works like Cary's was in some ways a poor reflection of the flesh-and-

blood women who inspired it. The managers of charitable institutions displayed a savvy in their public dealings that was at odds with the image of benevolent women as unostentatious and unobtrusive. Many of them were minor celebrities, familiar to their communities from their rounds of solicitations and from appeals in the newspapers. And when it suited them, they did not hesitate to remind the legislature and the public alike of their accomplishments.

The pride felt by Virginia's first generation of benevolent women is attested to in an 1834 legislative petition by Eliza Carrington, cofounder and secretary of the Female Humane Association of Richmond. Ostensibly, the petition had nothing to do with the subject of female charity. It spoke to a different issue of great concern to Richmonders—the status of free blacks. In 1834, Reverend John Buchanan died, leaving a will that emancipated one of his slaves, William Caswell. The will was a mixed blessing for Caswell, since an 1806 law required all free blacks to leave the Commonwealth of Virginia within one year after they were granted freedom. The General Assembly did, on occasion, make exceptions to this law, and it was just such an exception Eliza Carrington sought, for William Caswell was her carriage driver.[14]

Caswell should be allowed to remain in the Commonwealth, Carrington argued, because his "fidelity" had enabled her "to carry on the direction of a very beneficial and laudable institution denominated *The Female Humane Association of the City of Richmond for the Relief of Female Orphans*, which was many years ago incorporated and patronized by the Honorable Legislature of Virginia." Carrington, herself elderly and in ill health, feared that if Caswell left the state, she would be unable to find another driver in whom she could "confide," and "consequently the wonted intercommunication between the Members of the Society, will cease, to the great inconvenience of the Institution." The General Assembly saw merit in Carrington's argument, and gave Caswell permission to remain in the state.[15]

Eliza Carrington's petition speaks volumes about the attitudes and conduct of the female pioneers of benevolence in Virginia. Carrington and her coworkers depended on the labor of slaves and free blacks to furnish them with the leisure and mobility they needed to carry out their round of meetings, visitations, and solicitations.[16] And yet black girls, slave and free, were excluded from the Richmond asylum and from its counterparts. The managers of female orphan asylums in Virginia have not left explanations for their exclusionary policies. Perhaps, in a society that routinely separated whites and free blacks, it never occurred to white women to admit blacks into their institutions. Perhaps, historian

Suzanne Lebsock has speculated, they accepted the standing assumption that "poverty was almost inevitable and licentiousness natural" for black women, and feared that social contact between white and black girls would corrupt the former. Shut out of white charities, free blacks in antebellum Virginia formed their own network of mutual aid societies, to furnish aid to the free and enslaved alike; after 1832, only those which received white sanction, such as the all-male Poor Saints Committee of the First African Baptist Church of Richmond, were allowed to operate openly. Interestingly, the Poor Saints Committee, founded in 1848, included among its managers William Caswell.[17]

Implicit in Eliza Carrington's 1834 petition on Caswell's behalf is the idea that she and the "honorable legislature" of Virginia had entered into a sort of informal partnership — the association managers provided an invaluable service to the community and the legislature had the duty to facilitate the women's efforts. But just how far did that partnership extend? In the coming decades, Carrington's successors would find that the legislators and citizens who were quick to bestow praise on benevolent women were often slow to heed the women's advice or to fund their enterprises.

In the 1830s and 1840s, a new generation of benevolent women established a new set of charitable associations, designed to supplement and improve on the work of the older societies. The most ambitious new charity was the Union Benevolent Society (UBS), founded in Richmond in 1836. Its stated mission went far beyond that of the older Female Humane Association. While the humane association concerned itself with the care of poor girls, the UBS directed its attention to adults. The managers pledged themselves to "ascertain the habits and circumstances of the poor, the causes of their poverty, to devise means for the improvement of their situation." To that end, the UBS divided the city into twenty districts, with two visitors assigned to each. The society's first annual report explained that the visitors had identified 111 poor families, among them many "worthy females who were suffering *extreme* want, from their inability to procure employment."[18]

Early on, the managers of the society were contacted by "several gentlemen" who convinced them that the UBS would be more successful if men managed it. The women agreed to relinquish management, but after waiting a few months and finding "nothing would be accomplished by the gentlemen," they decided to retain control of the enterprise and to go ahead with plans to open a "Depository of Work" for poor women. At the depository, poor women received raw materials which they could turn into marketable products. The proceeds from the sale of clothes and other products funded the continued operations of the society. The depository initially provided work for 100 women.[19]

The managers enlisted the aid of some of the city's foremost clergymen, who took up donations in their respective congregations and addressed the UBS membership at the society's annual meetings. Those annual meetings received coverage in Richmond's secular newspapers and in the religious press as well. Despite this support and publicity, the UBS found itself proverbially short of funds, so short that it had, in 1838, to restrict the number of women at work in the depository to thirty. The managers of the UBS were highly critical of the community in their public reports. "Oh! Could we persuade the rich and prosperous to accompany us to the abodes of poverty and ignorance, and suffering. . . . Instead of receiving *one dollar*, when we present our annual subscription paper," the second annual report proclaimed, "we should behold their silver and gold *poured out* to be dispensed among their needy and afflicted fellow creatures!" Subsequent annual reports informed Richmonders that their donations were "entirely inadequate to supply the wants of the suffering poor" and called on them to "give with greater liberality than ever before." [20]

When cajoling the community did not work, benevolent women found some very creative ways to solicit funds. Julia Cabell, a manager of the UBS, raised money by writing a book. In 1852 she published *An Odd Volume of Facts and Fictions: In Prose and Verse*, a collection of stories and poems she had written on a wide array of topics, from foreign travel to temperance. The proceeds of the book were dedicated to the UBS. As the UBS's first annual report had, Cabell's book criticized men for their inaction. While "*all* acknowledged the necessity" of building a workhouse in the city, Cabell proclaimed in her preface, no one, including "that *august* body of our esteemed townsmen, the City Council," had taken any steps to erect it. So women stepped in to fill the breach. In order to inspire her fellow citizens, Cabell began her book with short biographies of three female pioneers of benevolence, including her own mother, Abigail Mayo, who served as a manager of the Female Humane Association.[21]

The UBS managers' frustration at the lack of support from the community—and from male leaders—was shared by benevolent women in other towns. In 1845, the managers of the Norfolk Female Orphan Asylum chastised the minister of the local Methodist Church for failing, for an entire year, to take up a collection on behalf of the orphans. That same year, the managers of the Lynchburg Dorcas Society went so far as to write a letter to the "gentlemen of Lynchburg and vicinity" imploring them to donate money for the founding of an orphan asylum. "Did we believe it necessary," the letter threatened, the Dorcases "would walk through the length and breadth of this town, and in *person*, receive at your hands what we must believe you intend to give." [22]

Benevolent women sought the financial support not only of their communities but also of municipal and state officials. While charities for adults, such as the Union Benevolent Society, relied exclusively on private donations, those charities that doubled as schools solicited financial assistance from the public coffers. The major female orphan asylums in the Commonwealth received small sums from the city councils in their respective locales. Gaining direct access to state funds was a far more complicated process. State aid for education came out of the Literary Fund, which had been established in 1810 for "the encouragement of learning." Assorted "escheats, confiscatures, and forfeitures" collected by the state (including the revenue from the sale of manumitted blacks who did not comply with the aforementioned 1806 law) went into the fund for distribution by the General Assembly directly to institutions it deemed deserving. In 1818, the General Assembly passed a law requiring each county court to appoint school commissioners, who would parcel out the share of the fund which had been allotted to their respective counties. These funds were meant to support the education of poor children. Some commissioners used the money to set up new schools; some used it to send poor children to privately run "pay schools"; some allocated the funds to "indigent schools." [23]

The system created by the legislature for the support of pauper education depended on the highly subjective assessments of the county school commissioners. Rather than rest content with that system, the managers of the Fredericksburg Female Orphan Asylum, in a remarkable series of petitions spanning the years 1833 to 1842, tried to reform it. The Female Orphan Asylum was founded in 1833, by a group of sixteen women who evidently believed that the Female Charity School, founded some thirty years earlier, could not itself meet the demands for shelter and education of a growing population of indigent white females. In December of 1833, the orphan asylum's managers sent a letter to Carter L. Stevenson, their county's delegate to the General Assembly. The letter included a constitution of their organization and a petition to the General Assembly, which they wished Stevenson to present on their behalf in Richmond. The managers sought from the legislature both a corporate charter and an appropriation of $600 directly out of the Literary Fund. They felt "confidence" in asking for money, they explained to Stevenson, since Virginia's "Sister States," New York and Pennsylvania, had each made appropriations to similar institutions.[24]

The 1833 petition spelled out the idea, implicit in earlier petitions, that a partnership existed between women and the legislature. The orphan asylum managers urged the legislature to "view them as Co-workers with you in Your humane, patriotic and benevolent efforts to extend the blessings of a good and virtuous education to all the destitute children." The General Assembly's response, however, revealed the limits of the partnership. As it had when the Female Charity School appealed to it some three decades earlier, the legislature bestowed a charter —but no "pecuniary aid"—on the petitioners. Unlike their forebears, the managers of the Female Orphan Asylum persisted in their campaign for state support. After three more unsuccessful petitions, the managers decided that in order to succeed, they needed the advice of powerful male allies. So in November of 1837, Catherine Lomax, manager of the orphan asylum, wrote to her friend Martha Hunter, sister of former state senator Robert Mercer Taliaferro Hunter, in order to enlist Robert's help. Lomax was a devout Presbyterian and sister of one of Fredericksburg's most distinguished citizens, Judge John Tayloe Lomax.[25]

Lomax offered Martha Hunter a detailed explanation of the orphan asylum's predicament. The managers were forced to petition for state aid, she explained, because the portion of the Literary Fund allotted to Spotsylvania County was insufficient to support the school, which took in orphan girls not only from Spotsylvania but from adjacent counties as well. Lomax wanted R. M. T. Hunter to draw up a petition on her behalf, since, as a former legislator, he would know "how to, and in what form, to approach that *Honorable Body*." The legislature had found it easy to disregard the women, Lomax wrote to her friend, but she hoped her persistence would pay off: "We have found it a difficult case to get access to them with acceptance—but I think they will find me like the *importunate widow* and in self defence they will have to grant my request [of money for the asylum] to get rid of me." Lomax's letter provides rare insights into the private thoughts behind the public actions of a benevolent woman. Sarcastic and self-conscious, Lomax implicitly acknowledged that she and her coworkers had ventured deep into the territory of politics—while women like herself had little problem getting "access" to the legislature, Lomax suspected that only a politician, who knew the system intimately, could win "acceptance" for the women.[26]

No record of Hunter's reply exists, but in 1838 the managers did try appealing to the legislature through male proxies. One hundred and five men from Spotsylvania petitioned the General Assembly for pecuniary aid on behalf of the women. The male petition, similar in tone and argument to the female ones, was likewise rejected. The legislature was evidently loath to set a precedent of making a special disbursement out of the Literary Fund to a female pauper school—it likely feared that other schools would demand similar favors.[27]

Finally, in 1840, the managers' persistence paid some dividends. Rather than asking for an allotment from the Literary Fund, their petition of January 8, 1840, asked for a modification in the law. Under the existing laws, the managers explained, the school commissioners of each county could allocate funds only to schools within their county limits. Local officials outside of Spotsylvania would gladly send their poor girls to Fredericksburg, if they could also allocate some of their county funds to the Fredericksburg Orphan Asylum. The managers suggested that the law be amended to allow for such reallocations of each county's funds. The General Assembly saw the logic in such a measure, and it passed "A bill for the support and education of poor girls within this commonwealth." Henceforth, school commissioners from around the state were authorized to use their allotment of the Literary Fund to send indigent children from their counties to the female asylum in Fredericksburg (or to female asylums in other towns).[28]

The Fredericksburg bill represents a major accomplishment—it set up a system that made urban institutions accessible to rural children. The orphan asylum managers had much reason to be proud of the new law and some cause to be sanguine about the future prospects for female education in Virginia. The passage of the bill was one of many signs that Virginians were doing more than ever before to promote the cause of female education. The same year the orphan asylum's bill was enacted, the General Assembly took under consideration a massive report from the Commonwealth's school commissioners on the "Progress and State of the Primary Schools under their Direction." While some commissioners stated plainly that they considered the education of boys to take precedence over that of girls, the vast majority of commissioners reported that, when funds were sufficient, "no distinction is made between the sexes, both being equally entitled to the charity of the commonwealth."[29]

In 1847, benevolent women made one more attempt, the last in the antebellum period, to bypass the school commissioners altogether and lay claim to money from the Literary Fund. That year, the managers of the Orphan Asylum and Female Free School of Alexandria petitioned the General Assembly for a corporate charter and "pecuniary aid." Their memorial came closer than any of its predecessors to broaching the subject of politics. First the managers reminded the legislature that the county of Alexandria had for many years been a part of the District of Columbia, and had just recently been retroceded to Virginia. They then made the case that their community had labored under "political disabilities" when it was part of the District—while the U.S. government and city officials had supported its sister charities in the city proper, Alexandria's benevolent societies had been slighted by "an Administration adverse to its true interests." Now that Alexandria was in Virginia again, the managers hoped to fare better. They could make a strong case that they were deserving of support—in the fifteen-year history of the organization, forty orphans had found a home in the asylum and 308 children had been educated in the free school. The petition won the school a corporate charter, but no disbursement.[30]

The Union Benevolent Society's annual reports, Julia Cabell's book, Catherine Lomax's letter, and the Alexandria petition all testify that the second generation of benevolent women was willing to go further than the first—further in criticizing their communities, and especially the men in them, for inaction; in approaching prominent men for assistance; in soliciting state aid; and in asking Virginia to live up to the standard of benevolence set by Northern states. And yet the second generation was not accused, any more than the first had been, of overstepping the bounds of the female sphere and encroaching on the sphere of politics. The class status and social prominence of benevolent women surely facilitated their dealings with politicians and with the public. So, too, did the limited scope of their operations. Community-based, female charities were not vulnerable to charges of Northern (abolitionist) infiltration. Since they excluded blacks, they posed no threat to the racial caste system.

The language employed by benevolent women also served as a shield from criticism. In their public rhetoric, women cultivated an image of themselves as exemplars of piety, disinterested empathy, and civic-mindedness. Prescriptive literature continued in the last decades of the antebellum period, as it had earlier, to support this image—and to remain silent about the range and conspicuousness of women's public activities. An 1855 address by the Reverend David Doggett on "The Mission and Destiny of Woman" declared that "Chambers of afflication, schemes of benevolence, [and] the cause of education" were all appropriate fields for female exertion; there, "in the retirement and modesty of their sex," women could "perform offices uncongenial to man." The practice of "visiting," which took women from their own domestic circles into those of others, was singled out by Virginia commentators as the quintessential act of benevolence. In 1855 a Richmond journal called *The Family Christian Album*, edited by one Mrs. E. P. Elam, featured an article on the "unostentatious charity" of Richmond ladies. It told the story of two members of the Female Humane Association (never mentioned by name) who went on an "errand of mercy" to a poor woman in their neighborhood; the woman's husband was dying of lung disease. Determining that she was worthy of charity ("there was a composure and almost refinement in her deportment"), the ladies gave the poor woman money to help support her children.[31]

Perhaps a greater testament to the impact of women on civic life than the narrow praise that came their way is their success in inducing male private citizens to take up the cause of charitable work themselves, in the 1840s and 1850s. Increasing male involvement in what had been women's work had mixed results. In Petersburg, in 1858, the Methodist orphan asylum was co-opted by men, who took over control of its operations. Women in other cities and towns, however, continued to manage poor relief organizations in the 1850s. In Richmond and Norfolk, female charities worked alongside a host of newly formed male charities. In 1844, for example, men in Richmond formed the Gentlemen's Benevolent Society. The expressed goal of the new society was to serve as an "auxiliary" to the Union Benevolent Society; rather than co-opting the female organization, the male auxiliary remitted funds to the UBS. The UBS received remittances as well from the local YMCA, Sons of Temperance, and Knights Templar. Men in Norfolk founded the Howard Association in 1855, in response to the yellow fever epidemic. In 1861 the Howard Association disbanded and turned over its "inmates" to the Female Orphan Asylum; it agreed to pay $2,500 per year to the asylum to sustain its new charges.[32]

Suzanne Lebsock, in her penetrating study of women in Petersburg, Virginia, has interpreted men's entry into charitable activity as a kind of "backlash" against women's increased autonomy in the private sphere, and as evidence of a new "togetherness" in men's and women's organizational lives. As Lebsock herself notes, the backlash thesis is difficult to substantiate. It is not clear that the managers of female charities perceived men's efforts as an unwanted intrusion into female affairs; they may just as well have welcomed men's contributions to what they considered vitally important work. Men's efforts were, after all, an implicit acknowledgment that the kind of work women had been doing for decades was significant.[33] The togetherness thesis is problematic as well, for the tradition of female association-building which benevolent women pioneered persisted throughout the nineteenth century. Women's charities served as models for a host of other nineteenth-century Southern organizations established and managed by women—associations to honor Whig politician Henry Clay; to preserve Mount Vernon and promote sectional harmony; to boycott Northern goods after John Brown's raid; to support the Confederate war effort; and to preserve the memory of the "Lost Cause." Each of these associations would include benevolent women among its managers, would mimic benevolent societies in its organization and operation, and would appropriate and reconfigure the ideology of benevolent femininity.

Furthermore, the organizational model of "togetherness"—of male-run associations in which women played auxiliary but highly valued and publicized roles—itself had a long history, reaching back to the 1810s. It is to that history that we now turn. While the image of benevolent women as apolitical beings had some basis in reality in the early years of the nineteenth century, by the mid-1820s it was fast becoming a fiction, as the leading benevolent women in the state, along with thousands of their female fellow-citizens, took up the banner of moral reform.

In the aftermath of the Second Great Awakening, Evangelicals around the country organized, to quote historian John Kuykendall, "for the deliberate conversion of their nation and the world into an empire under the governance of Christ." The empire took on a distinct institutional form. Northern and Southern Evangelicals from each of the four major Protestant denominations established thousands of religious societies across the country in the first two decades of the nineteenth century. Bible and tract societies distributed religious publications. Education societies provided seminary education to young men, whom missionary societies helped to place in communities that needed their services. Sunday school unions fostered the religious instruction of children. The activities of these societies were coordinated and systematized by a network of five national organizations, founded in the period 1815 to 1826: the American Bible Society, the American Tract Society, the American Education Society, the American Home Missionary Society, and the American Sunday School Union. Each had its headquarters in a Northern city. Together they followed a grand strategy for propagating the Gospel. The "Big Five" supplied publications and agents to local societies; local societies in turn provided national ones with money, progress reports, and delegates to their annual conventions.[34]

Women played a prominent role in staffing and supporting the local societies that constituted the evangelical "united front." In the 1810s,

Virginia women began organizing, in rural areas, towns, and cities alike, a wide array of voluntary associations dedicated to promoting piety. Women's missionary organizations, such as Richmond's Baptist Female Missionary Society and Petersburg's (Presbyterian) Woman's Missionary Society, were typically based in individual congregations and considered themselves auxiliaries to male-run associations in their respective denominations. Women's education, Bible, and tract societies—such as the Female Cent Society of Eastern Shore Parish, Princess Anne County, which distributed Bibles to the poor—also had their roots in particular churches and denominations. Women collaborated with men in founding Sunday schools, some sectarian and some interdenominational. Men and women in the town of Lovingston, Nelson County, for example, founded a school "for the purpose of gratuitously instructing, on the Sabbath, any (whites) who might be disposed to embrace the offer." [35]

Like the nonsectarian charities that preceded them, evangelical societies provided women with opportunities for leadership within their communities. The founders and managers of religious societies were typically active in a broad range of benevolent causes. The leading female contributor to the missionary cause in Richmond's Monumental Church (Episcopal) was Margaret Harvie Robinson, who also participated in "the distribution of Bibles and tracts; the temperance society; [and] the Union Benevolent Society." Norfolk's Margaret Tucker helped form an interdenominational Sabbath school in that city, and also served as a manager of the Dorcas Society and Female Orphan Society. As they did on behalf of secular charities, these women drafted constitutions, elected officers, and solicited donations. Their organizations occupied a conspicuous place on the public calendar. Fourth of July celebrations in Richmond, Norfolk, and other cities and towns, for example, regularly featured processions by Sabbath school pupils and their teachers. [36]

By the late 1810s, Virginia's evangelical societies had begun to formalize their links to each other and to the national movement. In 1817, women founded the Female Bible Society of Richmond and Manchester, an interdenominational auxiliary to the male-run Virginia Bible Society, itself a branch of the American Bible Society. Female Bible societies were founded in Lexington, Staunton, and dozens of other places over the next three decades; they routinely received publicity and praise in the annual reports of the state society. The Richmond Tract Society was founded in 1820 as an auxiliary to the American Tract Society; more than half of the RTS's life members, as of 1837, were women. In that year, at the request of their female counterparts in New York, Virginia women embarked on a fund-raising effort "both in town and country," and raised more than $500 for the American Tract Society. Sunday school unions were another manifestation of the spirit of interdenominational and intersectional cooperation. Presbyterians and Methodists founded the Richmond and Manchester Sunday School Union in 1819 as an auxiliary to the American Sunday School Union. By 1832, Virginia had more Sunday schools (157) — many of them staffed and some managed by women — affiliated with the American Sunday School Union than did any other Southern state.[37]

The growth of the evangelical empire was charted in the variety of tracts, journals, newspapers, and books turned out by Richmond's thriving evangelical publishing industry. These publications made the case that the work of religious societies was essentially charitable in nature — that the organizations provided moral sustenance to the poor and the heathen. Evangelical writers argued that, given its charitable nature, work on behalf of religious societies was specially suited to women. John Holt Rice's *Virginia Evangelical and Literary Magazine* conscientiously reported on the activities of female associations and of the "Big Five," and made the case that running Bible, tract, and missionary societies was every bit as natural an avocation for women as presiding over orphan asylums and charity schools. Rice's magazine featured articles that trumpeted the moral and religious influence of women and thanked them for contributing such a large "proportion of charitable resources" to the "sacred treasury." Like Rice, Reverend David Doggett of Randolph-Macon College took approving note of women's evangelical activism. In a speech on "The Proper Ornament of Woman," Doggett praised women for relieving the poor and "forming, amongst [their] own sex . . . meetings for prayer, plans of usefulness, and especially missionary and Bible societies." Henry Keeling, editor of the Baptist *Religious Herald*, wrote a pamphlet promoting Sunday schools in which he urged women to take an active part, saying "teaching is your appropriate business."[38]

Despite their strenuous efforts to associate evangelism with charity, the advocates of the "united front" met with fierce opposition in Virginia. The most common criticism of evangelical societies was that they served to undermine rather than promote the cause of religion, by emphasizing works over grace as the path to redemption and by dividing congregations into separate interest groups. In 1823, Alexander Campbell of Buffalo, Virginia, began a reform movement within the Baptist Church. Campbell's anti-mission movement virulently opposed all benevolent societies as "the engines of priestly ambition," of salvation by works rather than by faith. The "Campbellites" attracted a significant membership, claiming 123 of 486 churches and 6,657 of 77,000 Virginia Baptists by 1845. While "hardshell" Baptists like Campbell did not single out women's participation as a particularly objectionable feature of religious benevolence, other critics did. John Randolph, U.S. congressman from Charlotte County, wrote in 1825 that one of the most baleful effects of evangelical "fanaticism" was that Virginia women were "running mad after popular preachers or forming themselves into clubs of one sort or another that only serve to gratify the love of selfishness and notoriety." [39]

The most strident critique of female benevolence came from the pen of Anne Royall. Royall, a fascinating and little-understood character in American history, was a prolific writer and gifted political publisher and editor. Born in Maryland in 1769, Anne Newport grew up on the Pennsylvania frontier. As a teenager, she moved to western Virginia, where she married Major William Royall and settled into his Peters Mountain estate in Botetourt County. Royall spent the years after her husband's death in 1812 engaged in a heated court battle over his estate, which thoroughly alienated her from her Virginia in-laws. In 1823 she began a tour through the United States, which resulted in her first publication, *Sketches of History, Life and Manners in the United States* (1826). Between 1827 and 1831 she produced four additional books on her travels. In two of those, *The Black Book* (1828) and *Mrs. Royall's Southern Tour* (1830–31), Royall commented extensively on Virginia women.[40]

Royall's main goal in her travel writings was to warn readers of the spread of a pernicious force in America—evangelical religion, or "Priest-craft," as she called it. Virginia, and Richmond especially, she believed to be thoroughly cursed with Priest-craft. The city was virtually parceled out, she complained, between Episcopalians, Baptists, Methodists, and Presbyterians. What horrified Royall was her sense that "the *women* all belong to the Priests"—at their ministers' behest, women all over the Commonwealth "were setting up Missionary, Bible and Tract Societies." Royall did not believe these women to be motivated by true faith. Rather, "they all wanted to get their name in the papers," she charged, while the "priests" were intent on nothing less than amassing personal fortunes and eventually taking over the government of the United States.[41]

Royall herself was not popular in Virginia—too many of its inhabitants were "incensed" by her insulting treatment of them. But the antimission sentiment to which she gave voice was a persistent obstacle to the endeavors of evangelical reformers. Western farmers, for whom

Royall considered herself a spokesperson, seem to have been particularly resistant to missionary work; many believed in the existence of an "eastern conspiracy" of urban reformers intent on imposing their values on rural folk.[42]

Equally threatening to the cause of evangelical reform in Virginia was the charge that the Big Five national agencies—based in Northern cities, presided over by Northern leaders, funded primarily through Northern contributions—had a Yankee bias. The fact that prominent abolitionists, such as Arthur Tappan, were also zealous supporters of the Big Five did not help the reform cause in the South. Nor did the fact that many Evangelicals, Northern and Southern, proselytized among blacks.

According to historian Anne Loveland, the rise of the united front precipitated a "quickening of interest in the religious instruction" of blacks, made manifest in the establishment of missions to and Sabbath schools for them. The conservative case for education, one that had significant support among defenders of slavery, was that religious instruction would both make blacks more disciplined and docile, and counter the abolitionist charge that slaveowners cared nothing for the welfare of their bondspeople. More controversial was the case, made by reformers such as John Holt Rice and Episcopal bishop William Meade, that slaves had a right to knowledge of the Gospel and the promise of salvation.[43]

White women contributed to black education primarily through the institution of the Sunday school. During the 1810s and 1820s, the evidence suggests, the Commonwealth contained scores of Sunday schools for blacks, some run by blacks and others by whites. These generally offered black children instruction in reading and writing in segregated settings. White women not only contributed to church-based schools but also established their own. Ann R. Page and Louisa Maxwell Holmes Cocke, for example, ran Sabbath schools for the slaves on their respective plantations in Frederick and Fluvanna Counties. Both supporters of African colonization, they saw education not as means for preserving the subservience of slaves but rather as a way to ensure their spiritual salvation and prepare them for eventual emigration to Liberia.[44]

The period of relative tolerance for such educational efforts came to a tragic end in 1831, when, in an attempt to consolidate slaveholder rule in the face of the abolitionist challenge, the Virginia legislature passed a law prohibiting blacks from assembling to learn to read and write. The following year, in the aftermath of the rebellion led by the slave preacher Nat Turner, the legislature forbade blacks to conduct their own religious assemblies and ruled that only licensed white ministers could offer them religious instruction. In Virginia and in other Southern states, such laws ushered in what historian Carter G. Woodson has called an era of "religion without letters" for African Americans. In the face of mounting public hostility, many Sunday schools closed down, and Northern agents of the American Sunday School Union were silenced. Those schools that remained were permitted to offer only oral instruction to black students.[45]

Whites and blacks alike testify to the chilling effects of the 1831–32 laws. In his autobiography, Virginia abolitionist Moncure Conway remembers that it had been his mother's practice every Sunday to gather her household's white and black children together for Bible instruction. When word of "this equal treatment of slaves got out," some "officious men came with a report that my mother was teaching negroes to read." Though the charge was not true, his mother ceased the "mixed teaching," to avoid "even the suspicion of such an offense." Willis Augustus Hodges, a free black from Princess Anne County who went on to be a prominent abolitionist, recounts in his autobiography having been taught to read and write by both white and black teachers, including a "poor white woman whose name was Wilson." In the wake of Turner's Rebellion, white men forced their way into Hodges's home, took his schoolmaster Mr. Blanchford to jail, and seized the family's books, papers, and Bibles.[46]

Interviews with ex-slaves from Virginia illustrate how the ranks of white women — which supplied so many teachers of blacks — could also furnish enforcers, within the domestic sphere, of the 1831–32 laws. Julia Frazier of Spotsylvania County remembers that when she cleaned her master's rooms, "Ole Missus used to watch me mos' times to see dat I didn't open no books." Levi Pollard recalls that Miss Nanny Smith, a relative of his master's, broke up the local black Sunday School run by a Quaker preacher. Her words stuck in his memory: "I don't want you niggers ter learn how ter read en write; niggers ain't got no right ter know."[47]

Despite the vigilance of public officials and private citizens, a great deal of instruction went on in defiance of the law. Most clandestine teaching was carried on by blacks themselves. In the late 1840s, for example, Mary Peake of Hampton taught black children and adults to read in her home. A presumably small but nevertheless significant number of whites refused to be deterred by the legislature's measures. In Fredericksburg, for example, a certain Mrs. Beecham and her daughter held secret classes for black scholars, keeping "splinters of wood and a chemical preparation handy so that they could appear to be making matches if anyone tried to see they were teaching."[48]

Mary Berkeley Minor Blackford of Fredericksburg, well known to her community for her antislavery views, lamented in her private journal that legislative measures and public opinion alike forbade teaching. But, she explained in a letter to a friend, "I obey a higher law than the laws of man, when I teach [blacks] on Sabbath afternoon to read their Bibles, in my own room." Such illegal teaching was widespread enough to warrant the passage of a new law in 1848, levying stiffer penalties than before on those, black or white, who offered instruction in reading and writing to African Americans. An 1855 article in the Richmond *Daily Dispatch* reminded whites of these strictures, saying, "The law forbids your instructing [blacks] to read or write, either in Sabbath schools or any other kind, and if you violate it, you do so at the hazard of your liberties." [49]

The most celebrated and revealing case of a white woman defying the law is that of Margaret Douglass. A longtime resident of South Carolina, Douglass moved to Norfolk, Virginia, in 1852. After observing women in Norfolk's Christ Church conducting a Sunday school for free black children, Douglass established a school of her own, which operated on weekdays as a supplement to the Sunday school. On May 9, 1853, eleven months after her school had opened, Douglass was arrested, charged with the crime of teaching free black children to read. In the court case that ensued, Douglass mounted her own defense, claiming that if she were guilty of a crime, so, too, were the women of Christ Church, whose actions she had emulated. While members of Christ Church called to testify emphatically denied that they taught blacks to read, their testimony was contradicted by witnesses who averred that free black children in the Sunday school *did* read—from the same books Douglass distributed to her scholars. Douglass further argued that she was no abolitionist, but a loyal Southerner who thought that slaves should be instructed in religion, "that they may know their duties to their masters." Neither tactic worked. Douglass was convicted, and sentenced to a month in jail. After serving her term, she moved to Philadelphia and wrote a memoir of her experiences.[50]

Douglass's case reveals the hidden assumptions embedded in the concept of female benevolence. While evangelical literature declared that benevolent deeds were the "proper ornament" of woman, clearly women of the social elite were given more leeway than others in defining what constituted acceptable acts of charity. Norfolk residents saw the teaching activities of the elite ladies of Christ Church as harmless. The activities of Douglass, a lower-middle-class woman who made little effort to cultivate friendly relations with her white neighbors, were seen as threatening to the social order. According to her biographers, Douglass paid the price for being an outsider in a community that was "increasingly in a panic about secret enemies." Douglass's own testimony only heightened the perception that she was an outside agitator—her professions of loyalty to the South were overshadowed by her critique of white Southern males, whom she accused of harboring "criminal passions" for slave women.[51]

Douglass's case also offers a new perspective on a process that has received a great deal of attention from scholars—the fading of the "benevolent consensus." Historian John Kuykendall, in his study of how the Big Five fared in the South, has concluded that despite their diligent efforts to maintain neutrality on the slavery issue, the evangelical enterprises were inevitably politicized, in the minds of critics, by their connections to abolitionism. Once serving as important institutional links between the North and South, the national societies gradually curtailed their efforts in the South and abandoned the rhetoric of a united front. Local societies were left to decide how and to whom to administer charity.[52]

Scholars agree that this retreat from reform by evangelical societies in the South—like the schisms in the evangelical churches—was an important harbinger of political disunion. But they fail to appreciate the extent to which Southern women were implicated in the politicization of religious benevolence. Foot soldiers in the evangelical campaign for souls, Southern women such as Margaret Douglass were profoundly affected by shifts in the rules of engagement—in this case, the restriction of black education. When Douglass claimed to "glory in works of benevolence and charity to a race down-trodden," the *Daily Southern Argus* of Norfolk fumed, she aroused the "righteous indignation" of the community. The paper called her a "martyr to the cause of benevolence."[53] Though isolated, Douglass was not alone. By the 1850s, Virginia was littered with female martyrs to benevolence, who clung to controversial causes long after they had lost their popular mandate. One of those causes was temperance.

The temperance movement got its official start in Virginia in 1826, when a handful of Baptist and Methodist ministers founded the Virginia Temperance Society (VTS). The avowed goal of the Virginia Temperance Society was to woo the populace away from the evils of liquor consumption. In 1829 the VTS joined the American Temperance Society, the organizing body of the national anti-liquor movement, on the condition that Virginians would continue to direct the crusade in their own state. The Virginia Temperance Society was soon joined by a host of local organizations around the state. Most had their roots in evangelical congregations but were not officially affiliated with any one sect; most but not all were auxiliaries to the VTS. Like women's charitable and religious associations, temperance societies located themselves outside the political sphere, in the realm of benevolence. Anti-liquor groups propagated their ideas not through critique or coercion but by appealing to public opinion. Moreover, the anti-liquor cause was, according to temperance men, inseparable from the cause of religion. Each of the major denominations endorsed the temperance cause as a vehicle to promote piety. The evangelical newspapers in Virginia made the case that temperance societies were similar in nature and design to missionary, Bible, and tract societies.[54]

From the start, the temperance cause attracted the support of women, in rural as well as urban areas. The Lexington Union Temperance Society was organized in 1833 by "a number of persons of both sexes." Sixty-one men and women signed its constitution, and pledged themselves to total abstinence. That same year fifty men and women formed the Laurel Grove Temperance Society in Sussex County. Women were voting members and signed the constitution. The Henrico Union Society for the promotion of temperance had ninety-three members and six managers — three male and three female. Over the course of the 1830s, Virginia women joined temperance groups in Augusta, Campbell, Fluvanna, Norfolk, and dozens of other counties around the state.[55]

According to the public rhetoric of the movement, women embraced temperance because they desperately desired to protect the domestic sphere from male drunkenness. Though innocent of the sin of intemperance, a male member of the Louisa County Temperance Society averred, women were its principal sufferers. Drink made of men tyrants who terrorized their wives, mothers, daughters, and sisters; women were naturally interested in a "plan that may save their sex from so much sorrow." In a letter to the *Southern Religious Telegraph* in 1830, a correspondent named Elizabeth argued that "the great law of Christianity which requires every one *to do good* — requires all ladies to . . . inform the public that they do not countenance the use of strong drink." She noted that women "are no more departing from their station, in joining a temperance society, than they are in joining a Bible society or any other benevolent association." The Virginia Temperance Society apparently agreed. In 1834, it passed a resolution "invoking the continued cooperation of the ladies in [the temperance] cause." That cooperation was substantial—by 1835, the Old Dominion boasted one hundred temperance societies with a total of 35,000 members, about half of whom were women.[56]

Women's personal papers reveal that they had diverse reasons for joining the movement. Some women, such as Jane Chancellor Payne of Parkersburg, had experienced the ill effects of alcoholism in their own families. Payne's diary contains poignant and recurring laments over her husband's intemperance. He pledged to stop drinking a number of times but always returned to his destructive ways; Payne herself took up teaching to provide a living for the couple's children. "Will the tears and intreaties of a faithful and fond wife prevail against [intemperance?]" she wrote in 1835. "No she is either accused of usurping authority or put off with broken promises from time to time till all confidence is lost." Payne believed that "if females would unite in their exertions in putting down this bane . . . society would soon feel its happy riddance of the worst of evils."[57]

Other temperance women were motivated not by personal tragedy but by charitable impulses. Presbyterian reformer Margaret Rutherfoord of Richmond taught Sabbath school and distributed temperance tracts and food to the residents of poor neighborhoods in her native city. Louisa Cocke, the wife of the leading temperance man in the state, John Hartwell Cocke, frequently attested to her warm support for the temperance movement in her extensive diary, making note of the rounds of temperance conventions, addresses, barbecues, and other events she attended. The Cockes, supporters of African colonization, actually organized a temperance society among their slave men and women, as a way of improving the "moral character" of bondspeople. On the other side of the political spectrum, ardent defenders of slavery, such as Edmund Ruffin, promoted temperance among slaves for the purpose of improving discipline—of lessening, as Ruffin saw it, the "thefts & other offences which are induced principally by the habit of drinking." Whites organized temperance societies for blacks in dozens of communities. A temperance society for blacks in Portsmouth, for instance, had 532 male and female members.[58]

From its very inception, the temperance movement generated controversy. Indeed, the movement provoked more hostility in the South than in any other section of the country. Opposition to temperance had economic, religious, social, and political components. Naturally, communities that were renowned for their distilleries and wineries or dependent on the crops used in alcohol production proved resistant to temperance reformers; so, too, did "hard-shell" Baptists, like the followers

of Alexander Campbell, who believed that temperance was another reform that emphasized "works" over "grace." According to Ian Tyrrell,
advocates of total abstinence alienated many planters from the temperance cause by "threatening the freedom of the social elite to drink wine."
Indeed, contemporary observers and modern-day scholars agree that
the temperance movement in Virginia was dominated by the middle
class, and shunned, by and large, by the upper and lower classes alike.[59]

By the mid-1830s the Virginia temperance movement had become
mired in controversies, both internal and external. In 1836 it affiliated
itself with the newly formed American Temperance Union, successor
to the earlier American Temperance Society. The ATU was committed
to total abstinence from all liquor. Fierce debates developed over abstinence versus moderation and over whether to prohibit the use of wine.
An anonymous clergyman enumerated his reasons for not joining the
temperance crusade in an 1836 pamphlet. Unlike "Bible Societies, Tract
Societies, Sunday School Unions and other institutions of the kind,"
temperance societies, by demanding abstinence, promoted "intolerance
of the worst kind."[60]

More damaging to the cause than infighting were developments in
the North. In the mid-1830s, temperance came to be linked to abolitionism — many temperance leaders in the North advocated immediate
emancipation, and claimed that liquor and slavery were twin evils from
which society must be liberated. Virginia's anti-liquor men lamented
the association of temperance with Northern radicalism and reiterated
the "benevolence" of their cause. At its annual meeting of 1834, the
VTS passed a resolution that temperance societies "are Moral agents
acting on public opinion, and that it is unwise to use them for political purposes." Robert Peyton, founder of the Salem temperance society,
asserted in his annual report of 1837 that "the object of the Society is
simply and entirely benevolent"; he noted despairingly six months later
that some members of his community were "deterred by the fear of cen-
sure" from supporting the cause.[61]

Buckling under internal and external pressures, the VTS collapsed in
1839, bringing to a close the first, or "evangelical," stage of the temperance movement in Virginia and ushering in the second, or "popular,"
phase. Surprisingly, the organizations that replaced the VTS would build
a following not by repudiating politics but by embracing it. Temperance
was revived in the 1840s by two new organizations, the Washingtonians
and the Sons of Temperance, which, with the blessing of Evangelicals,
took over the leadership of the crusade. These organizations effected a
democratization and a politicization of temperance, trends which had

mixed results for temperance women. Founded in 1840 in Baltimore, the Washingtonian movement quickly received the endorsement of the American Temperance Union, and soon Washingtonian total abstinence societies were displacing older temperance groups.[62]

Appalled by the way alcohol flowed during William Henry Harrison's "hard cider" presidential campaign of 1840 and yet intrigued by the techniques political parties used to reach mass audiences, temperance advocates vowed to agitate against "political drinking," to work for the defeat of intemperate politicians, and to enlist sympathetic politicians to their side. The Washingtonians adopted one of the tactics of mass politics that the Whig Party used to great effect in the 1840 campaign — enlisting orators to make stump speeches before huge audiences of men and women for the purpose of converting people "by counties" rather than individually.[63]

By 1842, a number of highly effective Washingtonian orators were touring Virginia, urging crowds to take the pledge of total abstinence. In January, Washingtonians held a series of meetings in Richmond; at one of them an orator "addressed the female portion of the audience" in particular. By the time the Washingtonians left town, some 900 Richmonders of both sexes had signed the total abstinence pledge. Women heeded the Washingtonian call in other locales as well. Half of the 250 members of the Total Abstinence Society of King William County, for example, were women. Female members of the Fredericksburg Total Abstinence Society were credited by one temperance orator with having helped temperance men to "control the public sentiment of this town." [64]

Judging by the *Journal of the American Temperance Union*, temperance continued in its popular stage, as it had in its evangelical one, to appeal to women's benevolence. "Let woman then come forward as she never has in this great cause," one issue of the ATU journal exhorted in 1841 — "all this may be done . . . with the same propriety, as their efforts in the Missionary, Bible or Tract cause." A later article declared that since women were "not governed by love of popularity, nor moved by the prospect of political preferment," they were better suited than men to temperance work. Many Washingtonian songs, which were sung at meetings, praised and encouraged women. "Come join the Washingtonians / Ye dames and maidens fair / and Breathe around us in our path / Affection's hallowed air," rang one verse of a tune entitled "The Washingtonian Call." [65]

Though they had succeeded in reviving and reorienting the temperance movement, the Washingtonians were eclipsed in the mid-1840s by a new mutual benefit society, the Sons of Temperance. Organized in 1842 in New York to shore up the Washingtonian movement, the Sons eventually made their way to Virginia, where they soon became the most popular temperance group, coexisting with some older societies but replacing most. The Sons, whose leaders included editors, lawyers, businessmen, and politicians, outpaced the Washingtonians in the sophistication of their organization — they established a series of divisions which had regular meetings, permanent headquarters, and full-time staff. The ascendancy of the Sons was a mixed blessing for temperance women. On the one hand, as the number of independent temperance societies (those unaffiliated with the Sons) declined, so, too, did the opportunities for women to serve as leaders of temperance groups — women could not be full members, let alone managers, of the Sons. The fact that the Sons excluded white women and blacks from full membership may have reassured those Southerners who were suspicious of Northern efforts to empower those groups.[66]

On the other hand, the Sons did consider white women indispensable allies. By 1850, there were 353 divisions of the Sons in Virginia, with a total of 15,000 male members. Writing in that year, the leading temperance man in Virginia, Lucian Minor, asserted that "as many females, as males, became members of Temperance Societies," a claim seconded by the foremost modern historians of temperance in Virginia; Minor evidently counted as members women who publicly supported the work of the Sons but were not formally affiliated with the organization. In 1854, the Sons officially recognized women's contributions by ruling that women could be associate members, with the title "lady visitors." Some Virginia localities, such as Petersburg and Mount Crawford, adopted rituals for the admission of women into their chapters.[67]

Even more than the Washingtonians had, the Sons of Temperance specialized in public pageantry. The parades, barbecues, and conventions which the Sons sponsored were elaborate affairs that received detailed coverage in the press, and conspicuously featured female participants. In 1849, for example, the women of Lexington presented a "splendid banner" to the Lexington division of the Sons. Robert J. Taylor spoke on behalf of the women. The banner was a public testament to the fact that women — the "Representatives of virtue," as Taylor put it — approved of the cause and were ready to cooperate in "cultivating and adorning the moral wilderness." Women publicly expressed their support for temperance in other ways as well. Julia Cabell, president of the Union Benevolent Society of Richmond, penned a temperance song, on behalf of the Sons, for *Godey's Lady's Book*. Sarah Whittlesey, a popular poet, included a poetical "Address to the Sons of Temperance" in her

1852 anthology, *Heart-Drops from Memory's Urn*. Mary Virginia Terhune's first published work under the pen name Marion Harland was a
temperance tale entitled "Kate Harper," which appeared in the *Southern Era*, a journal owned by the Sons of Temperance.[68]

Not only public sources but private ones as well testify to women's
participation in the movement. As it had in its "evangelical" stage,
temperance attracted not only those women who were the victims of
alcoholism but also those who were motivated by benevolent impulses.
Anna Maria Weisiger, a devout Methodist from Chesterfield County,
taught a Sabbath school class, belonged to a sewing society, made occasional visits to the poor house, and went to temperance meetings. For
Weisiger, the temperance cause was inseparable from the cause of religion. In 1844, she lamented that the church was in a state of decline,
and speculated that too many members "drown their reflections in the
intoxicating bowl." Sidney Sophia Gore, a Baptist from Back Creek Valley, taught Bible classes for blacks in her neighborhood and belonged to
the local temperance society. "Intemperance," she wrote in 1849, "is the
curse and mildew of our land. It is coming upon us like a flood, a river
of fire consuming all who madly rush into its course."[69]

Even as the temperance movement solicited the aid of benevolent
women, it moved further away each year from the tactics of moral suasion. Inspired by similar efforts in the North, the Virginia Sons began
in 1845 to circulate petitions for local option laws, allowing cities or
counties to ban or restrict the sale or barter of liquor. To the objection
that petitioning was a political act, leaders of the movement countered
that the tactic of moral suasion was no longer enough. Temperance was
indeed a political issue, asserted an orator in Winchester. "What are
politics for," he asked, "but to guard the civil and social interests of the
community?"[70]

The years 1846 to 1853 witnessed a series of great petition drives on
behalf of prohibitory legislation. In Virginia, women participated in
these drives not only by lending their names to men's memorials but also
by drafting and circulating petitions of their own. Twenty-six women
of Cabell County submitted a temperance petition to the General Assembly in 1849. They first reminded the legislature—their "Fathers and
Brothers"—that they were "[w]ithout any other mode of redress, than
that of petition, to you who have the power to enact such laws, as will
protect virtuous females." They asked for the abolition of the laws that
granted liquor licenses, and if that request were deemed unreasonable,
for a law that would "curtail the profits of the venders [*sic*] of liquor."
Forty women from Wythe County submitted a similar appeal for prohi-

bition; liquor, they asserted, was the cause of much violence, pauperism, and crime. Both petitions were summarily dismissed by the General Assembly. In 1851, forty-three women of Pocahantas County submitted their own memorial. "We would ask that you would at least suffer the subject to come before the people," the petitioners proclaimed, "to say if they wish the curse of drunkenness to continue." The legislature was not impressed by the women's arguments. One legislator even quipped, to the great amusement of his colleagues, that the petition should be referred to "the grand division of the Daughters of Temperance [as it] would be more suitable there than here." Male petitioners fared no better; the first wave of anti-license sentiment produced little effect.[71]

Despite the support of thousands of Virginians, the petition campaign ended in bitter defeat for the temperance cause. Temperance advocates in the state conceded that in the wake of the defeat of the prohibition drive, temperance began a precipitous decline in Virginia. This time the decline was due not to internal dissension or weak organization but to a sea change in the political climate. The rise of the Northern woman's rights movement, the intensification of sectional tensions, and the demise of the Second Party System fed the public opposition in Virginia to anti-liquor laws.

Historians Jed Dannenbaum, Ian Tyrrell, and others have explained how the shift from moral suasion to legal prohibition in the North had the effect of galvanizing the woman's rights movement. Understanding that only voters could have a direct impact on the law, Northern temperance reformers, including Susan B. Anthony and Elizabeth Cady Stanton, argued that the cause would succeed only if women were granted the right to speak in public and to exercise the franchise. By 1852, Northern temperance conventions were often occasions for debates over woman's rights. After a few years, women did gain some ground—public speaking by Northern temperance women was commonplace in the mid-1850s—but the prohibition campaign itself had run aground. Some women, disappointed with the failure of that campaign, resorted to extralegal vigilantism. From 1853 to 1859, women in dozens of Northern and Western communities mounted violent attacks on saloons, aimed at destroying their liquor stocks.[72]

Temperance's chief supporters in Virginia were alarmed by these developments and hoped to reinstate "conservative" control over the movement. John Hartwell Cocke, president of the American Temperance Union, wrote to George Fitzhugh the following account of the 1852 World Temperance Convention: "You have doubtless seen in the newspapers the struggle we had with the strong-minded women . . . in the

World Temperance Convention.... We gained a perfect triumph, and I believe we have given a rebuke to this most impudent clique of unsexed females and rampant abolitionists."[73]

Even as the behavior of Northern radicals caused anxiety for temperance advocates, it provided ammunition to the movement's growing ranks of detractors. The campaign for prohibitory legislation was, according to its critics, a Yankee-inspired attempt to curtail individual freedoms. The *Daily Richmond Enquirer* attacked Virginia supporters of the license law for associating with such radical agitators as Horace Greeley and Lucy Stone. So, too, did the leading states-rights organ in the state, Roger Pryor's *The South*. One of Pryor's editorials fumed that temperance has "ceased to be a moral agency, mild, persuasive and unobtrusive in its course . . . and become a political despot compelling obedience to its arbitrary decrees by the strong arm of the law."[74]

Moreover, the temperance cause lost an ally in 1852 with the demise of the Whig Party, which had been somewhat more supportive of prohibition than the Democrats. The American Party, the Whigs' successor, embraced temperance as part of its anti-immigrant platform, but in Virginia, the association of temperance with the unpopular "Know-Nothings" hurt the movement. Sara Pryor, wife of Roger Pryor, attacked Know-Nothingism in her reminiscences by accusing its partisans of "outrageous lawlessness," citing as an example the fact that "Bands of women made raids on bar-rooms and smashed the glasses, broke the casks, and poured the liquor into the streets."[75]

Despite such associations between Northern temperance and female radicalism, the Virginia Sons of Temperance did not repudiate their female supporters. In September of 1856 the Springfield Division of the Sons of Temperance held a meeting which "embrac[ed] a goodly number of those fair and constant friends of the Temperance cause, the ladies." On at least one occasion, a woman even made a public address on the subject of temperance. In 1856 the ladies of Harpers Ferry presented a "splendid banner" to the Cadets of Temperance in that town. A speech was made by a Miss Chambers, who declared that if the cause flourished then "our alms-houses, jails and penitentiaries will stand as empty, silent, monuments of the degradation and misery which Intemperance produced . . . and the hearts of thousands of wives, mothers and sisters, will beat in unison as they realize the blessings of a temperance millenium."[76]

Perhaps the most outspoken female temperance activists in Virginia were editors E. P. Elam of Richmond and Rebecca Brodnax Hicks of Petersburg. Elam edited her own journal, the *Family Christian Album*, and Hicks her own weekly newspaper, the *Kaleidoscope*. Both publications were aimed at women and devoted to the cause of education; both featured articles and editorials on temperance. Elam chastised men who abandoned or harmed their families for the "sake of indulging a degraded and vitiated appetite" for liquor. "Zealously would we labor in the war of extermination, as far as our position and sex would allow," she promised her readers, "and devoutly do we trust that at no very distant period this liquid poison will be by law confined to the shelves of the apothecary." In the pages of the *Kaleidoscope*, Hicks proclaimed the temperance movement to be in a bad state, and pledged herself to revive it. Her appeals, she declared, were directed "not to those only whose privilege it is to go to the polls, but to their wives, and sons and daughters, whose influence will, in due time, reach and govern party leaders and legislators." [77]

Despite the best efforts of temperance activists, by the end of the decade the movement was in shambles. In 1858, a correspondent to the *Richmond Enquirer* declared that temperance societies had been annihilated, as a result of revulsion against prohibitory laws; a few months later, a correspondent of the *Virginia Free Press* bemoaned the lack of women at a recent rally: "We regretted the absence of many wives and mothers who ought to have been there. The ladies — young and old — should not forget that they are most deeply interested in all Temperance movements." The political events of 1859–60 only served to undermine the cause further. Alfred Beckly, speaking at the annual meeting of the Grand Division of the Sons of Temperance of Virginia in 1860, declared that temperance meetings were designed to foster "the breaking down of sectional prejudice, and . . . the perpetuation of our *Union*." But he and his colleagues concluded that John Brown's raid and the fall elections had rendered "efforts to enlist the people in the Temperance cause, in many sections, entirely abortive." In 1860, the Grand Division of the Sons of Temperance of Virginia had a total of 9,966 members (7,351 men and 2,615 lady "visitors") — a sad commentary on a movement that had once boasted some 35,000 male and female adherents.[78]

When considered together, the records of women's poor relief, evangelical, and anti-liquor activities bespeak the existence of a long tradition of public collaboration between white men and women in Virginia. Over the course of the antebellum period, a distinctive sexual division of civic labor took shape. Men did the work of public speaking, legislating, and voting. But women had duties of their own. By 1830, male and female reformers in Virginia had forged a consensus that women's superior morality—their disinterestedness, compassion, piety, and purity —fitted them to serve as "representatives of virtue" in the public sphere. As managers, teachers, fund-raisers, publicists, petitioners, lobbyists, and spokeswomen for benevolent causes, women brought "feminine" virtues into the public sphere and, so the argument went, purified it in the process.

Virginians, no less than their Northern counterparts, explored the political implications of the doctrine of female benevolence. While local female charities maintained a suprapolitical status, those voluntary associations connected to the national reform movements became embroiled in sectional politics. Within Virginia, the rise of sectionalism pitted the adherents of two political philosophies against each other. Those who remained committed to national reform causes such as temperance believed that the greatest threat to Virginia's stability and stature lay within her, in the form of moral decay. The critics of reform, by contrast, believed that what the Old Dominion had most to fear was not moral decay but aggression from Northern radicals. Women were deeply implicated in the transition, within Virginia's political culture, from a focus on moral decline to a focus on external enemies. For neither moral reformers nor their critics could do without women's support. A broad consensus prevailed throughout the antebellum period that women should serve as public "representatives of virtue." But as sectional tensions mounted, Virginians debated ever more fiercely the issue of where, on the political map, virtue lay.

"Slavery is indeed a fearful evil; a canker in the bud of our national prosperity; a bitter drop in the cup of domestic felicity." So began Virginia Cary's chapter on "domestic management," the twenty-eighth of her *Letters on Female Character*."[1] Cary's book, as we have seen, was a widely acclaimed articulation of the ideology of domesticity. Cary urged women to accept subordination to their husbands, to content themselves with the domestic sphere, and to pursue the path of Christian virtue. But why did Cary include in her domestic handbook such a stark condemnation of slavery?

White women, according to Cary, had the duty to create orderly domestic environments in which Christian piety could flourish. Slavery bred domestic chaos. As mistresses of slave households, white women, exposed daily to the temptations of absolute authority, too often became slaves to their own tempers, and white children who were raised without sympathy for their fellow beings became unruly despots. Slaves, whom she referred to as "helpless fellow beings," Cary saw as malleable, as good or as bad as their masters made them. If whites taught them the rules of morality, slaves would act with dignity and respect. But Cary was fundamentally pessimistic about human nature. Because of the tendency of absolute power to corrupt those who held it, the evils of slavery could be mitigated, but not overcome. Only in the absence of slavery, Cary implied, would Virginia women be able to fulfill their calling as religious exemplars. Until the day when "heavenly Mercy" would dismantle the slave system, white women had to struggle to submerge the tyrant in the "true woman."[2]

Cary's assertions — that slavery was not the Old Dominion's fault but had been "inflicted" upon her by the "parent country"; that slavery had a detrimental effect on the morals of the white population as well as the black; and that in time, under divine guidance, the institution would be dismantled — were Virginian to the core, firmly within the tradition of Jefferson, Madison, Monroe, and other statesmen of the Commonwealth who saw slavery as a "necessary evil." Rather than identifying herself with any political tradition or party, however, Cary addressed the subject of slavery purely in her capacity as a domestic manager. After calling slavery "a great national evil," she left aside the issue of the political legitimacy of the peculiar institution. How and when slavery ended was God's business; in the meantime, it was women's province to ameliorate the conditions in which whites and blacks coexisted.[3]

Cary's book is a fitting place to start a discussion of female colonizationists in Virginia, for although she did not explicitly endorse the scheme of sending free blacks to Africa, many of Cary's views on slavery were shared by women who supported the American Colonization Society. In recent years, scholars have debated whether white Southern women were "covert abolitionists," more inclined to antislavery sentiments than their men, or proslavery partisans, who equaled or even surpassed men in their zeal for the peculiar institution and in their capacity for cruelty toward slaves. This debate has focused on Mary Boykin Chesnut of South Carolina, who, in her extensive Civil War diary, described slavery as a "monstrous system," lamenting that it made white women and slaves alike victims of the absolute power of white men. Anne Firor Scott argued in her seminal work *The Southern Lady* (1970) that Chesnut's lament was but one of many manifestations of white women's discontent with and even opposition to the system of slavery. More recently, Elizabeth Fox-Genovese has made the case that Chesnut was no abolitionist: Chesnut criticized the abuses of the system of slavery, particularly miscegenation, and not the system itself. According to Fox-Genovese, even such mild critics of slavery as Chesnut were "few and far between" in the antebellum South; the vast majority of slaveholding women understood that they were beneficiaries and not victims of slavery.[4]

While it is incontrovertible that slaveholding women were as a class committed to upholding the institution of slavery, the tendency of scholars to categorize them either as abolitionist sympathizers or defenders of slavery is misguided. Such a view takes little account of the differences between the upper and lower South or between the early and late decades of the antebellum period. Most important, Southern women's historians, focusing on private letters and diaries, have overlooked women's contributions to public debates over slavery. Hundreds of white women in antebellum Virginia publicly expressed their opposition to slavery—in newspapers, journals, petitions, broadsides, and addresses—and publicly worked to dismantle the slave system. The vast majority of these women supported African colonization as the solution to the problem of slavery. Female colonizationists, like their male counterparts, covered a broad political spectrum: some, out of fear of or loathing for blacks, sought to "rid" the Commonwealth of them; but others were motivated by sympathy and even affection for blacks, whom they understood to be the victims of brutal oppression. To dismiss these women because they fell short of the paradigmatic moral vision and courage of the abolitionists is to overlook a rich and illuminating piece of the historical record.

The American Colonization Society was founded in 1816 to promote the emigration of free blacks to Africa. Throughout the first decade of its existence, the ACS tried to prove that colonization was both "politically legitimate, and religiously benevolent and right." Political legitimacy rested on the case that although the ACS wanted to enlist the aid of the federal government, it contemplated no interference with the Constitution and no legal coercion of slaveholders. The political goals of the ACS, its advocates contended, were benign — to provide a "middle ground" between the philosophies of radical abolitionism and proslavery ideology, on which all moderate people could meet, and to export republican institutions and ideals to Africa. Religious legitimacy rested on the case that the ACS was fundamentally a missionary society, dedicated to bringing the "glorious beams of christian revelation" to Africa.[5]

Both the political and religious cases for colonization were readily accepted in Virginia. The Virginia General Assembly appropriated money for the colonization society, and male-headed auxiliaries to the ACS were established across the length and breadth of the state. The most prominent auxiliary, the Richmond and Manchester Society, was presided over by such political luminaries as John Marshall, James Madison, and James Monroe. Each of the four major Protestant denominations endorsed the ACS and took up collections on its behalf. The religious press categorized colonization as a cause which, like Bible, tract, and temperance societies, deserved the active support of all Christians. A small but significant group of Afro-Virginians embraced the cause of evangelizing Africa. In 1815, black members of Richmond's First Baptist Church formed the Richmond African Missionary Society. In 1821, in cooperation with the ACS, the missionary society sent its charter member, preacher Lott Cary, and his wife and family, to West Africa; Cary would earn a reputation as the chief black missionary in Liberia.[6]

ACS leaders solicited and celebrated white women's contributions to the organization. Because colonization was a charitable enterprise, these men suggested, women had a special affinity for it. ACS vice president Henry Clay, speaking in Kentucky in 1829, declared that colonization had been "countenanced and aided by that fair sex, which is ever prompt to contribute its exertions in works of charity and benevolence, because it always acts from the generous impulses of pure and uncorrupted hearts." Virginia lawyer Peachy Grattan paid tribute to women at a meeting in Rockingham County. "Our mothers, our wives, and sisters, always foremost in every benevolent and charitable design, are with one heart, and one voice, enlisted in its service," he said of the ACS in 1825.[7]

Abundant evidence of female zeal for colonization can be found both in ACS publications and in the private papers of Virginia women. Throughout the 1820s, scores of Virginia women donated time and money to the colonization cause. Female contributions, which were publicized in the ACS monthly journal the *African Repository*, took a wide variety of forms. Some women acted through their churches, typically by purchasing membership in the ACS for their pastors. Some made outright donations in their own names; some bequeathed money to the ACS, or provided for the manumission and emigration of their slaves in their wills. Beginning in 1825, a number of informal networks of female colonizationists were converted into female auxiliaries to the ACS. These organizations proved to be highly effective at soliciting contributions for the cause. The Female Liberian Society of Essex County, for example, raised the sum of $170 in a six-month period in 1825; theirs was, according to the *African Repository*, "an example worthy of imitation." Colonization women favored a fund-raising tactic that would later be adopted by female abolitionists — raising money by selling goods at fairs. In May of 1830, the women of Charlottesville raised $500 for "the benevolent objects of the American Colonization Society," by holding a colonization fair at a local hotel.[8]

A common thread running through writings by and about female adherents of the ACS is their view that colonization was a religious scheme, not a political one. Colonization women saw themselves as missionaries, drawn to the ACS out of a sense of religious duty. They would spread the Gospel among slaves in order to prepare them to promote Christianity in Africa. Historian Donald Mathews has given a name — "Evangelical womanhood" — to the Southern evangelical incarnation of benevolent femininity. According to Mathews, Evangelical womanhood served as a rationale for women to practice benevolence outside the confines of their homes. Well before the emergence of an organized abolitionist movement, Mathews has argued, "Evangelical southern women had already established their peculiar and most important act of benevolence by becoming tribunes, teachers, and missionaries to slaves."[9]

For Virginia's most prominent female colonizationists, the conviction that Africa should be Christianized went hand in hand with the conviction that the institution of slavery was sinful and should, on moral grounds, be gradually dismantled. Anne Rice, wife of John Holt Rice, shared her husband's enthusiasm for reform causes and for the ACS. According to Rice's niece Mary Virginia Terhune [Marion Harland], a popular novelist of the 1850s, Rice was a fervent "convert" to colonization, and imagined herself as "the leader in a crusade that would wipe the stain of slavery from her beloved state." In 1848 she manumitted her oldest slave, Anderson, and his family, and sent them to Liberia; "in the fullness of time," Terhune writes, Rice arranged the emigration of five families, and "well nigh impoverished herself" in so doing.[10]

Louisa Cocke shared Rice's sentiments. A devout Presbyterian, she believed that slavery was an evil institution, and that whites would have to "render an account hereafter for our injustice" to slaves. She made a series of donations to the colonization cause in the 1820s and 1830s. In 1833, her husband John Hartwell Cocke manumitted Peyton Skipwith, his wife Lydia, and their six children and sent them to the ACS colony of Liberia; the Cockes and Skipwiths maintained an extensive and often poignant correspondence throughout the antebellum period. Like many colonizationists, Cocke practiced selective manumission. He sent fourteen other freed slaves—only a small fraction of the total number in his control—to Liberia over the course of the antebellum period.[11]

Ann R. Page, an ardent Episcopalian from Frederick County, hoped the colonization movement would break the "evil power of slavery." Page felt, her biographer asserts, that she was called by God "to a great missionary work in her own country, and at her own home." "To see Western Africa seasoned with divine salt, from American Christians," Page confided to her cousin and fellow colonizationist Mary Lee (Fitzhugh) Custis, was her fondest wish. Page lamented the effects of absolute power on the souls of masters and mistresses. In 1823 she wrote that "we are especially tempted to make the poor subservient to our own indulgence when those poor are our bond slaves and we can do as we like with them, and hush their murmurs by authority or by selling them." Debt, the proverbial nemesis of would-be emancipators, eventually compelled Page to do the very thing she decried. In order to satisfy the creditors of her late husband, Page sold more than one hundred slaves in 1826. The rest she worked zealously to prepare for freedom and for emigration to Liberia; between 1832 and 1838 she sent an estimated twenty-three manumitted slaves to the colony.[12]

The most prominent female colonizationist in Virginia was Mary Berkeley Minor Blackford, a staunch Episcopalian. Mary had learned her devotion to the ACS at the knee of her mother, Lucy Minor, who sent nine manumitted slaves to Liberia in 1826. As children, Mary and her brother Launcelot, who went on to serve as a missionary in Liberia, were accustomed to depositing their savings in a joint money box, "whose contents were carefully hoarded to aid the benevolent designs of the Colonization Society." In 1825, Mary married William Blackford, a promising young lawyer. The couple settled in Fredericksburg, where William became an influential newspaper editor and leader of the local Whig Party. The Blackfords were the archetypal middle-class slave-owners; their slaveholdings fluctuated but probably never exceeded six. William shared Mary's passion for the colonization cause, but not her antislavery views: while Mary hoped that colonization would pave the way for the gradual emancipation of the slaves, William saw the scheme primarily as a means to remove the "vicious and degraded" free black population. After years of entreaties, Mary finally persuaded William to free and provide for the emigration of one of their slaves, Abram, in 1844.[13]

In 1829, Blackford founded the Fredericksburg and Falmouth Female Auxiliary to the ACS, soon to become Virginia's most active female society. The Fredericksburg auxiliary distributed ACS tracts throughout the countryside, and tried to provoke the languishing male auxiliary to good works. By May 1830, such efforts had netted the ACS $500 and eighteen new female "life members"—including Dolley Madison, wife of ex-president James Madison, and Catherine Lomax, manager of the Fredericksburg Female Orphan Asylum. The work of her auxiliary, Mary Blackford wrote to ACS secretary Ralph Gurley, was carried on "in the domestic circle, around our own or the firesides of our neighbors, without the sacrifice of time or the proprieties of our sex."[14] She and her coworkers were merely exerting their benign influence in popularly sanctioned ways—using familiar vehicles for benevolence such as fairs and the distribution of tracts to exhort their neighbors to good deeds.

While male and female colonizationists alike trumpeted the religious benevolence of the cause, their claims did not insulate the ACS from political criticism. By the late 1820s the ACS was meeting with considerable political opposition in Virginia from proslavery men who thought it an abolitionist front, and from states-rights Jacksonians who saw colonization as part of an effort by nationalists like Henry Clay and John Quincy Adams to extend the power of the federal government. Hoping to win the support of Virginians who were wary of the Northern ties and nationalism of the ACS, the Richmond male auxiliary reorganized in 1828 as the Virginia Colonization Society (VCS), an independent state society which continued to remit its funds to the ACS, but took over the job of publicizing the cause in Virginia. While some VCS leaders still believed in gradual emancipation, they reasoned that in order to win converts and legislative support in the Commonwealth, they needed to focus on the removal of free blacks rather than encouraging manumissions.[15]

The formation of the VCS was the first in a series of events that would expose the fallacy of the notion that women could work on behalf of colonization without addressing the politics of slavery. The ideology of religious benevolence could not protect the ACS from criticism — nor could evangelical womanhood protect colonization women. Some women construed their benevolent duty narrowly: to ameliorate the conditions of slavery within the domestic sphere. But others, such as Page and Blackford, believed that they should serve as agents of the cause of gradual emancipation. These women chose, after the formation of the VCS, to work through the national society rather than to work with the new state society. They evidently believed that the parent society was more sympathetic to their goals than the VCS; they found an ally in the secretary of the ACS, Presbyterian minister Ralph Gurley. Page, discouraged by her neighbors' disapproval of her efforts, confided her hopes for colonization to Gurley. "The cause has for so many years been the chief object of my heart and life," she wrote, "that I require one, who sees it in the light you do, to bear with me." Blackford revealed to Gurley that while the "more liberal and benevolent" among men supported her auxiliary's efforts, others looked upon the women "as intruders into a subject we have no business to meddle with." Blackford's frustration motivated her to begin a long and fruitless search for a male agent who could act on behalf of the auxiliary.[16] The daunting task of balancing the need for propriety with the need for publicity was only going to get more difficult.

On August 21, 1831, in Southampton County, Virginia, a slave preacher named Nat Turner led a revolt which sent shockwaves of fear through the white population of the Old Dominion. Moving from farmhouse to farmhouse, Turner and his band of men left some sixty whites dead and others maimed and terrified in their wake. The Virginia militia and federal troops caught up with the rebels and put down the outbreak on August 23. But they could not restore order and peace — already, furious whites had begun indiscriminately massacring dozens of innocent blacks. Martha Jefferson Randolph, Thomas Jefferson's daughter, spoke for many elite Virginians when she advanced the opinion that

Nat Turner's Rebellion was the result of abolitionist agitation — particularly the distribution of David Walker's stirring booklet, *An Appeal to the Colored Citizens of the World* (1829), and William Lloyd Garrison's antislavery newspaper *The Liberator* (founded in 1831). The rebellion confirmed Randolph in her belief that "exportation [of the slaves] must be the consequence of emancipation." She lamented that raising money for colonization was a "very slow business" and that in response to Turner's rebellion, whites were rendering the conditions of the slaves "more insupportable." [17]

Virginia governor John Floyd put a distinct spin on this conspiracy theory in a letter of November 1831. The "most respectable . . . females," he opined, had paved the way for the Southampton incident by teaching blacks to read and write and by distributing Northern religious tracts proclaiming the spiritual equality of blacks and whites. Floyd was himself eager to see the slave system dismantled, but he, like many others, thought that Virginians should do the dismantling themselves, free from Northern interference. [18] The work among slaves that colonization women saw as "benevolent," Floyd viewed as subversive. The notion that women were both unwitting dupes, especially vulnerable to Northern heresies, and effective agents of political propaganda would be echoed in the coming years by proslavery Virginians who were unsure about the allegiance of Virginia women to the slave system. Floyd seems to have grasped what many contemporary historians have overlooked — that the political battle over slavery in Virginia which Turner's rebellion sparked was a battle for the hearts and minds of white women as well as men.

Floyd believed that Virginia had to act immediately, during the legislative session of 1831–32, to prevent another uprising, and the leading politicians and editors of the Commonwealth agreed. As the General Assembly began its deliberations, the colonization movement, which had languished in the late 1820s, experienced a revival. The VCS met in Richmond in January of 1832 for the first time since 1828 and vowed to secure further legislative support for the removal of free blacks. Colonization petitions poured into the General Assembly from around the state, mostly from the Tidewater counties that had large numbers of free black inhabitants. The majority of these memorials called attention to the dangers posed by the presence of free blacks in the Commonwealth. [19]

Three of the petitions intended for the legislature had a special agenda — to provide white women's perspectives on the slavery issue. The "Memorial of the Female Citizens of the County of Fluvanna" was drafted in the winter of 1831. While the petitioners did not explicitly identify themselves as colonizationists, the ACS hailed the petition as an example of colonization sentiment and published it in the *African Repository*. It is likely that the authors of the petition were members of the Fluvanna County colonization auxiliary.

The petitioners began by saying that they had never before "had occasion to appeal to the guardians of their country's rights for redress of any national grievance." But, they continued, "a blight now hangs over our national prospects, and a cloud dims the sunshine of domestic peace throughout our State." They argued that the "increasing evils of slavery" undermined "domestic discipline." Evoking a scenario meant to strike terror in the hearts of the legislators, the petitioners suggested that as men tended to public affairs, white women were left vulnerable to harm from the slaves. In the name of family and country, they concluded, the legislature must take steps to abolish slavery: "We now conjure you by the sacred charities of kindred, by the solemn obligations of justice, by every consideration of domestic affection and patriotic duty, to nerve every faculty of your minds to the investigation of this important subject—and let not the united voices of your mothers, wives, daughters, and kindred, have sounded in your ears in vain!!"[20]

The Fluvanna petition connected domestic peace and national prospects—if slavery were not abolished, the petitioners implied, the result would be not only domestic violence but national decline. In their formulation, gradual emancipation was no longer merely the business of churches and voluntary associations. It was the business, indeed the responsibility, of the state. The petitioners did not restrict themselves to reminding men of their domestic responsibilities, but invoked their "patriotic duty" as well.

The "Female Citizens of Fredericksburg" could "not refrain in uniting with their sisters from Fluvanna." So wrote Mary Blackford in a second female petition to the General Assembly on the subject of gradual emancipation. Blackford, too, reminded the legislature of women's vulnerability—their "defenseless state in the absence of our Lords, in times of apparent peace." Whereas the Fluvanna petitioners had urged the legislature to empathize with white women, Blackford also spoke of the interest of the slaves. "We would not amid a crowd of selfish considerations, forget the interests of an unfortunate people. We would supplicate for them, from your body, such an attention to their welfare and happiness."[21]

Blackford closed her petition with the secular image of female civic duty in times of crisis. Women appealed to the legislature not only as mothers and Christians but as patriots as well: "The example too of the Females of every great people, from the virtuous wife of Coriolanus to our own Revolutionary Matrons teach us that in times of great interest to their Country, women may come forward, meekly and humbly, to do what they can to strengthen the hands, and inspire the hearts of their wise and brave country men." Unlike the Fluvanna petition, Blackford's never made it to the legislature. Blackford admitted that she was too "weak and timid" to circulate the petition. It rests in her family papers, with only one signature, that of her friend Lucy Gray.[22]

The Shenandoah Valley produced a third female petition, one signed by 215 women. The January 19, 1832, memorial of the women of Augusta County begged the legislature "for the adoption of some measure for the speedy extirpation of slavery from the Commonwealth." The petitioners, many of whom were Presbyterians of Scots-Irish origin, lived in a region of the state in which large-scale plantation slavery had never taken root and reservations about slavery ran high. While the Augusta women did not specifically endorse colonization as a remedy for the slavery problem, they included in their number some relatives of male officers of the Augusta colonization auxiliary. The petition was presented to the legislature by delegate John McCue, a Presbyterian minister and avid colonizationist.[23]

The Augusta petitioners began by explicitly locating themselves within the political sphere: "although it be unexampled, in our beloved State, that females should interfere in its political concerns . . . yet we hold our right to do so to be unquestionable, and feel ourselves irresistibly impelled to the exercise of that right by the most potent considerations and the perilous circumstances which surround us."[24] That the women considered their intervention "unexampled" is revealing. For thirty years, women had been active in charitable enterprises, temperance, and colonization; they had even submitted petitions to the legislature on behalf of their charities. The petitioners could have chosen, as many colonizationists had before, to identify reform of the slave system with other moral reform movements. But in the minds of the Augusta women, slavery was no longer simply a domestic issue, a local one, or a religious one. It was now the subject of national controversy, and demanded a political remedy.

The petition went on to elaborate upon the "perilous circumstances." Like that of the Fluvanna women, the Augusta appeal was animated by fear of, not empathy for, slaves—it bade the legislature to remember "the late slaughter of our sisters and little ones, in certain parts of our land," an event which the women suspected was part of a larger plot. The petitioners evoked the specter of their destruction at the hands of the "bloody monster" that lived at their "own hearths." They attested that they would rather do without slave labor than live with those hardships "we now endure in providing for and ruling the faithless beings who are subjected to us." Favorable reports, they noted, came back to them from friends who had fled the South and resettled in free states.[25]

Eventually the petitioners returned to the question of their "right" to intervene in politics. In a remarkable passage, they laid out their interpretation of the relation between the private and public spheres:

> We are no political economists; but our domestic employments, our engagements, in rearing up the children of our husbands & brothers, our intimate concern with the intercourse & prosperity of society; we presume, cannot but inform us of the great & elementary principles of that important science. Indeed it is impossible that that science can have any other basis than the principles that are constantly developing themselves to us in our domestic relations. What is a nation but a family upon a large scale?[26]

Rather than advancing the notion that woman's sphere operated according to rules and values all its own, the women of Augusta portrayed the domestic sphere as a microcosm of the public one. Like the Fluvanna and Fredericksburg petitions, the Augusta memorial reminded men of their patriotic duty. "We implore you," the petitioners concluded, ". . . by our female virtues, by the patriotism which animates and grows in our bosoms . . . not to let the power with which you are invested lie dormant. . . . This we pray and in duty bound will ever pray." Only the extinction of slavery would preserve the peace and ensure the prosperity of future generations.[27]

Taken together, the three petitions shed light on how the events of August 1831 had transformed the public discourse over slavery. While Blackford and her counterparts in Fluvanna and Augusta came at the slavery issue from different angles—Blackford's petition evinces sympathy for the plight of slaves while the other two petitions bespeak antipathy—the three petitions used similar language to justify political intervention by women. One of the effects of Nat Turner's Rebellion, the petitioners implied, was to politicize domestic life. The Fluvanna and Augusta women challenged the validity of the domestic metaphor for slavery—that slaves were obedient members of the patriarchal household—and argued instead that blacks and whites lived in a state of protracted domestic warfare. Without help from the legislature, the memorials suggested, women simply could not fulfill their mandate of preserving domestic harmony. Blackford, too, evoked martial imagery in her elaboration of female duty. But her memorial, alone among the three, recognized that slaves were the true victims of domestic warfare between blacks and whites.

The Augusta and Fluvanna petitions, like other antislavery petitions, were taken into consideration by the special legislative committee charged with recommending a course of action to the General Assembly. These antislavery memorials received a good deal of publicity. John McCue presented the Augusta memorial to his colleagues along with a stirring antislavery speech, which was reprinted in the *Richmond Enquirer*. He told the select committee that "if an opportunity had been afforded, [the petition] would have been much more numerously subscribed by the ladies of the county." The Augusta petition also drew the notice of a proslavery correspondent to the *Enquirer*, with the pen name "Appomattox" (Richmond lawyer Benjamin Watkins Leigh), who calculated that some 2,000 people had signed memorials asking the legislature to take up the slavery issue. According to Leigh, though the petitioners ran far ahead of public opinion, they exercised a significant influence on politicians and editors alike.[28]

Women were present not only by proxy but in person at the famous debates in the House of Delegates. Louisa Cocke, for example, went to the Capitol to hear "Mr. Brown of Petersburg on the all engrossing question of emancipation which is now agitating the whole country." After weeks of deliberation, the select committee on slavery decided that it was inexpedient for the legislature to take any measures to dismantle the slave system. Alison Goodyear Freehling has convincingly argued that the 1831–32 slavery debate, rather than representing the triumph of proslavery forces in Virginia, was rather another chapter in the "perennial political quest for a 'middle ground' between slaveholding and non-slaveholding interests." While the legislature rejected immediate emancipation, a procolonization majority, including many conservatives, endorsed gradual emancipation. The House of Delegates resolved that state funds should be used to support the voluntary emigration of free blacks and manumitted slaves. The Senate, dominated by proslavery planters, then voted to postpone consideration of the "colonization bill" until a later date.[29]

Freehling's contention that the 1832 legislative session did not put an end to meaningful debate over slavery in Virginia is borne out by the testimony of women on both the pro- and antislavery sides. Mary Eliza Rives, a proslavery plantation mistress, agreed with many editors and politicians that by discussing slavery in public, the General Assembly had opened a Pandora's box. She believed that open debate on slavery would not preserve the public peace but undermine it. In April of 1832, she sent to her sister-in-law Judith a letter accusing advocates of gradual emancipation of "agitating a question which will be like a lighted faggot in the state, and which perhaps will not be extinguished in twenty years, and then not without bloodshed."[30]

Rather than being discouraged by the legislature's pronouncements, colonization women redoubled their efforts to promote the cause. In July of 1832, sixty women in Albemarle County formed a female auxiliary society to the ACS. Its secretary, Susan Terrell, stated her belief that the society would soon have "almost every lady in the county" and boasted that its efforts had won the approval of "some of our best men." The Albemarle auxiliary raised $500 in 1832; female societies in Powhatan, Louisa, Warrenton, and Richmond likewise made healthy remittances to the ACS that year.[31]

Blackford's Fredericksburg society continued to be the best-publicized female auxiliary in the state. In order to dispel the "mists of ignorance and prejudice" surrounding the society, Blackford penned the first annual "Report of the Board of Managers of the Fredericksburg and Falmouth Female Auxiliary Colonization Society" and had it published as a broadside. The report, which was also published in the Methodist *Christian Sentinel*, urged Blackford's sisters throughout the state to come forward and aid in the work of "this most important charity." Blackford conceded that some prejudices still existed against women who were active in charities, particularly in colonization, which "divides public sentiment, and is, in some respects, a political question." But she had this to say to opponents of female activism:

> . . . we would ask whether, because the scheme of Colonization involves ultimate political interests, our sex is to be forever precluded from any agency in its promotion? . . . The same course of reasoning would go to exclude female agency from the promotion of the Sunday School, the Missionary, or the Bible cause — for who will pretend to say that each of these schemes of amelioration is not pregnant with the highest consequences to the peace and prosperity of the State[?] [32]

Blackford turned the popular argument that colonization was like other benevolent enterprises, and therefore not political, on its head. Since religious benevolent societies, like the colonization society, involved "ultimate political interests," she argued, it was wrong to exclude women from either sort of enterprise.

While she worked in public to promote her auxiliary, principally by distributing literature to her neighbors, Blackford undertook, in the fall of 1832, a new project: a private journal entitled "Notes Illustrative of the Wrongs of Slavery." Her preface states that the "Notes" constitute a challenge to those who maintain "that Slavery is in accordance with the will of God." The entries that follow the preface are anecdotes about the horrors of slavery — not of "isolated instances of wrong and oppression but daily occurrences so common as scarcely to excite remark." What render Blackford's observations into an analytical indictment of the system are the themes that tie them together: the notion that the necessary setting for the exercise of Christian virtue is a republic in which everyone's fundamental rights are protected by law; that slavery "hardens the heart" to human suffering; and that blacks have the same innate capacity for "tender feelings" as whites.[33]

On a clear October evening, as she walked in shame past a jail kept by slave traders "to confine men whose only crime is that they wish to return to their families," Blackford thought to herself, "Thank God! . . . that I live in a land where no white man at least can be unjustly thrown into confinement until just cause can be shown why. . . . And may I live to see the time when the poor down trodden negro too shall enjoy this great privilege!" By denying blacks the protection of the law, Blackford observed, the institution of slavery undermined the exercise of virtue by whites and blacks alike. She inveighed against the measures which prohibited blacks from holding religious assemblies or learning to read and write. To illustrate the ill effects of such laws, she described a horrible scene in which a group of slaves who attended a Baptist meeting in Hanover County were "all whipped, old and young, Men & women," by an armed patrol. Nor did she shy away from the subject of sexual abuse. Black women, she understood, were the special victims of a system in which "the conjugal tie can be broken at the will of the Master at any time." Telling the story of a "wretched Mother" who had been impregnated and then abandoned, destitute, by a slave trader, Blackford noted that black women often became "the prey of the brutal lust of their oppressors."[34]

"Mercy is not in man when interest and power unite in drawing him from it," Blackford concluded from observing the intractable racism of her neighbors. She recounts an incident in 1832 in which she interceded on behalf of a black woman, whose son, about to be sold south by a slave trader, was incarcerated in the trader's cellar. The mother begged her son's guard to let her see the boy one last time. When she was refused, Blackford wrote, the mother "came over the street to our house. . . . [I] asked her if she thought my intercession would do any good. She answered, perhaps it might. So I put on my bonnet and went over with her, she waiting at the gate while I went to the door." Getting nowhere with the guard, Blackford asked to see the wife of the trader, "hoping from one of my own sex to find mercy that I looked for in vain from a man." The trader's wife denied any responsibility in the matter. Blackford tried again to influence the guard: "I fixed my eyes steadily upon the hard hearted being before me and . . . warned him that such cruelty could not long go unpunished and reminded him of the affair at Southampton [Nat Turner's Rebellion] which had just occurred." Blackford's efforts achieved nothing; some weeks later, she saw the young prisoner led off in chains.[35]

While Blackford believed that the system of slavery had also produced a "hardening effect" on the minds of its black victims, she marveled that "it had not produced the effect in a greater degree," and devoted the bulk of her journal to examples of blacks who rose above the moral level of their oppressors. The story of a slave woman whose husband escaped from the clutches of a slave trader and crossed 500 miles on foot to return to his wife Blackford saw as "one of the many proofs that such feelings exist among the negroes, notwithstanding the course of treatment pursued by the whites toward them in continually slighting their marriage ties." Perhaps the most wrenching section of the "Notes" is the story of Betsy, a slave whose "simple narrative" Blackford transcribed. Betsy recalled being kept in a slave trader's jail in which old and young were routinely cobbed—beaten with a board with holes in it. After hearing the cries of a young girl undergoing this torture, she lamented to Blackford, "I sometimes think the world will not stand much longer, there is so much wickedness in it." Her own children were soon sold away from her. In an editorial postscript to the narrative, Blackford averred that this heartbroken woman had transcended bitterness and served as a beloved mammy to the young daughter of her new master.[36]

Blackford's journal is both a unique document, without counterpart in Southern antislavery literature, and an embodiment of the limitations of and contradictions in the colonization movement. With the exception of the abolitionist publications of South Carolina's exiled Grimké sisters, Blackford's journal is the most thoroughgoing attack on slavery penned by a white Southern woman in the antebellum era. First and foremost a plea for empathy, Blackford's journal implores the reader to "Think what it is to be a Slave!!!," to conjure the "nameless horrors" of being deprived of one's rights as a human being. It shares a number of themes—the prevalence of sexual exploitation, the breakup of families, the assault on marriage ties, the suffering of mothers and children—with slave narratives produced by women. The narrative of Bethany Veney, who had been a slave in Virginia, poignantly put into words a sentiment that Blackford struggled to express: "hearts that love are much the same in bond or free, in white or black." [37]

But for all the merits of her analysis, there were distinct limits to Blackford's powers of empathy. Like other colonizationists, she did not reckon among blacks' rights the right to live in freedom in their native country, nor did she imagine that blacks and whites could coexist as equals. Having been kept in "profound ignorance" by whites, she argued, blacks were "not prepared" for immediate emancipation and full participation in the American republic. Only in Liberia would they be safe from prejudice and united in communities of common interest. There, she noted in a letter to Ralph Gurley, "the delightful consciousness of freedom and equal rights may like a sculptor's tools, bring forth hidden qualities" in the race. Moreover, Blackford, unlike white and black abolitionists, seemed reluctant to acknowledge white women's full complicity in the brutal enforcement of the slave system. "Slaveholding ladies," ex-slave Austin Stewart of Prince William County wrote in his memoirs, not only looked on the punishment of bondspeople "with approbation" but often used "the lash and cowhide themselves, on the backs of their own slaves, and that too on those of their own sex!" Blackford must surely have known of such instances, yet she reserved her harshest criticisms for white men, slave traders in particular. Finally, like so many other Southern colonizationists, who saw fit to emancipate some — but not all — of their slaves, Blackford herself relied on the labor of slaves. Beginning with the birth of her first child in 1826, Blackford suffered physical disabilities that worsened with each of the six pregnancies that followed. Her husband, William, believing that the chronically infirm Mary needed help tending to the children, bought a slave girl named Peggy in 1846 to serve as "mammy." In spite of Mary's "abhorrence of slavery," the Blackfords kept Peggy in bondage throughout the antebellum period; the family assumed, conveniently, that the affection they held for "Ma'm Peggy" was mutual. [38]

Isolated in an increasingly hostile proslavery environment, Blackford remained steadfast in the belief that the American Colonization Society, while it claimed only to "send free people of color by *their own consent* to Liberia," was "gradually preparing a Country for the whole unfortunate race when Slavery shall be abolished." Unfortunately for her and other like-minded colonizationists, the doctrine of gradual emancipation came under withering attack in the early 1830s. In the minds of abolitionists, the antislavery credentials of Southern slaveholders such as Blackford were highly suspect. William Lloyd Garrison's "Thoughts on African Colonization" (1832) and his journal *The Libera-*

tor rejected the notion that colonization was "benevolent," and argued instead that the ACS was a slaveholders' tool, meant to undermine support for immediate emancipation. Moreover, Garrison noted that free blacks had vehemently rejected the colonization movement. He produced as evidence nineteen proclamations by free blacks in Northern cities, expressing opposition to the ACS.[39]

Indeed, as historian Marie Tyler-McGraw has demonstrated, the changing composition of the Liberian emigrant pool signaled free blacks' growing unwillingness to migrate: while the majority of emigrants in the 1820s were free black families, by the early 1830s the majority were manumitted slaves from large estates. Free blacks had come to believe that "colonization was less an opportunity presented to them than a judgment placed upon them." Most damaging to the cause of emigration in Virginia, Tyler-McGraw argues, were the grim reports of economic hardship, appalling death rates, and internecine warfare that black emigrants, such as Richmonders Edward and Helen Lewis, brought back from Liberia. Well aware that the Virginia Colonization Society was in the hands of proslavery forces, free blacks, in the wake of the Virginia legislature's 1832 rejection of gradual emancipation, rejected colonization in turn.[40]

By the mid-1830s, white women were playing a prominent role in the abolitionist critique of colonization. In 1836, the Grimké sisters launched a speaking tour of antislavery societies in New England and New York, giving women unprecedented visibility in the abolition movement. A national convention of antislavery women met in New York in 1837, initiating a petition drive to convince Congress of the need for immediate abolition. The Southern press took notice of these activities, branding them as subversive and unfeminine. Angelina Grimké specifically targeted Southern women in her 1836 *Appeal to the Christian Women of the South*. She argued that Christian women should act as "instruments of reform" by advancing the antislavery cause as a "matter of *morals* and *religion*, not of expediency or politics." To those, like Blackford, who believed that immediate emancipation without colonization would leave blacks vulnerable to prejudice and lacking in resources, Grimké replied that "duty is ours and events are God's." To those who feared that such bold actions would alienate them from their communities, Grimké responded that women must find the moral courage to endure persecution. In later works, Grimké would call the ACS an "EXPATRIATION Society" that hid the "monster of prejudice" behind the "mantle of benevolence."[41]

Even as abolitionists attacked colonization and urged Southern women to abandon it, Thomas Dew, a Virginia professor, dealt colonization a crippling blow from the other end of the political spectrum. Dew's 1832 essay, *Review of the Debate in the Virginia Legislature of 1831 and 1832*, portrayed colonization as an abolitionist plot, and a "totally impracticable" one at that. Since Liberia was a failure, Dew averred, manumitted blacks would stay in Virginia, posing a threat not only to slaveholders but to nonslaveholding whites as well. Dew devoted a section of his essay to the "influence of Slavery on the female sex." He constructed what would become a popular argument among proslavery theorists — that white women benefited from the institution of slavery, for the labor of the slave was a substitute for that of the woman. Dew not only addressed slavery's impact on white women but also their attitudes toward slavery. Southern women, Dew lamented, did not seem to recognize that slavery was responsible for their "elevation" in society. Instead, filled with "benevolence and philanthropy" and "fine feelings unchecked by considerations of interest or calculations of remote consequences," women were inclined "to embrace with eagerness even the wildest and most destructive schemes of emancipation." Woman's influence was powerful and would be exercised either for the "weal or woe" of Southern society. Southern men, Dew cautioned, should take an interest in the moral and intellectual development of "*her* in whose career we feel so deep an interest." [42]

Colonizationists, one historian has noted, were slow to join the battle against their foes. In late 1832, at Ralph Gurley's request, Jesse Burton Harrison of Lynchburg penned a response to Thomas Dew, denying that there was any connection between colonization and abolition. All over Virginia, colonizationists repudiated abolition. At its 1833 annual meeting, for example, the secretary of the Lynchburg Colonization Society proclaimed that like Bible, missionary, and education societies, the ACS was benevolent, intent on "snatching from the depths of the most cheerless and hopeless poverty a class of beings, who . . . are proverbially heedless of the future." An 1833 editorial in the *Christian Sentinel* claimed that Christians should not "engage in the political controversies which may arise out of the subject of slavery as existing in our country." But to support colonization was acceptable, because "it meddles with no State policy . . . but receives all free colored persons who may offer themselves voluntarily to emigrate to Africa." Christians, the editor suggested, should resist the attempts of "designing and interested individuals" to make colonization a "political question." [43]

Unfortunately for those who sought to cloak colonization in the mantle of benevolence, the "designing individuals" who saw colonization as a "political question" included not only the movement's critics but also some of its most prominent supporters. By the mid-1830s, Northern colonization societies, such as those in New York and Philadelphia, were trying to increase public support for the cause by arguing that colonization principles did indeed embrace emancipation. Southern state societies, such as the VCS, countered with bitterly sectional rhetoric, in which colonization became a weapon in the South's battle against Northern aggression. At the seventh annual meeting of the VCS, in 1838, Henry Wise denounced the abolitionists for trying to "demolish all social relations." No longer was there room in the VCS for those who hoped colonization was a wedge to general emancipation—while abolitionists favored "Philanthropy to the SLAVE!," colonizationists favored "Friendship to the SLAVEHOLDER." [44]

On the subject of white women's part in the slavery controversy, male colonizationists in the South sent out mixed messages. The notion that women were easy prey for the abolitionists had its share of advocates. James Garland of Virginia, for example, declared at an ACS meeting in 1837 that Garrison and his cronies waged their warfare on the South "aided by the misguided support of *priest-ridden* women and children." In his speech at the state society's 1838 annual meeting, VCS president John Tyler fumed that the abolitionists "seek to enlist woman—she who was placed upon the earth, as the rainbow in the heavens, as a sign that the tempest of the passions should subside. Woman is made an instrument to expel us from the paradise of union in which we dwell." [45]

What part did Virginia's white women take in the debate over colonization and abolition? Unwilling to disavow the goal of philanthropy toward the slave or to embrace immediate emancipation, Virginia's staunchest female colonizationists adopted a new tack in the mid-1830s, focusing their energy on the promotion of female education in Liberia. Such a strategy had many merits—it allowed Virginia women to build bridges to their counterparts in other states and to women in Liberia, while at the same time distancing them from the radical tactics of female abolitionists.

By 1834, Blackford had become thoroughly disillusioned with the "unaccountable apathy ... benumbing the public mind." The cause was languishing, she wrote Gurley, for want of "someone to speak to the people and interest them," adding, "Our sex forbids this." That Blackford ruled out public speaking is not surprising. It was literally unheard of for Southern women to deliver speeches on the subject of slavery. None of the leaders of the VCS or ACS ever condoned public speaking by women; judging by the evidence, colonization women never addressed "mixed" public assemblies of men and women. Unable to change the minds of her neighbors, Blackford announced in the *African Repository* in 1834 that her auxiliary was reconstituting itself as a female African education society; "it would seem to us that it is peculiarly befitting our sex to be thus engaged," she noted. After searching fruitlessly for an appropriate outlet for its funds, Blackford's group began in 1837 to support a girls' academy run by Presbyterian missionaries in the Maryland colony, Cape Palmas. In its third annual report, the Ladies' Society of Fredericksburg and Falmouth, for the Promotion of Female Education in Africa, reemphasized the missionary aspect of colonization: "We would make it our main object to promote the knowledge of God."[46]

The Richmond and Manchester female auxiliary adopted a similar strategy. In order to reassure the public of the benevolence of their aims, the Richmond women changed the name of their auxiliary in 1834 to the Ladies Society for Promoting Female Education in the Colony of Liberia. The society eventually hired an African American teacher, Mrs. Cyples, and opened a school for orphan girls in Monrovia, Liberia (it had thirty-two pupils in 1836). The actions of the Fredericksburg and Richmond auxiliaries reflect a national trend. Margaret Mercer, who served as a teacher at girls' academies in Essex County and then in Cedar Park, Maryland, devoted the proceeds of her Cedar Park Liberian Society to promoting the founding of a high school in Liberia. Female education societies were formed in such places as Louisville, Kentucky, New York City, and Philadelphia; the Richmond and Philadelphia enterprises cooperated closely. Such efforts won the hearty approbation of male colonizationists, who saw in them a refutation of the abolitionist charge that colonizationists cared nothing for the fate of those who emigrated.[47]

As promising as it may have seemed, however, female colonizationists' change of tack did not ultimately revive their beleaguered movement. The schools sponsored by women proved prohibitively expensive to maintain. "The Society is now in great want of funds," the Richmond society's 1837 annual report declared. "Without them our school must suffer, and our benevolent operations must remain stationary or be curtailed." Apparently these appeals fell on deaf ears—the auxiliary's 1838 annual report declared that its orphan school was "languishing." Liberian women increasingly addressed the needs of dispossessed females by forming their own benevolent associations, such as the Ladies Benevolent Society of Monrovia; it included among its leaders Mrs. Colin Teague, one of Richmond's first emigrants. While it may well have gratified white women to see, as the *African Repository*'s editor put it, that "the same spirit of benevolence which animates them is manifested by their colored sisters on the other side of the Atlantic," the grinding poverty of Liberia proved a formidable obstacle to women's collective exertions. By 1850, the *African Repository* was declaring that despite women's efforts, "the facilities for a thorough education are not afforded to the youth of Liberia."[48]

Nor ultimately could Virginia's colonization women reverse the political trends in their home state. All over the Commonwealth, the fate of gradual decline befell women's auxiliaries in the 1830s. The Albemarle auxiliary, described in the *African Repository* in 1833 as a "flourishing institution," was, by 1836, in trouble. Susan Terrell, its secretary, attributed the decline in receipts to Northern agitation: "Many of [the auxiliary's] members since the great Abolition stir of the North have become apparently indifferent while a portion are more zealous in the cause than ever." In the heart of the Shenandoah Valley, too, colonization sentiment among women was evaporating. The VCS mounted an unsuccessful petition drive for legislative aid in 1837. Only thirty-five women signed a colonization petition of February 10, 1837, from the citizens of Rockingham and Augusta Counties—an alarmingly small number compared to the 215 women who had signed the 1832 antislavery petition from Augusta.[49]

In what appears to have been a last-ditch effort to improve the prospects of the cause, the leading female colonizationists of the Richmond area formed the Female Colonization Society of Virginia (FCS) in 1840. The society was designed to replace the VCS as the hub of female auxiliary activity and to serve as a model for other such organizations: "This we believe to be the first State Society formed by the Ladies, and we hope that not only will the Ladies of every city, town and village in Virginia, form Societies auxiliary to the State Society, but that in every State of the Union, the ladies will go and do likewise." The female society would be the medium through which auxiliary donations were forwarded to the ACS. Its eight female officers came from Richmond, Fluvanna, Goochland, Chesterfield, and Rappahanock and represented each of the Protestant denominations in Richmond and Manchester. As the Richmond female auxiliary had over a decade earlier, the new female society described colonization as a missionary scheme. And it passed a resolution requesting that the editors of religious newspapers publish its constitution and circular.[50]

In 1845, Catharine Ellis willed her estate to the Female Society, but the bequest was void, since the society had not been incorporated. After 1845, the society received no further mention in ACS publications.

Whether the FCS disbanded or continued to carry out its mission in obscurity is unclear. Over the course of the 1840s, references to Southern colonization auxiliaries, male and female, dwindled in the religious newspapers which had helped to promote colonization in its heyday. The declining visibility of Southern colonizationists in the press reflects the Southern evangelical retreat from politics in the wake of the denominational schisms in the Presbyterian, Methodist, and Baptist Churches. Despite the fact that the ACS continued to have some powerful allies among Virginia's clergymen, such as Presbyterian minister William Henry Ruffner, donations from churches, especially Methodist and Baptist ones, slowed to a trickle in the 1840s.[51]

A small band of stalwart female supporters of the cause kept up a stream of individual remittances, but on the whole, female donations fell off steadily in the late 1840s. Moreover, group remittances by Virginia women became rare; colonization seems to have provided women with fewer opportunities for autonomous organization than it had in previous decades. No longer did the *African Repository* publicize the work of the "tenth legion" of female auxiliaries. Women's colonization organizations in Rockbridge, Albemarle, Fredericksburg, Warrenton, and elsewhere disappear from the historical record.[52]

By 1850, the American Colonization Society was firmly under the control of a Northern-dominated board of directors, while the Virginia Colonization Society, by contrast, was an unabashedly proslavery organization. One of many signs that the gulf between antislavery and proslavery colonizationists was growing ever wider is an 1852 petition to the legislature, from an anonymous "Virginian." "From what the writer has seen and known personally," the petitioner stated, "he honestly believes that the female free negroes keep their husbands and families from emigrating to Liberia. For while we know of many men among them ready and willing to go, they are held back by a stubborn refusal of their wives to accompany them." In a move that would have appalled the likes of Blackford, the petitioner proposed the passage of a law that would sell free black women "into perpetual slavery upon condition they do not emigrate to the land of their forefathers." Whether his observation that women were less willing to emigrate than men has any basis in reality is unclear. It is clear, however, that white antipathy to free blacks rose steadily as the free black population grew; Virginia lawmakers seriously debated measures for the outright expulsion of free blacks in the 1850s.[53]

Many women evidently approved of the rhetoric of the VCS — dozens contributed money to the state society in the 1840s and 1850s. Interestingly, however, none of the women who have left a historical trail in the form of letters, diaries, memoirs, and the like subscribed to the view that the sole purpose of colonization was to deport free blacks. On the contrary, women's correspondence with ACS officials and with emigrants evinces their belief in the cause of gradual emancipation and their concern for the fate of manumitted slaves. It may be that antislavery colonizationists went "underground": they continued to contribute to the ACS as individuals, but they no longer used auxiliaries as vehicles for their work, and they no longer sought publicity for collective efforts.[54]

The ranks of gradualists included Mary Custis Lee, wife of Robert E. Lee. A longstanding supporter of the ACS, Lee corresponded in the 1850s with her ex-slaves, William and Rosabella Burke, who had settled in Monrovia. The Burkes provided Lee with details of their daily lives and assessments of Liberia's prospects, and she in turn gave them the news of their friends and relatives in Arlington; Ralph Gurley frequently served as a go-between for the two families. Elizabeth Van Lew of Richmond, who, after her father's death in 1843, prevailed upon her mother to emancipate the family's nine slaves, reached out to ACS secretary William McLain for advice on how to send supplies to Liberia. Mary Brown of Elm Grove sent ten dollars to McLain with her "sincere thanks for your long continued services in behalf of our poor collered [sic] brother."[55]

Helen Grinnan, Mary Blackford's coworker and confidante in the Fredericksburg auxiliary, looked to ACS officials to confirm her belief in the righteousness of colonization. After reading the 1846 letter of Virginia emigrant Willis Helmn (sic), a manumitted slave who complained that starvation and disease were the main features of life in Liberia, Grinnan worriedly contacted William McLain for clarification; McLain explained that Helmn was a malcontent and reassured Grinnan that most of the emigrants were satisfied with conditions in the colony. Despite troublesome developments in Africa and at home, Grinnan remained committed to the cause of gradual emancipation, writing Blackford in 1849 that if the abolitionists would only "hold their peace . . . we should in time, do our duty" and emancipate the slaves.[56]

Another diehard gradual emancipationist was Margaret Mercer. The daughter of Governor John Francis Mercer of Maryland and cousin of Virginia colonizationist Charles Fenton Mercer, Mercer had in 1829 freed sixteen of her slaves and sent them to Liberia. An educator by profession, Mercer used her lectern as a bully pulpit for colonization. In 1836 she purchased an estate, Belmont, from fellow colonizationist Ludwell Lee and relocated from Maryland to Virginia. She ran the estate using only free black labor or neighboring slaves whom she remunerated for their work. She also opened a new school in which she continued her colonization work; the students made handicrafts to raise funds for Liberia. Hard economic times and growing public suspicion of reformers made Mercer's work difficult. But she remained adamant in her belief that colonization was "the only possible means of reconciling the South to the subject of emancipation."[57]

The most detailed accounts of the changing fortunes of the colonization movement come from the pens of Anne Rice and Mary Blackford. In 1848 Rice sent her oldest slave, Anderson, and his family to Liberia, and in 1851 she sent four additional servants there. Dire news of sickness and war in Liberia led her to wonder, in 1856, whether she had done the right thing in sending them. Rice's letters to ACS officials in the 1850s bespeak her growing isolation. In an 1857 letter to McLain, she offered a critique of the radicals on either side of the slavery issue—"I think both sides go too far & are on extremes and such as I know will not receive any information but what suits their own views." The next year she reported that more and more Virginians were asserting that slavery was a positive good. By 1859, Rice was so sensitive about her antislavery views that she apologized even to her friend and ally Ralph Gurley. After declaring that "our good, & wise, & pious now seem to set down content, with consciences quite relieved that [slavery] is the very best state for the coloured race," she excused herself for writing so indiscreetly on the subject.[58]

As for Blackford, in the 1840s she concentrated on a very personal matter—the safe emigration of her slave Abram. In 1844, she convinced her husband, William, to fulfill a longstanding promise that he would free Abram as soon as it became financially feasible. William thought that Abram would be better off as his slave than in Liberia, but Mary believed it possible to provide Abram with all the requisite resources for success in the colony; at her behest, Abram spent 1843 with Blackford's brother Lucius, honing his skills as a farmer and handyman. On the eve of Abram's departure, Blackford pumped Gurley and ACS treasurer William McLain for information about the colony, asking, "Will you also tell me what he had best be provided with? How long he will receive support from the Society after he arrives? Will he be well attended to while he is sick? How much land will be given him?"[59]

Blackford felt amply rewarded for her efforts on Abram's behalf when she received a letter from him on September 9, 1844, from Monrovia, reporting that all was well. She kept up a warm correspondence with Abram and with her mother's former slaves, James Cephas Minor and

Mary Ann Minor, during the 1840s and 1850s. Abram's letters bespeak his pride in his newfound freedom and his concern for those in Virginia. In letters to Mary Blackford and to Susan Wheeler, a black friend in Fredericksburg, Abram reported that the whites he met in Monrovia were polite, and respectfully referred to him as "Mr. Blackford." "It is much Bether than to be in the state [where the practice is] for them to call you Boy," he wrote to his former owner. In an 1846 letter, he conveyed his respects to the Blackford family and asked Mary to write his mother and tell her he was well. Historian Randall Miller, in analyzing the correspondence of the Cocke family and its manumitted slaves, the Skipwiths, has observed that since former slaves were still dependent on the philanthropy of their masters when provisions in Liberia proved scarce, "we can never know how much, if at all, the emigres lifted their masks" to express their true feelings. He finds nonetheless that the Cocke/Skipwith correspondence "implies something of trust and affection"; the same can be said of Mary Blackford's exchanges with Abram.[60]

While Abram's was a success story, Liberia's reputation among prospective emigrants continued to worsen in the 1840s. After Abram's emigration, Blackford found herself lacking in willing recipients of her charity. She wrote to McLain in 1845 that there was "no chance of persuading any of the free people here to emigrate to Liberia, as their partialities lean toward Ohio and other Northern States." When she and her family left Fredericksburg for Lynchburg in 1852, Blackford's career as a public advocate for the ACS came to an end.[61]

Separated from her female auxiliary in Fredericksburg, Blackford scaled down her activities, occasionally sending in small remittances of no more than a few dollars. As sectional tensions mounted, she felt increasingly alienated, not only from her community but also from her husband and sons. William Blackford, who had always emphasized the degradation rather than the possible redemption of the free black population, became more sectional in his outlook, and wooed his sons to his way of thinking. Blackford lamented this state of affairs in a letter to her mother in 1853: "The object nearest to my heart is to do these boys good, but as they grow older my influence weakens, [as] they think my notions womanly." To Blackford's notion that "it is patriotic for the North and South to go among each other and cultivate kindly feelings," her husband and sons counterposed that Southerners should be free to solve their own problems without instruction or interference from the North.[62]

In August of 1856 Blackford sent a series of despairing missives to longtime friends McLain and Gurley. One letter enclosed a five-dollar contribution. "How I wish it was five hundred," she wrote, "for never did the cause seem so important as now, for it would afford a mighty remedy for the greatest evil that hangs over our country, if its benevolent and patriotic objects could be carried out." A few weeks later, Blackford lamented the growth of proslavery sectionalism in Virginia: "I cannot express what I feel at the state of things in our country. It has really become a reproach to advocate human liberty, and I hear statements so high handed and oppressive, that I can hardly believe I live in a free government. . . . Oh that something could be done to arouse the people of Virginia, but the good old patriots that would have done it, have passed away, and their opinions on the subject are laughed at." In Blackford's view, Virginia was in a state of moral decline. To her, the remedy for sectional tensions lay in the values and virtues of her parents' generation, which had been committed to the idea of gradual emancipation. Blackford had once seen herself as a standard-bearer not only of Christianity but of the Revolutionary legacy. On the eve of secession, she felt like a relic of a world that had passed away. The failure of the Union she interpreted as the failure of women like herself to transmit the legacy of the founders to the next generation.[63]

It is tempting to relegate the likes of Mary Blackford to the file marked "loser's history." Women proved, ultimately, to be ineffectual agents for the colonization cause. Their numbers dropped off as controversy over colonization heated up, and they could not insulate the movement from crippling attacks from either end of the political spectrum. To be sure, even the most sympathetic of female colonizationists bear up poorly in a comparison with abolitionists.

But the fact that women like Blackford failed in their self-appointed task of proving the righteousness and viability of colonization is no reason to write them off. For, together with their male allies, colonization women offered up an influential argument about women's civic duty, one which resonates to the present day in the scholarly debate over Southern women's "covert abolitionism." In essence, colonizationists made the case that Southern women had a special moral perspective on slavery. Because of their role as domestic managers, women had a unique awareness of the threat slavery posed to the maintenance of orderly homes and communities. Because of their piety and sensitivity, women had a particular sympathy for the plight of slaves. Because of their role as mothers and teachers, women had the special ability to mold the opinions of the next generation on the issue of slavery. Because of their disinterestedness — their selfless concern for the common good—and moral integrity, they had a unique ability to inspire those around them to good deeds.

This vision of women received its most sustained articulation in biographies of Ann R. Page and Margaret Mercer, published in the North in 1848 and 1856 respectively. Page's biographer, Charles Andrews (an ACS agent for Virginia), presented his subject as the very personification of the spirit of charity, of the virtues of "self-denial" and "disinterestedness." Andrews believed that Page had had a great impact on antislavery sentiment in Virginia. "In an extensive tour through the state in the year 1836," Andrews heard the "remark from many persons, that they had never felt any particular interest in the condition of the slaves, or had their consciences awakened respecting them, until they heard of the efforts of Mrs. Page." Andrews also quoted Ralph Gurley's biography of ACS missionary Jehudi Ashmun, which featured a stirring tribute to the influence of Virginia women: "In a future world, the fact may stand revealed, that from the sacred retirement of a few devout ladies in Virginia, who at the Savior's feet had learned better lessons than this world's philosophy can teach, emanated a zeal and charity in behalf of the afflicted Africans, which has widely spread, and inspired ministers and statesmen with an almost divine eloquence in their cause." [64] Gurley held that women, by virtue of their piety—their attention to God's word rather than to "this world's philosophy"—could lead men by example to patriotic deeds.

Equally laudatory of women was Caspar Morris's biography of Mercer. Like Page, Mercer was commended for her "disinterestedness" and "self-denial." She was not only a great Christian but a "patriot woman, [who] lived and suffered and virtually bled and died in the service of her country." Furthermore, Morris saw Mercer's career as a rebuke to those who claimed that the real aim of the colonization movement was to "rivet more closely the bonds of the slave." Mercer was a "shining testimony of the fact that the society was countenanced in its origin and supported to the present hour by persons who were ready at any cost . . . to promote the good of those in whom they recognized the traits of common brotherhood." In short, Gurley, Morris, Andrews, and the scores of other men who lauded women's contributions to colonization made the case that women were effective organizers, who brought needed converts and funds into the organization, and moral exemplars, who proved by their very association with colonization that it was a benevolent scheme. [65]

By the mid-1850s, only a small minority of Virginians would have endorsed Andrews's and Morris's view of colonization. But ironically, rather than rejecting the notion that women had a special moral perspective on slavery, many defenders of slavery accepted it. Some of Virginia's most zealous advocates of Southern rights feared that antislavery feeling ran high among the ranks of Virginia women. Southern nationalists such as Edmund Ruffin and Roger Pryor routinely lambasted colonization as a Northern-inspired attempt to undermine the Southern social order. An 1859 letter from Ruffin to the *South* (Richmond), a states'-rights paper, portrayed women as especially vulnerable to antislavery heresy: "The teachings and arguments of the agents & mouthpieces of the [Colonization] Society, and their efforts have mainly operated on morbidly tender consciences and weak minds of benevolent men, and women more especially, to induce them to emancipate their slaves." Pryor, editor of the *South*, agreed that Southern security depended on the inculcation of a *"proper sentiment"* on the slavery question among women. "If, especially, the mothers of the Southern country were all sound on the question," he suggested, "there would be less occasion for combined effort on the part of our citizens to put down the insolent schemes" of the abolitionists.[66]

Indeed, in the 1850s a chorus of voices argued that women must be taught the "proper" views on slavery and educate their children in turn. In the pages of the *South*, a proslavery colonizationist claimed that Southern patriots needed to "educat[e] the public mind until every man and woman shall come to know and feel that slavery is not only right in itself, but that for most of the negroes held in slavery, manumission would be a curse and a cruelty." The proprietors of the Southern Female Institute in Fredericksburg urged the General Assembly to support their female academy in order to promote "Southern" values among women. Southern daughters, at a time in their development when "their feelings are stronger than their reason," were too often exposed to Northern teachers who "infected [them] with that sickly sentimentalism which . . . generates such monsters as the Abby Kellys and the Fanny Wrights who stand now . . . upon the platforms of Anti-slavery societies and women's rights conventions."[67]

A similar case was made by Alexander H. Sands, commencement speaker at the 1859 graduation ceremony of the Hollins Female Institute in Richmond. Sands called on proslavery women to educate their misinformed sisters:

I do ask you to look well to the surroundings of this question — to read and understand the argument used in behalf of slavery, and to correct a false sentiment, which I fear is already too prevalent among females, that the institution is wrong. It is not wrong ... and our educated women ought to know it that they may imbue their children with it and educate in the truest and best method a popular sentiment in conformity to right reason and to the word of the Living God. This is one of the duties (and but one) which an educated woman at the South owes to the State.[68]

Whether or not "false sentiment" on slavery was more prevalent among Southern women than among men, we will never know with certainty; few people of either sex left records as rich as Blackford's. But the fact that the most prominent female colonizationists endorsed the broad interpretation of colonization as a wedge to gradual emancipation even as the leaders of the VCS repudiated it is surely significant. ACS ideology continued to resonate with women long after sectional tensions had undermined public support for colonization. The ACS had defined a host of activities, from education to manumission, as philanthropy, and had defined philanthropy as the special province of women. In the minds of Blackford, Rice, et al., the architects of ACS ideology— Gurley foremost among them — understood women's concerns and appreciated women's contributions.

With the rise of sectional tensions, the ACS case for the involvement of women became politically suspect in Virginia. Men like Ruffin feared that women still clung to the hope of gradual emancipation and still believed that individual acts of kindness, such as manumission, were moral imperatives. Rather than simply bemoan the fact that some women were not "sound" on the slavery question, proslavery apologists began to construct a counterargument. George Fitzhugh, Alfred Taylor Bledsoe, and a host of others followed Thomas Dew's lead. They conceded the moral superiority of women over men — of *Southern* women, that is; Fitzhugh averred that the "judgment of women is far superior to that of men." But, in Fitzhugh's opinion, Southern women's moral refinement was a product of the institution of slavery, and their superior perceptions should lead them to support, unequivocally, the peculiar institution. As we shall see in Chapter 4, many Virginia women in fact rallied to the defense of slavery and Southern values in the 1850s. A new generation of female authors took it upon themselves to prove that masters and mistresses were humane and well-meaning. Women's special moral perspective, these writers would argue, allowed them to describe Southern domestic relations with objectivity.[69]

In short, the Virginia sources suggest that the question of whether or not Southern women were "covert abolitionists" is the wrong one to ask.

White Virginians of both sexes, the subjects of this chapter included, re-soundingly rejected abolitionism. But the rejection of abolitionism did not preclude meaningful debate over slavery or over women's part in the slavery controversy. The "moderate" position on slavery—that the institution was wrong and should be slowly and cautiously dismantled—was the victim of a protracted siege. As it fell, so too did a particular vision of women's civic duty, one so eloquently expressed by Blackford. In the 1850s, the notion that white women were the special victims of the slave system gave way to the idea that they were the special beneficiaries of it; and the argument that women had the public duty to work for gradual emancipation gave way to the notion that they had the public duty to defend slavery.

Long before Virginia women took up their pens on behalf of slavery, however, they entered the public sphere to participate in a different political cause—the advancement of political parties. Only by examining the realm of party politics can we put the experiences of colonization women in historical context. The decline of antislavery sentiment in Virginia did not mark the retreat of women from the political sphere. In the 1840s, many of the men and women who had joined together to promote the causes of temperance and colonization rallied behind the banner of the Whig Party. How did the Whigs justify the inclusion of women in partisan rituals? By arguing that women had a special moral perspective on politics.

GENDER AND THE SECOND PARTY SYSTEM

The 1840s witnessed the emergence of what historian Joel H. Silbey has called a new "American political nation." Gone was the political world of the early republic, with its widespread antiparty sentiment, deferential behavior by voters, and political dominance by social elites. In the new order, two highly organized parties — the Democratic and the Whig — campaigned vigorously for popular support. Led by a new cadre of professional politicians, the parties pioneered the tactics of mass mobilization and demanded disciplined partisanship from the electorate. The "electoral universe" was in constant motion. Men participated in a frenzied cycle of party rallies, processions, committee meetings, conventions, caucuses, and elections. Partisan loyalties were fierce, and voter turnout high.[1]

What about women? What implications did the advent of the "second party system," as the new order has been dubbed, have for them? Historians agree that the Whigs' 1840 campaign marks the first time a political party systematically included women in its public rituals. All around the country women turned out at Whig rallies; on occasion they even made speeches, conducted political meetings, and wrote pamphlets on behalf of the Whigs. And yet, while many studies note these developments, none draw out their implications. Scholars generally present women not as political actors, but as "audience and symbol." The pioneering treatment of Whig women, Robert Gray Gunderson's 1957 *The Log-Cabin Campaign*, characterizes women's role at rallies as "conspicuous, but passive." A 1990 study by Mary P. Ryan makes a similar case: women who attended Whig political events in 1840 did so "not in public deliberation but as symbols," as "passive and respectable representatives of femininity." Arguing against this view, Jayne Crumpler DeFiore, in an article on Tennessee, credits women with active and intense participation in the campaigns of 1840 and 1844, but finds that their engagement in politics was short-lived: after entering the public sphere "for an instant in time," women "drop out of sight" in 1848. Robert J. Dinkin's recent synthesis of work in the field draws heavily on

DeFiore, asserting that in the South, the decline of the Whig Party in 1852 would "sharply reduce [women's] direct involvement in partisan electoral activities," for the remainder of the antebellum period.[2]

The Virginia evidence suggests that to characterize women's partisanship as passive or ephemeral is to obscure the transformation in women's civic roles that the election of 1840 set in motion. Newspapers, pamphlets, and speeches, taken together with women's diaries, letters, and reminiscences, chart this transformation. In the presidential election campaigns of the 1840s, Virginia Whigs made a concerted effort to win the allegiance of the Commonwealth's women by inviting them to the party's rallies, speeches, and processions. Though the Whigs never carried the state for their presidential candidates, they repeatedly claimed that the majority of women favored their party over the Democrats. Whig campaign rhetoric, as presented by the party's newspapers, and women's private and public expressions of partisanship articulated a new ideal of feminine civic duty, one that I call Whig womanhood. Whig womanhood embodied the notion that women could—and should—make vital contributions to party politics by serving as both partisans and mediators in the public sphere. According to Whig propaganda, women who turned out at the party's rallies gathered information that allowed them to mold partisan families; reminded men of moral values that transcended partisanship; and conferred moral standing on the party.

The Whigs' claim that there was a "gender gap," to use a modern phrase, between them and the Democrats, did not go unanswered. During the 1844 campaign, the Virginia Democrats made sporadic appeals to women. A full-scale public debate over women's partisanship erupted in the months after the presidential election of 1844, when the Whig women of Virginia formed the Virginia Association of Ladies for Erecting a Statue to Henry Clay. The Clay Association believed its work was the perfect expression of female patriotism. The Democrats disagreed, branding the association's activities unladylike and even rebellious. The debate fizzled out in a few months, with the Whigs apparent winners. Gradually, Democrats in Virginia adopted Whig tactics for developing female allegiance to their party. By the mid-1850s, the inclusion of women in the rituals of party politics had become commonplace, and the ideology that justified such inclusion had been assimilated by Democrats.

Before the campaign of 1840 comes under consideration, an overview of Virginia women's partisanship in the 1820s and 1830s is in order.

Evidence for this period can be found primarily in the letters of female relatives of politicians. Many a Southern lady harbored fierce partisan loyalties and served as an intellectual mentor and moral adviser to her politician husband. Judith Rives was one such woman. Mistress of a vast plantation in Albemarle County, Rives routinely discussed political matters in her correspondence with her husband, William Cabell Rives, who served as a Virginia legislator, U.S. representative and senator, and minister to France. Judith was considered by William his "wisest and best counsellor." He counted on her for advice and reassurance, and he reported on the deliberations of the state legislature and U.S. Congress in painstaking detail. Judith Rives, for her part, felt she was a partner in her husband's career. She wrote of one of his speeches that it "made us [their family] feel very proud of *our* contribution to the patriotism, the elevation, and the oratory of the Senate." Rives seems to have fancied herself her husband's political conscience — she urged that he not be motivated by "any motive of vain or worldly ambition," but instead consecrate his career to higher causes: "the good of your fellow men, and the glory of our almighty father."[3]

Like William Cabell Rives, state legislator James McDowell trusted deeply in his wife's political counsel, believing it to be "the only advice that governs, because always rendered from the most devoted feelings and from the *best* judgment." Susan McDowell both encouraged ambition in her husband and feared that success might come at the cost of moral integrity. McDowell frequently criticized her husband for his lack of drive. When she heard rumors in 1834 that a U.S. Senate seat was to open, she wrote to him: "you I suppose have already escaped to your *stall* or even hid in a *chicken coop* (the old temper still in you) lest some friend might propose your taking it [the seat]. Do creep out and do yourself and your family justice." At the same time, she believed that McDowell's position in the Virginia legislature brought "strong temptations." She warned her husband that he must ask God to help him withstand the "flattery of the world."[4]

Some women, particularly relatives of officeholders and those who lived near Washington, D.C., or Richmond, attended political speeches and legislative deliberations. Helen MacLeod, for example, a resident of Alexandria, sent firsthand accounts of congressional debates to her brother Martin in Glasgow, Scotland. In September of 1826, she witnessed a fiery speech by Virginia senator John Randolph. Randolph, she wrote to Martin, abused "the present administration in the most scandalous manner . . . ridiculing those who sided with him as being mean [and] . . . seeking his favor." To MacLeod's dismay, Randolph "even went so far as to insult the ladies who frequented the Galleries and indeed his language on some occasions was so gross that it became difficult for any *decent females* to be present during his speeches." Women were also on hand at debates of the Virginia General Assembly. Anne Newport Royall, whose views on evangelical benevolence are quoted in the previous chapter, left an account of the Virginia legislature's constitutional convention in 1829–30. Thronging the convention hall, she claims, was an "army of women" wearing gaudy "Convention-bonnets." The "line of bonnets" so disrupted the view of those sitting behind it that on the second day of the convention, the sergeant-at-arms requested that the ladies refrain from wearing large hats.[5]

Though they felt partisan allegiances and occasionally could be found in the audience at political speeches, women were, with a few notable exceptions, marginal to the discourse and rituals of partisan politics before 1840. Political parties made no systematic efforts to encourage or to publicize women's presence at campaign events. The rhetoric and symbolism of presidential election campaigns in the 1830s were predominantly masculine and martial. For example, the *Staunton Spectator* of October 20, 1836, featured the following exhortation to the voters of Augusta County: "Let every man then gird on his armour for the contest! Let the beacon FIRES be lighted on every hill, to give warning to all that the enemy is at hand! Let the WAR DRUMS beat a loud REVEILLE!"[6]

The only expression of partisanship by a woman found in the Virginia newspapers from the 1820s and 1830s sampled for this chapter is a poem to William Henry Harrison — one of the Whigs' three presidential candidates — that appeared in the *Staunton Spectator* on September 1, 1836. A "young lady" from Pennsylvania defended Harrison and chided his critics with these words: "Those who would thus *disgrace their land* / Are found in every age; / Not ev'n our Washington could stand / Untouch'd by *Party rage*." The *Spectator*'s editors said of the poet, "We are glad she is for Harrison — though we understand most of the Ladies are so."[7]

The *Staunton Spectator* editors were ahead of their time in suggesting that an affinity existed between women and the Whig Party; so, too, was Lucy Kenney of Fredericksburg, who made a similar claim. A single woman aspiring to be a professional writer, Kenney published a series of pamphlets in the 1830s, including one in which she proclaimed her support for Democratic president Andrew Jackson and his heir apparent, Martin Van Buren. In 1838 Kenney switched allegiances and became a Whig. A fervent supporter of slavery and states rights, Kenney believed that the passing of the Democratic torch to Northerner Van Buren—who had supported the Missouri Compromise and, so Southerners charged, had abolitionist supporters—boded ill for the South. But her defection from the Democrats was not purely ideological. When Kenney had called on Van Buren in 1838, asking that he and his party remunerate her for her efforts on their behalf, the president, much to her disgust, had offered her a mere dollar. Some "honorable Whigs," however, had a different notion of her worth and offered her one thousand dollars for her services.[8]

Kenney took the Whigs up on their offer, and later that year published a scathing pamphlet, *A Letter Addressed to Martin Van Buren*, in which she predicted that the 1840 election would strip Van Buren of the "usurped power" he had gained by "false pretences." Kenney's attack on the president prompted a response, in pamphlet form, from Van Buren supporter Eliza B. Runnells. According to Runnells, Kenney possessed none of the "elevated tone of feeling and celestial goodness, that has distinguished the female character." Kenney had been enlisted and armed for battle by "Whig magicians," and in the process "transfigured from an angel of peace, to a political bully."[9]

The exchange between Kenney and Runnells prefigures later developments. In 1840, as Whig recruitment of women began on a grand scale, Democratic commentators would echo Runnells's doubts about the propriety of women's partisanship. Stung by their loss in the presidential campaign of 1836, the Whigs in 1840 overhauled both their message and their strategy for taking it to the voters. In the South that message was, in the words of William W. Freehling, "safety on slavery and reversal of political immorality and economic chaos." Virginia Whigs included both states-rights men, such as Beverley Tucker, who bolted the Democratic Party during the nullification crisis and thought Van Buren soft on slavery, and anti–Van Buren nationalists, such as James Barbour, who believed Henry Clay's American System of national banks, national roads, and other internal improvements would benefit commercially minded planters and townsmen alike. Too ideologically divided in 1836 to settle on a single presidential ticket, the Whigs in this election cycle chose two sons of Virginia—William Henry Harrison and John Tyler.[10]

The new medium for the message was equally important. The Whigs decided that to win the election, they needed to "agitate the people"—and that the people included women. Leading Whigs around the country called for strong local organization and the use of "every lawful means" to bring men to the polls. Means for influencing the electorate included dinners, barbecues, picnics, and processions, with women as spectators and participants.[11]

The function of antebellum newspapers, which were the organs of political parties, was to make partisanship seem essential to men's identities. With the campaign of 1840, Whig newspapers took on the additional task of making partisanship seem essential to women's identities. Whig newspapers in Virginia, in lockstep with those in other states, featured invitations to women to attend the speeches and rallies of Tippecanoe and Tyler, Too clubs, and provided glowing reports of such events. The *Staunton Spectator* noted, for example, that the women of Mount Solon favored its Tipp and Ty club with their attendance, and "enjoyed very highly the display of eloquence" by the speakers. Whig rhetoric argued that the presence of women at such events bespoke not only their admiration for Harrison but also their opposition to the policies of the Democrats. In an article in the party's national organ, the Washington, D.C. *Daily National Intelligencer*, one Whig correspondent, commenting on the high turnout of women at Whig rallies, declared that they supported the Whigs because the "selfless schemings" of the Van Buren administration had "made themselves felt in the very sanctum sanctorum of domestic life."[12]

Anecdotes celebrating women's influence began to circulate in the Whig press. One such story, entitled "Another Conversion," told the tale of Miss Bond, "a warm Harrison woman," who refused to marry Mr. Provins, her Democratic suitor. After hearing a particularly convincing Harrison speech, Provins finally came around: "*he* declared for Harrison, and *she* declared for PROVINS on the spot." The very fact that the writer referred to Miss Bond as a "warm Harrison woman" reflects the new political climate. Women who felt partisan identities in the 1820s and 1830s were often referred to as "men": in 1827 James McDowell wrote to his wife, Susan, that his sister Sopponisha was an "Adamsman"; in 1834 William Cabell Rives referred to his friend Mrs. James Cocke as a "warm *Jackson-man*." In 1840, and in the presidential campaigns that followed, partisan women were commonly described, and described themselves, as "Whig women" and "Democratic women."[13]

According to the Whig press, women could contribute to the campaign not only by listening to speeches and exerting influence over men but also by making public presentations. On October 1, 1840, the "Whig Ladies of Alexandria" presented a banner with the motto "Gen. Wm. H. Harrison, the Glory and Hope of our Nation" to the local Tippecanoe club; male delegates of the club carried the banner in the grand Whig procession that took place four days later in Richmond. One native of Virginia wrote a song in honor of her party's candidate that ended with the refrain, "Down with the Locos / dark hocus-pocus / The banner of Liberty floats through the sky."[14]

The single most vocal female contributor to the Tippecanoe campaign was Kenney. She published two pamphlets, *The Strongest of All Government Is That Which Is Most Free* and *A History of the Present Cabinet*, in support of Harrison's 1840 campaign. In her view, Harrison had earned the "blessings of thousands of women and children" in his career as an Indian fighter. In keeping with a favorite Whig theme, Kenney asserted that Harrison's private character was as unassailable as his public record. He was an "honest and upright" and "chivalric" man who would restore America to "peace, plenty and prosperity." "Let the present party leaders remember that in November next we will shout the harvest home," she declared, sure of Harrison's triumph.[15]

The diaries, letters, and memoirs of Virginia women confirm that the 1840 campaign was different from its predecessors. "[F]ashionable topics seem to turn on politics more than anything else at present," Whig Judith Rives wrote to her son in February of 1840, from the family plantation in Albemarle County. "I never saw anything like the excitement here," Sarah Pendleton Dandridge of Essex County informed her sister; "we hear of nothing but Gen. Harrison." Jane Gay Roberts of Mount Pelier confided to her diary that she "found it impossible to avoid feeling the liveliest interest in the success of the Whigs" and the "deepest mortification" at the thought that her husband was considering voting for the Democrats.[16]

Girls and teenagers, as well as grown women, got caught up in the excitement. Sally McCarty Pleasants's reminiscences, *Old Virginia Days and Ways*, begin with a chapter entitled "Politics and Politicians." Daughter of an ardent Whig, Pleasants recalls that as a young child she was privy to the "endless political discussions" of adults. During the 1840 campaign, she marched with a group of little girls in a Whig torchlight procession in her hometown of Leesburg, and admiringly observed the local ladies fashion a banner in Harrison's honor. Sara Pryor, who grew up near Richmond, relates in her reminiscences that she knew of many a young girl who enjoyed singing the songs of the Log Cabin campaign. Thirteen-year-old Frances Ann Capps of Portsmouth attended a crowded Whig meeting at which she listened to a four-and-a-half-hour speech; she found the occasion "very pleasing."[17]

Private residences and businesses became sites for the consumption and production of partisan material culture. Women not only bought a vast array of Whig paraphernalia (such as stationery, songbooks, plates, buttons, glassware, and quilts bearing Harrison's name) but also made their own. In preparation for a Whig procession, Celestia Shakes of Alexandria made a model log cabin, which she placed in the window of her shop where everyone was sure to see it; "the Cabin pleased the Whigs very much [and] they cheered it," she wrote her sister.[18]

In the age of mass politics, even women's housekeeping could serve partisanship. Party conventions, rallies, and processions might bring thousands of visitors who had to be lodged, fed, and cared for. Naturally, women played a key role in providing these services and so facilitated the political process. One such woman, Mary Steger of Richmond, wrote to a friend in September of 1840 about her preparations for the upcoming Whig state convention:

> ... every Whig house in the city is to be crammed we expect to have 10 or 12 sleep here to say nothing of the stragglers in to dinner &tc you will think perhaps it needs not much preparation but we are all in a bustle. . . . it is no easy task in this filthy place to keep a three story house clean. . . . there are from 6 to 8 thousand Delegates and members of our Tippecanoe Club here determined to pay all their expenses. . . . Our Log Cabin is open almost every few nights (the regular meetings being once a week) to some speakers from a distance. the Cabin holds 1,500 and it is always full.

In all likelihood, Steger had been to the "Log Cabin" (the Whig campaign headquarters) herself to hear Whig discourses. It was quite impossible to remain aloof from politics, she told her friend: "I never took so much interest in politics in my life. . . . the fact is you have to know something about them for nobody here thinks of any else."[19]

For Whig women in Virginia, the crowning event of the 1840 campaign was Whig luminary Daniel Webster's visit to Richmond during the October convention. Susan Hooper, who achieved some renown as a writer during the Civil War, was at a reception for Webster on his arrival in Richmond and later wrote a detailed description of the event. Her father, a staunch supporter of Webster, "could not permit so golden an opportunity of his child's seeing his political idol to pass unimproved; so, girl, almost baby as I was, he hurried me down to the honorable gentleman's reception . . . that in after years I might boast of having heard Webster, the immortal."[20]

After giving two speeches to huge crowds of enthusiastic Whig men and women, Webster yielded to the "particular request of the ladies of Richmond" and agreed to deliver a special address on women's political role to them at the Whig campaign headquarters. On October 7, some twelve hundred women turned out for the event. Webster took issue with the popular maxim that "there is one morality for politics and another morality for other things," and he looked forward to the day when the standards of private life would govern public conduct. It was women's special duty, he suggested, to bring that day about. Because their moral perceptions were "both quicker and juster than those of the other sex," Webster continued, women could infuse society with the "pure morality" on which sound government depended. Mothers had to teach their children that "the exercise of the elective franchise is a social duty, of as solemn a nature as man can be called on to perform; that a man may not innocently trifle with his vote; that every free elector is a trustee as well for others as himself, and that every man and every measure he supports has an important bearing on the interests of others as well as his own." Webster refrained from analyzing specific political issues, not because he feared the women would not be interested but because, he said, "You read enough — you hear quite enough on those subjects."[21]

Webster's views were echoed by two of Virginia's leading Whigs, former governor James Barbour and Richmond lawyer James Lyons, who spoke to the crowd after Webster had finished. They made explicit what Webster had implied: women's civic duty was to create Whig families, and their participation in Whig events empowered them to fulfill that role. Barbour expressed delight at having seen throngs of women attend Whig rallies, throughout "the length and breadth of this land," during the year's canvass. Those women were "animated with the one holy purpose of redeeming from destruction those liberties earned for us by our fathers, which are equally dear to woman as to man, and which she, with us, is equally bound to transmit untarnished to our children for ages to come." With all the ladies against Democratic candidate Martin Van Buren, Barbour asked, how could he possibly win? James Lyons proclaimed that the "countenance" of the ladies was both a means and a guarantee of the party's success. Women were forging a "great Whig family": with Whig mothers there must be Whig sons and Whig daughters; with Whig daughters there would be Whig sweethearts, he asserted. Guarded by the "shield of female purity," Lyons concluded, the Whigs were sure to conquer.[22]

The *Daily National Intelligencer*, which reprinted the speeches in their entirety, praised Webster for celebrating the "vast influence" of women on the well-being of society. The *Richmond Whig* saw the turnout of women as evidence that "the better part of creation were and are, almost unanimously Whig." Women's support for the party "ought to sanctify the inevitable Revolution which is about to occur," the editors proclaimed.[23] The "Revolution" the editors had in mind was the victory of Harrison over Van Buren. But they, along with Webster and his colleagues, were helping to actuate another revolution — one in gender conventions.

Webster and his fellow speakers were in effect articulating a new theory of women's civic duty. That theory, Whig womanhood, attempted to reconcile women's partisanship as Whigs with the ideology of domesticity or "true womanhood." The canon of domesticity, like the Revolutionary-era theory of republican motherhood, celebrated woman's power and duty to mold the character of her sons, to instill in them civic virtue and a love for the Republic. At the same time, domestic doctrine held that the "true woman" was nonpartisan. Men embodied the "baser instincts" — selfishness, passion, and ambition — which partisanship expressed. By contrast, women were selfless, disinterested, and virtuous. Men pursued their self-interest in the public sphere; women maintained harmony, morality, and discipline in the domestic one.[24]

What was new about Whig womanhood was its equation of female patriotism with partisanship and its assumption that women had the duty to bring their moral beneficence into the public sphere. Whig rhetoric held that women were partisans, who shared with men an intense interest and stake in electoral contests. No longer was patriotism a matter of teaching sons to love the Republic. A patriotic woman would teach her family to love the Whig Party; she, after all, understood that the Whigs alone could ensure the health and safety of the Republic.

That very understanding was forged in public. Rather than affirm a cherished tenet of the ideal of domesticity, that women must avoid the contentious political arena in order to safeguard their virtue, Whig speakers argued that by attending campaign events, women could transform the public sphere, fostering "domestic" virtues such as fairness, harmony, and self-control in a larger setting. Women's "countenance" sanctified the Whig cause; their presence bespoke the party's moral rectitude. Not only did women legitimize partisan behavior, they helped to set limits on it — they guarded men with a "shield of purity" and made them understand the moral consequences of their actions. In a sense, Whig womanhood was the ultimate testament of faith in true womanhood. Its expositors held that *even* participation in party politics could not corrupt women, or erase the fundamental differences between them and men.

How well did Whig rhetoric about women conform to reality? The

Whigs' claim that the "ladies are all Whigs" was, of course, a fanciful fabrication. Despite Harrison's vigorous campaign, the Democrats still had the support of a majority of voters in Virginia in 1840. Private papers reveal that Democratic women could be every bit as ardent in their partisanship as their Whig counterparts. Democrat Margaret Randolph, granddaughter of Thomas Jefferson, wrote her sister in October that she regretted having married a Whig. Of her husband's allegiance to the Whigs Randolph had this to say: "You have no idea what a source of vexation it is to me. . . . We had several hot quarrels about it and determined not to mention the subject again however I took advantage of Williams being stretched on the bed with a mustard plaster on, the other day to try it again and we got in such a rage that he wanted me to come to the side of the bed & take it out in a fisty cuff & I felt sorely tempted to take the broom stick to him but was afraid of after consequences." Margeret E. Loyall of Norfolk wrote bitterly in late October that she had "never despaired of the reelection of Van Buren" until she read in the New York newspapers that the Whigs were accustomed to perpetrating "villanous" election frauds.[25]

Since women did not cast ballots, the Whigs' assertion that there was a gender gap in politics cannot be empirically proven or refuted — therein, no doubt, lay some of its viability as propaganda. The leading Democrats in Virginia did little to contest the Whig Party's assertion that it alone had the blessing of women. Some Democrats openly expressed their contempt for Whig tactics. The Richmond *Crisis*, a Democratic campaign paper, mockingly suggested to the Whigs that they might increase the "swelling pageant" at their state convention if they ran the following advertisement: "A meeting of the Babies of Richmond, with their Nurses, is respectfully requested this evening, at the Log Cabin, in order to form a Tippecanoe Infant Club." After Webster's speech to the Whig women of Richmond, a correspondent to the *Richmond Enquirer* lambasted speaker and audience alike, asking, "Are the ladies of Virginia so destitute of religious and moral instruction, that they need a thorough politician to enlighten them on the subject of the training of their children?" At least one Democratic paper took a different tack. When a woman in Charlottesville wrote to the *Warrenton Jeffersonian* with the news that the Democratic convention in her town had "caused some of the Whigs to lose their countenance," the editor of the newspaper held her up as a "good Republican." He responded to the Whig insistence that " 'All the Ladies are Whigs!' " by proclaiming, "We never believed it." But most Democratic editors chose to ignore rather than refute the Whigs' claims about women.[26]

Why was the Whig and not the Democratic Party the first to seize the opportunity to make, as one Democrat put it, "politicians of their women"? Answers to the question must be speculative, for neither Whig nor Democratic commentators explicitly accounted for this difference in the political tactics of the two parties. Studies of Whig ideology argue that women were central to the Whigs' worldview.[27] Although the Democrats sought to maintain a strict boundary between the private and public spheres and resented attempts to politicize domestic life, the Whigs invested the family—and women in particular—with the distinct political function of forming the stable American character on which national well-being depended. While the Democrats acknowledged the reality of social conflict, the Whigs preferred speaking of a society in which harmony prevailed; women's special moral and spiritual qualities, Whigs maintained, fitted them for the task of promoting such harmony.[28]

Historians Joe L. Kincheloe Jr., Ronald P. Formisano, and Richard J. Carwadine suggest that inclusion of women in partisan rituals was a by-product of the Whig Party's effort to blend religion and politics. Many Whig leaders were steeped in evangelical religion and applied what they had learned in the religious sphere to the political one. They practiced "secular revivalism"—the great rallies of the 1840s were, in essence, secular camp meetings. Using the evangelical idiom, Whig orators told crowds of enthusiastic men, women, and children that a presidential campaign was not simply a contest over political principles but a clash between good and evil.[29]

While some Whig men may have conceived of religious revivals as a model for partisan rituals, it is also likely that the connections of Whig leaders to benevolent reform movements predisposed them to recognize the value of women's aid. Scholars have long identified the Whig Party with benevolent reform. The Whigs believed, historians Daniel Howe and Lawrence Kohl have argued, in the malleability of human nature. They championed institutions that could help individuals achieve the self-mastery on which social order depended: schools, benevolent societies, reformatories, and asylums. All around the country, Whigs were leaders in reform movements. Henry Clay of Kentucky served as president of the American Colonization Society, and Theodore Frelinghuysen of New Jersey served as president of the American Tract Society and the American Bible Society. In Virginia, too, Whigs championed moral reform. Prominent Whigs such as Governor Barbour supported a variety of reform causes, from a conviction that public education and benevolent societies were a means to create a more harmonious society.[30]

By 1840, women had long been active in the sphere of benevolent reform. They had proved that they were effective organizers, skilled at mobilizing public support for their projects. In Virginia, as we have seen, men had enthusiastically enlisted female support in the temperance and African colonization causes, arguing that the participation of "disinterested" and virtuous females would legitimate those causes. In short, when reform-minded Whig leaders like James Barbour encouraged women to join in the party's glorious crusade, they were not inventing or advancing new arguments to justify public activism by women but rather recasting old ones, adapting the ideology of benevolent femininity to the new realities of mass party politics.[31]

On balance, Whig propaganda about women more closely resembled the rhetoric of disinterested benevolence than that of religious enthusiasm. Women's roles in the two settings, evangelical revivals and partisan rallies, differed in one essential way. Camp meetings were known for their high emotional pitch. Kincheloe asserts that women who attended them "screamed, participated in the 'exercises,' exhorted, sang, and did anything else that men could do." Women's role at political rallies, by contrast, was more to contain passions than to give in to them. Political passion, according to nineteenth-century rhetoric, was a sort of "blindness"; critiques of "blind party spirit" float through the campaign rhetoric of the 1840s.[32] Whig rhetoric implied that women—who were by nature more virtuous and gentle than men, exercised influence rather than wielding power, and brought no personal ambitions to politics—could resist this blindness. Whig men occasionally praised female enthusiasm, but they more often stressed Whig women's disinterestedness, dignity, and decorum.

In other words, the participation of women helped to relieve men's anxieties about changes in electoral behavior. Even as men likened partisan competition to warfare, they maintained an intense concern for setting behavioral constraints on partisans. This concern, it might be argued, ran especially high among Whigs in 1840, when they began their appeals to women. The Whigs wanted to have it both ways: to steal the Jacksonians' democratic thunder and to claim that the Whigs were a breed apart from the Democrats—and a superior one at that. The Whigs' 1840 campaign was masterminded by a new cadre of professional politicians who sought to beat the Jacksonians at their own game of rousing the common man. They hoped that the din produced by Harrison's Log Cabin campaign of 1840 would drown out the Democratic charge that the Whigs had no platform and no policies. Even as they stressed the humble origins of their candidate and claimed to be more democratic that the Democrats, the Whigs also sought to retain the mantle of patrician dignity. In contrast to the Democrats' excessive partisanship and executive corruption, the Whigs, so they claimed, represented disinterested virtue, a love of the Union, and a reverence for the traditions of the founding fathers.[33]

If this message seems dissonant, it was. Men such as Webster, Clay, and John Quincy Adams initially resisted the notion that the Whig campaign of 1840 should focus on "style, song and hysteria." When these "old guard" leaders began to taste victory, however, they came around, and played the demagogue to crowds of enthusiastic followers in places such as Richmond, telling them what they wanted to hear. The Democrats naturally charged that the Whigs' efforts to unleash voter enthusiasm were immoral and destructive to the public peace; particularly disturbing, Democrats charged, was the way the dispensing of hard cider by Harrison campaign workers encouraged intemperance.[34] But the Whigs had the perfect counterargument — the very presence of women at Whig events insured decorum and sobriety. With women on their side, Whigs could lay claim both to popular democracy and dignity.

The Whig Party's victory in the 1840 presidential contest proved to be short-lived. The death of William Henry Harrison within a month after his inauguration exposed the fault lines in the Whigs' fragile coalition. Seeking a consensus candidate in 1844, the Whigs chose a man, Henry Clay, whom their Northern and Southern wings could agree on. Clay, a Southerner, opposed the annexation of Texas unless it was on terms acceptable to the North. And he championed an American System of internal development that would bind the country together through commercial ties.[35]

The years between Harrison's victory in 1840 and Clay's campaign in 1844 afforded women and men alike fewer opportunities to display partisanship than the presidential campaign season had. Women did attend political speeches and debates in nonelection years.[36] But they were generally not included in the year-round succession of meetings, held behind closed doors, in which the state business of the Whig Party, such as the selection of delegates to state conventions, was conducted. Women's function in partisan life had clear limits: their role was not to choose Whig candidates but to affirm the choices of Whig men, particularly in high-stakes presidential campaigns; to help maintain party discipline; and bring new members into the Whig fold.

As soon as the presidential canvass of 1844 got under way, the tide of female partisanship rose again, to new heights. The Whig Party in Virginia flooded women with a virtual torrent of invitations to Whig events, including them in the meetings of Clay Clubs—local campaign organizations—which sprang up across the state. By the thousands, women turned out to hear lengthy speeches on subjects such as banking, tariffs, internal improvements, and the annexation of Texas. As in 1840, Whig men thought that the approval of the "ladies" legitimized and purified the Whig campaign. "If we doubted before," a correspondent wrote after seeing the large number of women at a Whig rally in Goochland County, "now we know the Whigs must be right and will be more than conquerers." The presence of Whig "maidens" at a rally in Buckingham lent "a chastening influence to the occasion," the *Lynchburg Virginian* reported. Such expressions of female partisanship led the *Richmond Whig* to draw a now familiar conclusion: "It is well known that the Ladies are Whigs, almost universally." Rather than ascribing ladyhood narrowly to plantation mistresses or members of the urban elite, Virginia newspapers were at great pains to point out that ladies attended Whig events in villages, county courthouses, and rural settings around the state. Reporting on a Harrison County rally, the *Whig* noted that "ladies in the remote and retired Mountain districts take the same interest in the success of the Whig cause, which they do everywhere else." [37]

As in 1840, anecdotes about female partisanship circulated through Whig newspapers. Particularly telling is a lengthy piece, entitled "A Famous Fine Girl," which originated in the *New York Journal of Commerce* and was picked up by the *Lynchburg Virginian*. In Charlestown, Virginia, so the anecdote went, the Democrats had recently attempted to disrupt a Whig procession by stretching a long rope across the street down which the Whigs intended to march. The almost certain effect of the subterfuge was to "bring on a general battle" as the Whigs were determined to breach and the Democrats to defend the makeshift roadblock. Fortunately, a "young lady, who, in the gentleness of her nature, could ill endure to see brethren fall out by the way," resolved to be "not exactly a mediator in the full sense of the term, but to interpose her kind offices in such a way as to extinguish the kindling flames of party spirit." She ascended to a nearby window and cut the "obnoxious" rope; conflict was avoided, the "sterner sex" having been subdued by this act of "heroism." The anecdote ends with a rhetorical question: To which party, if any, did the young lady belong? The answer: "The Virginia girl was a sterling Whig." [38]

No other story sums up as aptly the essence of Whig womanhood.

Men, according to the anecdote, are passionate creatures, ruled by base instincts, ever-ready to throw aside decorum, peace, and morals in pursuit of victory. The heroine, by contrast, combines gentleness and resoluteness, and displays courage born of sound moral judgment. Her presence in public, far from corrupting her, preserves the public order. She saves men from their own worst designs.

The Whig Party's campaign rhetoric conjured up an image of the ideal Whig woman: a chaste, honorable lady who attended political rallies to sanction the party, to dignify its proceedings, to affirm her loyalty, and to gather information that would allow her to transmit Whig culture to her family, friends, and acquaintances. Although often spoken of, Whig women rarely "spoke" for themselves at campaign events. On at least one occasion, a Virginia woman addressed a Whig crowd through a male proxy. On September 3 the *Richmond Whig* featured "AN EXAMPLE TO THE LADIES OF RICHMOND!," the story of Miss Martha Peake of Charlottesville. Peake presented a "splendid Banner" to the Clay Club of Charlottesville in September of 1844, along with a "chaste and beautiful letter" that one of its male members read aloud. When Clay is elected, she cautioned the Whig voters of the town, "forget not that those whom you have vanquished are your brothers, subjects of the same government, struggling as ardently and as honestly, as you, for what they believe, with mistaken judgment, in my poor opinion, to be the true path to national honor, happiness and glory." Only if the victorious Whigs were able to transcend the fierce emotions of party competition would the nation "bask in the sunshine of moral, social and political purity and peace."[39]

Webster and his fellow Whig luminaries undoubtedly would have approved of Peake's message, for she was imposing her superior moral sensibilities on the conduct of politics, admonishing men of the proper limits of partisanship. Apparently the *Richmond Whig* agreed that Peake successfully harmonized partisanship and true womanhood: she was bound to get married soon, the editors allowed, for her Whig credentials made her "pre-eminently qualified to confer domestic happiness" on some fortunate man.[40]

Virginia women's own accounts of the campaign of 1844 echo the party's rhetoric. Mary Virginia Terhune, who under the pen name Marion Harland achieved national fame as a novelist and author of domestic guidebooks for women, asserts in her autobiography that even as a child of thirteen, she was an avid Whig partisan and supporter of Clay. In 1844 the Whigs invited the women of her county to a political rally, the first time such an invitation had been extended to ladies, according to Terhune; the innovation "set tongues wagging," she remembers, and "practically guaranteed the county for Clay." Like Terhune, Missouri Riddick appreciated the Whig Party's hospitality. Mistress of one of the most prominent families in Suffolk, Riddick wrote to her husband in White Sulphur Springs on August 5, 1844: "Great preparations are making for the Democratic mass meeting, at Cowling's landings on the 10th. . . . We think, as no doubt you do, that it will be a poor affair . . . the ladies are not invited. I believe all of the ladies will attend the Whig Barbecue, as they are particularly invited, and tables and seats are to be provided for them." In her husband's absence, Riddick felt it her duty to stand in as the political head of the family. "I shall go [to the rally], as your representative," she told him.[41]

In the early stages of the 1844 campaign, Democrats made few overtures to women to join in partisan activities, but by the fall of 1844, the party was actively appealing to women and trying to counter Whig propaganda with its own claims. Hundreds of women attended a Democratic rally in Fairfax in September; twenty-eight young ladies carried flags bearing the different mottoes of the states. "About 100 ladies favored Mr. L. [Mr. Leake, the speaker at the rally] with their presence, and their approving smiles," wrote the *Daily Richmond Enquirer* of another Democratic meeting, "demonstrating the falsity of the charge that the 'Ladies are all Whigs.' "[42]

These appeals notwithstanding, some Democrats continued to be critical of female mobilization. According to one report, a Democratic speaker named Philip Mayo asserted at a party rally " 'that ladies were not capable of understanding the great Political questions, which now agitate the country,' and that they ought not to be allowed to by their husbands to visit the [Clay] Club House." Mayo's comment prompted an anonymous "Whig lady" to fire off a letter to the *Richmond Whig*. "I should like to see my husband try to stop me from going" to the Clay Club, she defiantly asserted, adding, "There is one lady ready to meet [Mayo] in debate at any time he may select." Describing a Whig procession in New York, a Democratic correspondent to the party's national organ, the *Daily Globe* (Washington, D.C.), declared that while the Whigs' "showy pageant" might "amuse the wives, daughters and sisters of our sovereign lord the people . . . it can neither buy, bribe, nor beat the staunch and sterling democracy of New York, when it comes to the matters of MEN." Such skepticism about the propriety and utility of Whig appeals to women was not confined to men. According to Serena Dandridge, a Democrat from Essex County, and kinswoman of Congressman R. M. T. Hunter, the reason the Whigs lost the election of 1844 was that they had "too many women & children in their ranks."[43] Ironically, the strongest articulations of Whig womanhood and the most strident attacks on it came after the election of 1844 had been lost. For it was then that Whig women in Virginia tried to snatch a symbolic victory from the jaws of defeat.

On November 17, 1844, Lucy Barbour of Barboursville, Orange County, sent to the *Richmond Whig* a seemingly innocuous letter which would touch off months of debate in the Virginia press. The letter proposed that the "Whig women of Virginia" give some "token of respect" to Clay, who had just lost his third bid for the presidency of the United States. Barbour anticipated that her appeal would raise eyebrows. "I know our sex are thought by many unstable as water," she wrote, "but after crowding the Whig festivals, and manifesting so much enthusiasm, few will be found so hollow-hearted as to refuse a small sum to so good—I had almost said, so holy a cause": the tribute to Clay.[44]

Barbour was a member of Virginia's social elite and an exemplar of her society's ideal of the Southern lady. She was born in 1775 to an influential planter family in Orange County. In 1795 she married her first cousin, James Barbour, a young lawyer and planter whom she had known since childhood. The couple settled in Orange County, where they came to preside over a vast estate of more than 5,000 acres and more than 100 slaves. Lucy Barbour gave birth in 1797 to the first of their seven children. A devoted and exacting mother, Barbour was intimately involved in the details of her children's moral development and education. But her life was marked neither by the domestic isolation nor the spirit of dependence that characterized the lives of many antebellum plantation mistresses. James Barbour's tenures as governor of Virginia (1812–14), U.S. senator (1815–25), secretary of war (1825–28), and minister plenipotentiary to England (1828–29) took the family to Richmond, Washington, and London, where Lucy Barbour earned a reputation as a gracious and popular hostess. James Barbour played an instrumental role in the creation of the Whig Party in Virginia, and was a close friend of party leader Henry Clay. While her married life nurtured her interest in politics, it was only after her husband's death in 1842 that Lucy Barbour translated her political concerns into public action, calling on women to honor her husband's defeated friend.[45]

Despite Barbour's social stature, the editors of the *Daily Richmond Enquirer* wasted no time in ridiculing the plan to honor Clay, asking, "[H]as it come to this, that the 'gallant Harry' has been turned over to the tender mercies of the ladies . . . ?" The *Enquirer* also printed a letter from one "Incognita," who thoroughly disapproved of the notion that Whig women should hold a meeting to decide on a strategy for honoring Clay: "a public meeting of political amazons! . . . Was such an event ever recorded, or before heard of, in the annals of time?"[46]

Barbour vigorously defended her project. In a second letter to the *Richmond Whig*, published on December 13, she stated that women deserved "freedom of thought even on political subjects; and the power of performing an act of justice to an injured statesman; when, doing so, we neglect no duty assigned to us by the most rigid." "We are the nursing mothers of heroes, statesmen, and divines," she continued, "and while we perform a task so important, we mean to be counted something in the muster-roll of man."[47]

Inspired by Barbour's appeal, a group of Whig women met on December 9, 1844, at the First Presbyterian Church in Richmond and formed the Virginia Association of Ladies for Erecting a Statue to Henry Clay; they elected Barbour as president. The statue was to be funded by membership subscriptions, costing no more than one dollar each. Men could make donations but not become members. Auxiliaries to the association, with women as officers and collectors, were organized all around the state and began the work of soliciting donations to pay for the cost of commissioning the statue. Thanks to the survival of a subscription book from around 1845–46 that lists contributors to the Clay Association by county, we can get a sense of the breadth and nature of the organization. The book lists the names of 2,563 subscribers, covering counties from Accomac to Orange; at least 2,236 of the subscribers were women. The association, which received national publicity in the *Daily National Intelligencer*, also had an auxiliary in Alexandria (204 subscribers) and Boston (215 subscribers). Additional contributions came from families in Vermont, Mississippi, and Georgia.[48]

The list of subscribers confirms that there was a strong connection between Whiggery and female benevolence in Virginia. Seventeen of the thirty-six members of the Female Humane Association of Richmond in 1843 subscribed to the Clay Association in 1845; so, too, did Lucy Otey of Lynchburg, Ann Clagett of Alexandria, and Julia Cabell of Richmond, directors of poor-relief organizations in their respective towns. Eliza Brend and Julia Nelson, officers of the Female Colonization Society of Virginia, subscribed, as did six future officers of the Mount Vernon Association, a national organization dedicated to preserving Washington's estate.[49]

The social prominence of the Clay Association's leaders did not insulate them from criticism. As auxiliaries sprang up around the state, so, too, did debate over the propriety of the association. On December 22, 1844, for example, two days after the Whig women of Lynchburg formed an auxiliary, the editors of the Democratic *Lynchburg Republican* attacked the Clay Association, suggesting with derision that "the name of every lady who mingles in this great work of generosity and patriotism will be handed down to posterity as a *partisan* lady." "Is not this whole movement conceived in a spirit of rebellion?" the editors asked. The Democrats mocked the notion that partisanship was appropriate for women — that partisanship and patriotism were synonymous. The Whiggish *Lynchburg Virginian* defended the Clay Association, commending it for advancing the Whig cause. "We shall not be surprised if the vehemence and universality of this female and most honorable sentiment," its editor mused, "will present Mr. Clay again as a candidate for the Presidency in 1848." A week later, two more male defenders of the association came forward, urging Whig women to stand their ground. A correspondent with the pen name "Peter Caustic" proclaimed, "There is too much firmness of character, and nobleness of soul about Virginia's daughters to suffer themselves to be intimidated by the denunciations of Locofocoism." The second defender agreed, stating that "the Whig ladies of Virginia consider themselves at least as well qualified to judge of their own acts as the Locofoco editor, who has undertaken to lecture them." [50]

Perhaps the most strident defense of the association came from a correspondent of the *Lexington Gazette*, who jumped into the fray after an auxiliary was formed in that town in January of 1845. The Democrats, he claimed, were being disingenuous: "The sneering democratic gentry who ridicule the idea of ladies meddling with politics, would not be so bitterly sarcastic if they could have a little of this meddling on their side of the question." "We are willing to avow our own opinion that woman's proper sphere is HOME," the writer continued. But "there are occasions . . . when her domestic duties themselves demand that she should enter the arena which man has considered his exclusive province." [51]

If some male defenders of the association stressed the propriety of female partisanship, others argued that the Whig women's mission was to counteract the dire consequences of "party spirit." The *Staunton Spectator*, for example, praised the association with these words: "Though blind party spirit may elevate the Demagogue, there are enough left to cherish and commemorate the many virtues and noble deeds of the bright genius of his country!" Women, the implication was, remained somewhat aloof from "party spirit" and therefore were better able than men to recognize virtue. [52]

Whig women themselves came forward on their own and Clay's behalf. In December 1844 a female correspondent to the *Richmond Whig* wrote that women had a duty to honor Clay since he had been "shamefully neglected by his countrymen." She had nothing good to say about the newly elected president, James K. Polk: "The more insignificant a man is, the greater are his chances, with the Democracy, for attaining exalted honors." The notion that the "sterner sex" had failed in its patriotic duty was also advanced by Mrs. N. K. Trout of the Staunton auxiliary, who was ashamed that Virginia—the "Mother of Statesmen"—had treated Clay "so unmaternally." One Mrs. King, of Waynesboro, refused to accept Clay's defeat. "I shall never *give him up* no *never*," she wrote to an association official, adding that she fervently hoped Clay would "adorn the White House" in 1848.[53]

Other women expressed the hope that the statue would have an enduring legacy. Susan Doswell, a plantation mistress from Hanover County and president of the local Clay auxiliary, asserted in an address to her colleagues that women "cannot but erect a statue . . . that our children may early learn well to distinguish the true difference between exalted worth and that cringing sycophancy, which, in a Republic, too often usurps its highest honors." Sarah French, vice president of the Warrenton auxiliary, wrote to Clay on February 27, 1845, asking him to visit her town (he graciously declined). The association's goal, she stressed, was to teach the young men of Virginia to imitate Clay's "noble deeds." Jane Baxley sent in a donation to association treasurer Eliza Riddle with a note asserting that the Clay statue should "show to nations, and succeeding generations" that Virginians prized their "noble Statesman & *Pacificator*."[54]

The women who spoke for the association tapped into two currents in Whig political culture: the party's social elitism and its emphasis on "statesmanship." The Whigs considered themselves the party of "property and talents." One prominent Virginia Whig recorded in his memoirs his belief that the Whigs "represented the culture and wealth of the state. . . . It had become an old saw that 'Whigs knew each other by the instincts of gentlemen.'" Furthermore, as historian Thomas Brown has pointed out, the Whigs claimed to stand for "statesmanship" over "partisanship." The Whig Party carried on the founding fathers' tradition of great statesmanship, transcending partisanship and sectionalism in the interests of national unity.[55]

Whig women such as Judith Rives, vice president of the Albemarle Clay Association auxiliary, believed that men of wealth and culture should run the state. In 1861, in her memoirs, she looked back on the early days of her husband's career. "In those days, education, talent, a noble nature, and even advantages of birth and fortune, instead of being disqualifications for the public service and favor, were considered the best requisites," she wrote. Another of Virginia's renowned female authors gave voice to Whig elitism. Mary Virginia Terhune recalled in her autobiography that as a child she thought it "monstrous" that poor white Democrats should have the same political rights as wealthy Whig gentlemen.[56]

One of the central issues in the 1844 campaign was Clay's stature as a gentleman and statesman. The Democrats assailed Clay's character, charging him with the unchristian practices of dueling, gambling, and womanizing. The Whigs countered that Clay was the epitome of a Southern gentleman, a model of gallantry and social grace. Just as women's support had helped Harrison establish a virtuous reputation, so, too, did it help, in Clay's case, to diffuse the "character issue." Women around the country flocked to Clay's speeches and showered him with gifts. "If nothing else, Clay had the women's vote," Clay biographer Robert V. Remini asserts, repeating a favorite theme of Whig rhetoric. According to the Whigs, Clay's public record was as spotless as his character. The man who had steered the Union through the nullification crisis, Clay was known as "The Great Pacificator." In 1844, Clay's reputation as a peacemaker had special meaning, in light of Whig fears that Polk's election would bring a bloody war with Mexico. Clay's antiwar stance, Whigs argued, endeared him to women. An article on the Clay statue that appeared in the *Richmond Whig* in March 1845 suggested that Clay represented the "love of peace which is the sweetest attribute of woman."[57]

The notion that Whig women saw Clay as a guarantor of peace finds additional support in the correspondence of Ellen Mordecai of Richmond. Mordecai believed that Clay's defeat was a horrible omen for the Union. On the subject of Polk's inauguration in March of 1845, she wrote: "I don't know that I am feeling too much apprehension for the welfare of my country, yet it appears even to me ... that dark clouds are gathering, which unless scattered by elements now unseen, will thicken and bursting, overwhelm us in misery."[58]

Even as Mordecai penned her lament, debate over the Clay Association was dying down. Perhaps it had become clear to Whigs and Democrats alike that the Whig women were determined to see their project through. In November 1845, barely a year after Barbour's initial appeal, the association commissioned sculptor Joel Tanner Hart to design and execute the marble statue; he was to be paid $5,000 for the project. Once sufficient money had been raised to pay Hart, the association's only purpose was to encourage him to finish the statue. Finally, in 1859, after a series of delays because of ill health, Hart completed his work. On April 12, 1860, the eighty-third anniversary of Clay's birth, the Clay statue was inaugurated in Richmond, amid great public celebration. Business in the city had been virtually suspended so that the entire community could participate in the inaugural ceremonies; an estimated twenty thousand spectators witnessed the unveiling. The Clay statue, which stood in an iron pavilion in Capitol Square until 1930, now stands in the Old Hall of the Virginia House of Delegates.[59]

The 1844–45 debates over the Clay Association, though short-lived, are significant for revealing the tensions inherent in Whig womanhood, a new variation on the time-worn and resilient doctrine of "indirect influence." This doctrine, which eventually emerged as a key argument against woman's suffrage, held that women's civic duty lay, not in casting a ballot, but rather in influencing men's opinions and behavior.[60] The Whig innovation was to suggest that in the era of mass party politics, women could not fulfill this mandate properly unless they were integrated into the culture of political parties. For all its homages to female influence, Whig womanhood still ultimately vested women's power in male proxies. An unanswered question at the heart of Whig womanhood was implicitly posed by Lucy Barbour. What if men, despite the benign efforts of women, simply failed to do the right thing? What if they elected the wrong man? What were women to do then?

In the wake of Clay's 1844 defeat, Barbour and her supporters offered an answer: women had the duty to restore the reputation of their party's rejected hero. Barbour conceived of women as opinion makers. They were not simply to affirm the choices of men but to advance their own ideas of what constituted political worth in men—before, during, and after campaign season. In attacking the association, Democrats worried out loud about the potentially radical implications of this view, and paid backhanded tribute to women's influence. When Whig men rushed to defend Barbour, they reminded Democrats that Whig women's partisanship came with the full approbation of Whig men; the women of the Clay Association were not challenging the authority of all men, only of Democratic ones. Rather than symbolizing female rebelliousness, the Clay Association came to symbolize the efficacy and propriety of political collaboration between men and women.

By the time the Clay statue was inaugurated, both Clay and the Whig Party were long gone. Clay had died in 1852, the same year that the Whig

Party—its fragile coalition of supporters torn apart by sectionalism—
ran its last presidential campaign. But in at least one respect, Whig
political culture, like the Clay statue that symbolized it, proved more
enduring than the party itself. For even as the Whigs disintegrated, their
policy of making "politicians of their women" became standard practice in Virginia politics.

The Mexican War (1846–48) and the territorial controversies it precipitated gave rise to what historians have called the "age of sectionalism"—a prolonged period, lasting from 1848 to the eve of secession,
in which the Second Party System collapsed and sectional relations
deteriorated. In Virginia, the age of sectionalism witnessed a series
of important and interrelated transformations in party politics. The
Democrats consolidated their dominance over the state. A small but
vocal faction of Southern nationalists emerged within the Democratic
Party and began slowly building popular support. Issues that had formerly separated the parties, such as tariffs and internal improvements,
faded in importance, and slavery became the dominant political issue
in Virginia.[61]

In the presidential campaign of 1848, the Whigs chose as their standard bearer Zachary Taylor, offering him up as the "no-party" candidate, whose principles and record of service put him above partisan and sectional loyalties. Taylor, like Harrison and Clay before him,
was a slaveholder and a Southern gentleman. His Democratic opponent, Lewis Cass of Michigan, Southern Whigs charged, was unsound
on slavery—he favored "popular sovereignty" in the territories of the
Mexican Cession. As in the previous two elections, the Whigs in 1848
made much of women's alleged loyalty to the party. A meeting of
the Always Ready Club (Taylor's nickname was "Rough and Ready")
in Fairfax, the *Alexandria Gazette* noted, included "a large number of
ladies who appear to have taken hold of the Taylor cause as they did that
of Harrison in 1840." A speaker at a Whig barbecue in nearby Alexandria sounded a familiar theme: he said that the ladies "were all Whigs"
and "begged that they would go heartily to work in the good cause."[62]

But for all the Whigs' efforts to evoke the spirit of 1840, the 1848
campaign was different. Whig commentators conceded that Taylor's
canvass was marked by less popular enthusiasm than the previous two
campaigns. The Democrats by contrast trumpeted the success of their
efforts to enlist men—and women—to their cause. A Democratic rally
in Fauquier Springs was "filled with fair women and stalwart men, who
had left their honest labors at home, and had come together . . . to cheer
one another in the glorious cause." The Rural Cass and Butler Associa-

tion of Alexandria held a meeting which was "graced with the presence of one hundred ladies," and a "glorious" political festival in Norfolk brought forth a large number of women as well as men.[63]

More often than before, the two parties sponsored joint events, usually debates between Whig and Democratic electors. The following notice in the *Richmond Enquirer* describes one such bipartisan event: "DISCUSSION IN ROANOKE —... we gave a public barbecue at the Cave Spring last Saturday — Whigs and Democrats uniting. There were in attendance between a thousand and fifteen hundred persons, and among them about 200 ladies." Invitations to these joint events were usually gender-neutral. The Democratic Association and the Rough and Ready Club of Henrico, for example, held a joint barbecue, "free for all citizens," featuring hour-long speeches by representatives of each party.[64]

The enthusiasm of the Democrats for feminine supporters and the use of gender-neutral campaign rhetoric reflect the growing acceptance of women's partisanship. That the Virginia Democrats chose in 1848 to harness women's partisanship rather than to criticize it is not surprising. They knew that Taylor, as a war hero and slaveowner, had distinct advantages over their own candidate. Democrats were probably loath to let the Whigs — with the help of women — build a "cult of personality" around Taylor as they had around Harrison and Clay. Moreover, Democrats had just witnessed the Clay Association's successful campaign for popular support. Whig women had not only demonstrated the positive good they could do for their party but they had also demonstrated that women could participate in politics without harm to their dignity or to propriety. None of the fears that Democratic commentators professed in 1844 — that Whig women would act like "political amazons" or French Revolutionaries or rebel against male authority — had been realized.

Even as Whig womanhood was absorbed into the political culture, the Whig Party began to unravel. Taylor's victory in 1848 was followed by what Southerners of both parties saw as his shocking betrayal of their trust. The new president's support for the admission of California and New Mexico as free rather than slave states not only alienated his Virginia supporters but also gave momentum to the newly formed "Southern Rights" wing of the Virginia Democratic Party. It argued that passage of the Wilmot Proviso, which declared that slavery could never exist in territory acquired from Mexico, would be cause for disunion. In the 1850s, the rhetoric of presidential campaigns was more bitterly sectional than ever before. The Whig Party portrayed itself in 1852 as the bastion of republican virtue, besieged on all sides by the "unholy alliance of Nullifiers, Free Soilers, Abolitionists, Secessionists, Southern

Abstractionists, and Northern Fanatics." The Democratic candidate, Franklin Pierce, was, Whigs claimed, an abolitionist in disguise. The Democrats, for their part, portrayed the Whigs as the party of Northern fanatics — charging that it was not Whig candidate Winfield Scott, a Virginia-born war hero, but New Yorker William Seward who was the true guiding spirit of the Whigs.[65]

In political appeals addressed to women, the campaign of 1852 continued the trends of the 1840s. The Whigs again tried to foster female enthusiasm for their presidential candidate. A Whig meeting in Danville was announced in the *Richmond Whig* as follows: "The presence of the *ladies*, is especially desired. . . . *Awake, thou slumbering spirit* of 1840!" As in 1848, the two parties frequently held joint rallies or debates. The Whigs of Waterford, for example, held a rally in August, to which "whigs and democrats, one and all, including the ladies" were cordially invited.[66]

One feature that distinguished the 1852 campaign from its predecessors was the frequency with which women made public presentations of campaign decorations, accompanied by brief public addresses, to Whig clubs. On September 23, 1852, the young Whigs of Portsmouth had a banner presented to them by Miss Mary E. Jobson, in behalf of the Whig Ladies of the town. Jobson and a Miss Texania Clarke addressed the crowd. A month later Whig men marched to the residence of a Mrs. Montague, where her daughter Miss Malvina Montague presented them with a silk transparency and "an appropriate address." Women gave addresses elsewhere in the South in the 1852 campaign. In Louisville, Kentucky, for example, a Miss Oliver presented a speech and a flag to the Young Men's Scott and Graham club.[67]

In 1852, for the first time, the Democrats matched the Whig's zeal for female support and participation. Granite Hill clubs (so named because Pierce hailed from New Hampshire, the "Granite State") invited women to their meetings. The rhetoric of Democratic women and men reveals how fully they had appropriated Whig ideas about female partisanship. The Whig argument that women both legitimized and purified partisan activities was now enthusiastically advanced by Democrats. Describing an October rally in Norfolk, a Democratic correspondent wrote: "There was no *fuss* — no disturbance. The ladies — guardian angels that control our natures — were around us with their illuminating smiles to cheer, and their bright countenances to encourage us on to victory." [68]

On occasion, even Democratic women were given to public speaking. At a Democratic meeting in Norfolk in September 1852, a certain Miss Bain addressed the crowd, urging men to support Democratic presidential candidate Franklin Pierce: "Patriotic sons of Patriotic sires! . . . Oppose with all power of rectitude that odious and destructive policy that would plant the seed of discord within our borders. . . . Battle with the foes of Pierce and King; use all proper exertions to defeat them. . . . You can inspire others with a love for the pure, uncontaminated tenets of democracy, the only principles which represent the best interests of our beloved Union."[69] Like Lucy Barbour before her, Bain fused partisanship and patriotism, but she associated the Democrats with sectional harmony and the Whigs with "discord."

Many Democrats hoped Franklin Pierce's victory would herald a new era of peace and prosperity. Sara Pryor, the wife of Democratic editor Roger Pryor, was one such woman. A native Virginian living in Washington, D.C. (where her husband edited the Democratic national organ, the *Washington Union*), Pryor, in her memoirs, confessed that it was exhilarating to be an insider in the nation's capital. Pryor's husband was called upon by Pierce to help the president draft his inauguration speech. Roger Pryor talked over the speech with Sara, and she felt after hearing "these mighty political secrets," that she belonged not to the "small world" of her female social circle but "to the nation." But her enthusiasm for Pierce soon waned, as she learned of his "vacillation" and "weakness."[70] Pierce's decision to support the Kansas-Nebraska Act in 1854—which provided for popular sovereignty in the new territories and therefore repealed the Missouri Compromise—stirred up the controversy over slavery anew, and precipitated the formation of new party structures. Northern Whigs resoundingly rejected the bill and thereby alienated their Southern counterparts. Many Southern Whigs felt compelled to join the ranks of the fledgling American Party.

The American Party—or Know-Nothing Party, as it came to be known—was formed in New York in 1854, and dedicated to ridding the government of all foreigners and Roman Catholics. In Virginia, the Know-Nothings' nativism and anti-Catholicism found few supporters. It was instead the party's "theory of Union" which attracted Virginians, most especially former Whigs. Each member of the party was required to take the "third degree oath," a pledge not to vote for anyone in favor of disunion. In 1856, the remnants of Virginia Whiggery opted to support Millard Fillmore, the American Party's presidential candidate. Virginia Know-Nothings portrayed themselves as defenders of the Union; according to their propaganda, Southern Democrats and Northern abolitionists were responsible for stirring up sectional animosities. The Democrats, for their part, accused the American Party of being Northern-dominated and unsound on the slavery question.[71]

Historian Jean Gould Hales has found that antebellum nativists believed in the "innate patriotism of American women" and therefore "welcomed women's assistance"; from Kentucky to New York, women participated in American Party rallies. The Virginia evidence supports her claims. Together, Whigs and Know-Nothings in the Old Dominion made the familiar case that women favored their candidate over the Democrats' and were out in full force at the meetings of Fillmore clubs. At one such meeting, the *Richmond Whig* reported, Mary L. Sibert presented a bouquet to party leader John Minor Botts with a note which read: "May his light grow brighter and brighter until the midnight of disunionism is driven from our land." A rally of the party in Kanawha County witnessed the presentation of a large flag by a Mrs. Ruffner, with a note attesting that she was "warmly attached to the principles of the American Party, and ardently desirous of their success at the approaching election."[72]

The Virginia Democrats, for their part, aggressively taunted the Know-Nothings for their relative lack of support, and bragged that Democratic rallies drew throngs of women. "Some five or six hundred ladies, the fair daughters of Page and the adjoining counties, graced the occasion [a Democratic rally] with their presence," the *Richmond Enquirer* noted in September. "We love our cause the more when it wins the approving smiles of the ladies," said Democrats of women's attendance at a Norfolk meeting.[73]

As in the two previous campaigns, the parties frequently sponsored debates to which the "public generally" were invited. Whig Robert Saunders and Democrat Muscoe Garnett, rival candidates for the Congress, debated in Tappahanock, Hampton, and a number of other places in the Chesapeake region. Peggie Nottingham of Northampton County heard them on October 6, 1856: "We arose quite early this morning filled with the thought of being allowed to listen to the political speeches from Messer. Saunders & Garnett. . . . We collected flowers and made a very large bouquet for Mr. Garnett. . . . [He] was a very excellent speaker I could have listened to him nearly the whole day. Mr S. made out very badly. at the close of speeches Mr Waddy came forward and handed the two bunches of flowers to Mr Garnett and after he thanked the ladies." We can surmise from the *Richmond Enquirer*'s coverage of a Saunders/Garnett debate in Northumberland County just what kind of arguments met with Nottingham's approval. Charging Saunders and the Virginia Know-Nothings of failing to defend the Old Dominion's "dearly cherished institution" of slavery, Garnett exclaimed, "I am for emblazoning the word slavery upon all our banners, setting it forth, in bold relief, in all our party creeds, and defending it, if need be with my life's blood; regarding it as I do, as next to the Christian religion, the best and most conservative institution ever vouchsafed from God to man."[74]

While Democratic women publicly sanctioned and upheld the principles of the party, a new generation of Democratic girls got caught up in the rites and rituals of the campaign. Martha Buxton Porter Brent of Portsmouth includes in her reminiscences an account of her first partisan act. As a little girl, she participated in the celebration of the victorious Democrats. All the Democrats illuminated their houses, and put wreaths of evergreen in windows, she remembers. She made her own contribution: "Some of my sister's beaux had brought me a little glass deer, beautifully tinted meaning 'Buck' of course, and, so Buchanan. I was very proud of it and put that into the window with the other decorations." As the procession reached her house, her family descended into the streets to join it, leaving her mother alone to watch the flickering candles. Sarah Virginia Weight Hinton, a ten-year-old living in Norfolk, wrote this simple entry in her diary on November 4, 1856: "The day of election—raining—our party victory 149 majority."[75]

Perhaps the single greatest testament to Democratic acceptance of female partisanship is the novel *The Life and Death of Sam, In Virginia*, which was published in Richmond in 1856. Authored anonymously by "A Virginian," the novel is a stinging indictment of the Know-Nothing Party and ringing endorsement of the Democratic Party. The author adapted a favorite Whig allegory—the tale of lovers kept apart by partisanship—to his own ends. The central drama of the novel revolves around the courtship of Fannie Bell (a Catholic and a Democrat) and her suitor, Maurice Meredith (a Know-Nothing).[76]

After a short courtship, Meredith proposes marriage to Bell, and she accepts. But the engagement is based on deception, for Meredith, who knows that Bell comes from a Democratic family, has hidden from her the fact that he is a Know-Nothing. Worried that Bell will renounce him if she learns the truth, Meredith tries to reassure himself with the rhetorical question, "What does a woman know or care about a man's political opinions[?]" But doubt plagues him, and one night he has a disturbing dream. In the dream, he approaches a bridge spanning a rushing river between two jutting mountain crags. The bridge is bedecked in Democratic mottoes and Bell is the gatekeeper, holding in her hands the scales of justice. Meredith watches as his political enemies, the Democrats, cross the bridge singing victory songs. When his Know-Nothing comrades approach the bridge, they are turned away by Bell, and sent tumbling off the rocks into the river. Woman, representing justice, has sanctioned the Democratic Party and condemned the American Party to failure.[77]

Bell eventually discovers Meredith's political identity and calls off their engagement. "Must I marry the man, whose political principles would lead him to no higher aim than the proscription of foreigners and Catholics?" she angrily demands of him. Meredith, who runs as a Know-Nothing candidate for Congress, is dealt a crippling defeat in the state elections. At the story's end, Meredith is a broken man: "He had lost Fannie; he had lost all prospect of rising politically." Bell meanwhile gets engaged to Mr. Dew, a promising young Democrat.[78]

The Life and Death of Sam, In Virginia reveals much about women's political roles at mid-decade. The author's assumption is that women do — and should — know enough about party politics to serve as men's consciences. Bell is both a partisan herself and an arbiter of partisan behavior by men. She is the figurative gatekeeper of political righteousness. Her message is that those who win the moral sanction of woman are right and win political power; those who deceive woman to evade her moral judgment are doomed.

Even as the Democrats succeeded in staving off the Know-Nothing threat, a new opponent established a small but significant presence on the Virginia political scene. Motivated by hostility to the politically powerful slaveholders of eastern Virginia, a group of white men from the west of the state, led by John Underwood, formed a Republican Association in August of 1856, held a state convention in Wheeling in October, and nominated John Frémont as their presidential candidate.[79]

Wherever Virginia's small band of Republicans tried to campaign, they were met with social ostracism, harassment, and violence. Maria Underwood (John's wife) made an elaborate Frémont flag and flew it over the house in spite of her neighbors' warnings that such a display of Republican partisanship was dangerous. Virginia newspapers, Know-Nothing and Democratic alike, reviled the Republican Party, reserving special venom for John Frémont's wife, Jessie. Celebrated in the North for her political pedigree, her beauty and intelligence, her daring decision to elope with John Frémont at the age of seventeen in 1841, and her antislavery convictions, Jessie Benton Frémont soon became the heroine of the Republican Party, and was prominently featured in campaign songs, stories, and paraphernalia. Democrats around the nation treated this development with scorn. A September 23, 1856, editorial in the Richmond *Daily Dispatch* associated Jessie with the dread Northern doctrine of woman's rights. "Jessie Circles," made up of "the old Amazonian phalanx, of which [feminist/abolitionist] Abby Kelly is Generalissimo," were springing up around the country, the paper noted disparagingly.[80]

Interestingly, the evidence on women's partisan oratory suggests that a sort of backlash against female "stump speakers" may have set in between 1852 and 1856. The campaign of 1852 presented women with more occasions for public speaking than any previous campaign. In the campaign of 1856, by contrast, individual women continued to make presentations to mixed assemblies, but when these women "spoke" in public, it was through male proxies. Suzanne Lebsock has argued that one mark of the male backlash against women in Petersburg was that by the mid-1850s, women were no longer extended the opportunity for public speaking.[81]

The reason that women were extended fewer opportunities for partisan oratory in 1856 than 1852 may lie in Southern perceptions of the rise of feminism in the North. Ironically, the very same newspapers which celebrated the contributions of partisan women and printed their speeches reported on the woman's rights conventions of 1852 with hostility and derision. After the 1848 Seneca Falls meeting, when feminists began holding regular conventions, Virginia papers followed the developments of the woman's rights movement carefully. More often than not, articles on woman's rights were hostile. The *Daily Dispatch* described delegates to the woman's suffrage convention in Syracuse, New York, in 1852, as "cackling geese," no two of whom "could agree as to any distinct proposition." The paper condemned the convention for endorsing the Whig presidential candidate, Winfield Scott. The Norfolk *Daily Southern Argus* said of the delegates, "They resolved to do innumerable silly things in order to keep pace with the progress of the age. . . . Their deliberations, from the opening to the close, exhibited one continuous scene of uproar and confusion." The *Alexandria Gazette* reported that women's-rights advocates would overturn St. Paul's injunction against women "preaching" in public. The paper reassured its readers that 999 out of 1000 women disagreed with the feminist position on female oratory.[82]

Why partisan women's opportunities for public speaking were curtailed remains a matter of speculation; no one explicitly addressed the issue. But the hypothesis is advanced here that the phenomenon was in no small part a consequence of sectionalism. In the partisan realm, the rise of sectionalism intensified the trends of the 1840s — Southern "ladies" preserved their image as moral agents specially able to discern where the interests of party, state, and Union converged. But it also intensified Southern anxiety about Northern feminism. With the ascendance of the Republican Party, Northern feminists had, or so Southerners feared, found a home. Torn between their desire to recruit women and their need to distance themselves from the Republicans, the political parties in Virginia seem to have settled on a compromise—while women were not encouraged to speak before mixed assemblies, they were encouraged to speak through male proxies. Women's perspective on public issues was valued, but the means by which women conveyed their messages were carefully regulated by men.

In the late 1850s, former Whigs and Know-Nothings in Virginia regrouped as the "Opposition" and portrayed themselves as moderate Unionists, steering a middle course between the "fanaticism" of the Northern Republicans and Southern Democrats alike. The dominant Democratic Party, for its part, fell more and more under the spell of "fire-eaters" such as Henry Wise, who advanced the Southern nationalist creed—that the North and South were distinct societies and cultures, that the North was to blame for the sectional impasse, and that secession was the only means of guaranteeing the permanency of slavery.[83]

Focused as they have been on men, histories of Southern nationalism have overlooked an important truth: Southern women, as consumers and producers of political discourse, were deeply implicated in the transition from partisanship to sectionalism. Through the medium of the political parties, women were exposed to sectional rhetoric and imbibed the notion that they could both express their partisanship in public and simultaneously promote the "feminine" values of harmony and moral virtue. Even as female oratory acquired the taint of radicalism in the 1850s, Virginia women elaborated new ways to express their political opinions. Using the media of fiction and prose, women entered the debates of the 1850s in the guise of sectional mediators, who could at once defend slavery and denounce "fanaticism," and thereby restore the equilibrium between the North and South. But they found that in the arena of sectional conflict, no less than in that of partisan conflict, true neutrality was impossible. One simply had to choose sides.

CHAPTER 4 *To Still the Angry Passions*

WOMEN AS SECTIONAL MEDIATORS AND PARTISANS

In the 1850s, as national moral-reform societies came under fire from Southern rights advocates and as partisan conflict became sectionalized, political moderates in the North and South argued with new urgency that it was woman's special duty to promote sectional peace. The notion that women should be sectional mediators, which had been present in the public discourse since the 1820s, was further developed in the 1850s in at least two forms—in "anti-*Uncle Tom*" literature that purported to ease sectional tensions by telling the "true" story of the South; and in the rhetoric of the Mount Vernon Association (MVA), an organization founded in 1854 to preserve George Washington's estate and his political legacy.[1]

Virginia women were relative latecomers to the literary defense of slavery and the South. Only one published defense of slavery by a Virginia woman appeared before 1848: Lucy Kenney's *A Refutation of the Principles of Abolition: By a Lady of Fredericksburg* (1830). She produced the proslavery pamphlet, Kenney claimed, at the urging of "some distinguished gentlemen of the South." Virulently racist, Kenney's tract asserted that blacks were characterized by "drowsiness, dullness, stupidness, inertness, or want of ability." Articulating the increasingly popular "comparative" defense of slavery, she contended that slaves were far better off than the "wretched poor emigrants which crowd the Northern cities." Abolition she attacked as a "diabolical scheme," adding, "I concur with those who believe that the incendiary spirit which is abroad can only be met and successfully opposed by a firm and united stand on the part of the slaveholding states." Details about Kenney's life and the reception of her work have proven elusive. Her proslavery pamphlet, like her later partisan tracts, render her somewhat of an anomaly; as we shall see, it was rare for women to choose the medium of the polemical essay to express their support for slavery. Much more popular was the medium of fiction.[2]

The 1820s witnessed the emergence of a new literary genre—that of plantation fiction. Disappointed that the Northeast had taken a decisive

lead over the South in literary output, and disgruntled by the negative portrayals of Southern life in the rhetoric of the nascent antislavery
movement, Southerners such as George Tucker and John Pendleton
Kennedy of Virginia and William Gilmore Simms of South Carolina
responded by developing the "Cavalier" myth in their fiction. They argued that the plantation South had a distinct culture — descended from
English Cavaliers rather than from the Puritan Roundheads who settled
the North — which needed to be promulgated in regional literature.[3]

The plantation tradition in literature has been the subject of extensive scholarly study. Plantation literature contrasted the harmony,
gentility, and moral virtue of Southern culture with the acquisitive-
ness, instability, and immorality of Northern culture. The genre's featured characters were benign planter-patriarchs, devoted slaves, and supremely moral and refined plantation mistresses. According to historian
Elizabeth Moss, plantation fiction by Southern men offered up the same
"prescriptions for ornamental femininity" as the proslavery polemics
of Thomas Dew and George Fitzhugh did: plantation novels emphasized feminine weakness and passivity. While authors in the genre paid
homage to woman's superior virtue and her mastery over the domestic
sphere, they demanded female obedience to male authority in return;
Southern women were, William Taylor has written, "offered half the loaf
in the hope they would not demand more."[4]

Female characters in the plantation genre were not necessarily igno-
rant of politics, but they were content to let their men speak for them
on political issues. Take, for example, the character of Delia in Nathaniel
Beverley Tucker's *The Partisan Leader* (1836). An eerily prescient novel
forecasting the secession of the South, *The Partisan Leader*, set in
Tucker's native Virginia, is also a romance — the love story of Delia, the
daughter of a pro-secession politician, and Douglas, her pro-secession
cousin and suitor. When, early in the novel, Delia's father is insulted in
her presence by a Unionist, she, though "conversant with the politics
of the day," does not defend her father but lets Douglas do the talking.
As a man, Douglas is "unrestrained by the considerations that imposed
silence" on Delia. By the novel's end, Douglas has proven himself a hero
in the South's quest for independence and won the hand of Delia.[5]

Only recently have scholars reminded us that another kind of female
character populated the Southern literary landscape in the antebellum
period. Even as Southern men developed the plantation genre, Southern women developed a literary tradition of their own — that of Southern domestic fiction. Southern women's domestic fiction, pioneered by

such authors as Caroline Gilman of South Carolina and Maria McIntosh of Georgia, represented variations both on the plantation novel and on Northern domestic fiction. Similar to plantation novels in cast and setting, Southern domestic novels, like Northern ones, featured intelligent and autonomous female heroines who overcame misfortunes to achieve self-fulfillment. While the plantation genre stressed female subordination, says Moss in her study of the five most influential Southern domestic novelists, Southern domestic fiction "explored the variety of options available to the female elite." In Southern women's fiction, women spoke out about politics — not only did female authors craft political dialogue and put it into the mouths of male characters, but female characters themselves often held forth on political issues.[6]

Moreover, Southern domestic novelists shared with their Northern counterparts a distinct political agenda — to promote sectional peace by telling the "truth" about life in each section. Scholar Nina Baym has argued that "women are given quite different patriotic work from men" in antebellum domestic fiction. Female authors in the North and South believed that it was women's special duty to serve as "guardians and implementers of the idea and ideals of nationhood" and thereby to preserve "civic stability." They favored plot devices such as intersectional marriages and "sentimentally negotiated rapprochements between northern and southern kin" to convey their message of political harmony. This mission of peacemaking, however, proved difficult to carry out, for women's "truthful" portrayals of sectional life were invariably colored by sectional prejudices. In works by Northern authors, such as Sarah Hale's *Northwood* (1827), the North on balance appeared to be superior in culture, morality, and industry to the South; Southern novels, such as Caroline Lee Hentz's *Lovell's Folly* (1833), suggested that the South was the repository of moral virtue and social stability — and that women should serve as the conservators of the region's values.[7]

The first Virginia woman to offer an extended defense of the South through fiction was Martha Fenton Hunter of Essex County: her "Sketches of Southern Life" appeared in the *Southern Literary Messenger* in 1848, under the pseudonym "F*****." Hunter was the sister of prominent politician Robert Mercer Taliaferro Hunter, a former Whig turned Democrat who served as a U.S. senator in the 1850s and vied with Governor Henry Wise for control over the Democratic Party. While residing at the Essex County estates of her father and brother, Hunter produced, usually under pseudonyms, an array of novels, short stories, and juvenile fiction in the 1840s and 1850s. Her efforts garnered her some praise;

the *Southern Literary Messenger* said in a review of her 1852 novel *The Clifford Family*, "Few of either sex in the commonwealth write in a more pleasing and flowing style."[8]

Hunter's "Sketches" begin with a conversation between two men, one from New York and one from Virginia. The New Yorker, Henry Livingston, harbors certain conceptions of the South which his friend Philip Seyton wishes to disabuse him of. So Seyton invites Livingston to visit his father's plantation, Oak Grove, in Virginia. When Henry arrives at the plantation, he is immediately taken aback by the kind relations between master and slave. One slave fervently defends his master's treatment of him, pointing out that the master never allows the overseer to mistreat the slaves, and even asserting that the master is perhaps not strict enough. Seeing a group of happy slave children playing outside, Henry finds it impossible "not to contrast them with the sickly children of the destitute poor, that he often met in the streets of N.Y., and feel an emotion of pity for the latter."[9]

Henry has an even bigger shock in store when he meets the mistress of the plantation, Philip's sister Fanny (their mother has died some years ago). Fanny is the very picture of the belle. She has a "natural grace of movement, . . . a light that beamed from the full, dark hazel eye, which seemed to emanate from the true, beautiful and tender spirit." But she is far from frivolous or spoiled. Fanny presides over a plantation of more than one hundred slaves with a firm but compassionate authority. Under her auspices, a fine dinner is presented to Henry, who, at the end of his first day at Oak Grove, finds it increasingly difficult to "reconcile his facts to his theories."[10]

Fanny is no ingenue when it comes to politics. She understands the importance of defending plantation ladies from the charge of indolence, and she is informed enough on history and current events to converse with and even advise men. Fanny, who is fiercely proud of her native state, tells Henry about how the typical plantation mistress spends her time, in order to "vindicate a class whose real position is so little understood—the daughters of the Old Dominion." After breakfast, Fanny explains, she gives "directions of all imaginable kinds to seamstresses, cooks, gardeners, housemaids, and an anomalous class denominated spinners." She then inspects their operations to make sure they are done properly. After describing to Henry her daily routine, Fanny impresses him with her knowledge of French history. Fanny even helps her cousin Frank, a politician running for a seat in the General Assembly, write a speech. Frank asks Fanny to look up some statistics in the *National Intelligencer*. "Ah, Fanny, if I had your quick eye and ready apprehension with me to aid my search over the long dull Congressional proceedings tonight, I should soon be as well off in facts as I am in quotations," he tells her. Henry, predictably, falls madly in love with Fanny by the story's end.[11]

Hunter's "Sketches" clearly contain many elements that were present in earlier works of Southern domestic fiction. Southern women, according to Hunter, infused plantation life with order and morality. Sectional peace depended not on a change in the South's understanding of the North, but in the presentation of "facts" about Southern life to undermine the North's invidious "theories." Each of these messages would take on a new urgency after Northerner Harriet Beecher Stowe countered Southern domestic novelists' vision of the plantation regime with her own.

Harriet Beecher Stowe, in *Uncle Tom's Cabin* (1852), irrevocably transformed the literary debate over sectionalism by doing what no other female novelist had done—she declared slavery a sin, and she brought slaves, who had remained in the background both of plantation novels and domestic fiction, into the foreground. Touching on themes such as miscegenation and sexual abuse that other literary women had ignored, Stowe presented an unrelenting picture of the injustice and cruelty that whites perpetrated on blacks. She did not deny that white Southern women could play the role of moral exemplars—Mrs. Shelby and little Eva were paragons of compassion—but Stowe made it clear that these female characters were, ultimately, powerless to bring virtue to an essentially immoral system.[12]

The Southern reaction to *Uncle Tom's Cabin* has been well documented. The novel caused a widespread public uproar, and prompted the South's leading literary lights to condemn Stowe for having committed the supremely unwomanly sin of fomenting discord. The most influential literary man in Virginia, John R. Thompson of the *Southern Literary Messenger*, offered up a typical Southern critique of Stowe. His October 1852 review of *Uncle Tom's Cabin* accused Stowe of meddling in public affairs. Stowe, Thompson charged, belonged to the school of woman's rights which "would place woman on a footing of political equality with man . . . [and] would engage her in the administration of public affairs."[13]

Moreover, *Uncle Tom's Cabin* served as a catalyst in the transformation of Southern literary sectionalism into Southern literary nationalism. Up until the 1850s, Southern writers, by and large, had believed that Southern literary sectionalism was compatible with American literary nationalism — that to promote excellence in Southern literature was to enrich the national culture. In the wake of *Uncle Tom's Cabin*, however, the competition between North and South for literary honors turned into open conflict. The South, the editors of the region's leading literary journals asserted, needed to achieve not only equality with the North in literary production, but cultural independence from the North as well. It was the duty of Southern authors, a contributor to the *Southern Literary Messenger* wrote, not only to dispel Northern fanaticism but also to "show that it is to the institution of slavery that we [Southerners] owe our superiority in morals, politics, religion and obedience to the law."[14]

After *Uncle Tom's Cabin*, as before it, Southern women participated in the literary debate over slavery in the role of mediators, who could restore sectional equilibrium by presenting truthful pictures of Southern life. But just as Southern literary sectionalism and American literary nationalism were becoming ever more difficult to reconcile in the 1850s, so, too, were women's twin duties — to defend the South and to promote harmony. Virginia women's writings on sectional issues ultimately better served the cause of Southern partisanship than that of sectional peace.

Within two years after the appearance of Stowe's work, some fourteen novels by Southern writers were published to rebut her claims. Five of those novels were written by Southern women, two by Virginians. The first — and generally considered the best — fictional proslavery response to *Uncle Tom's Cabin* was Mary Eastman's *Aunt Phillis's Cabin: Or, Southern Life as It Is* (1852). Born and raised in Virginia, Eastman spent most of her adult life outside the state, traveling in the West with her army-officer husband, and finally settling with their children in Washington, D.C. The couple collaborated on an influential book on Indian culture, *Dahcotah: Or, Life and Legends of the Sioux Around Fort Snelling* (1849), Mary providing the texts, and Seth, an accomplished artist, furnishing the illustrations. Appalled by the success of *Uncle Tom's Cabin*, Eastman in 1852 put aside her Indian writings and hurried into print her own novel on slavery.[15]

The plot of *Aunt Phillis's Cabin* centers on a Virginia family, the Westons, who live on a grand plantation populated by kind white folks and contented slaves. The main protagonist is young Alice, the niece of the plantation patriarch. Over the course of the novel, she falls out of love with the wrong man, Walter, agrees to marry the right man, Arthur, and learns the duties of the plantation mistress from her mother, Anna. Eastman's novel, like Stowe's, includes detailed depictions of slaves — only Eastman's depictions were meant to illustrate the harmony and morality of plantation life. Aunt Phillis, who appears halfway through the story, is the archetypal contented slave. A mulatto house servant with "free blood" in her veins, Phillis nonetheless refuses to accept freedom when it is offered her by her master. Phillis's household, Eastman relates, is nothing like the shabby slave dwellings described by Stowe. Rather, it is the picture of order: "not a spot of grease dimmed the whiteness of the floors, and order reigned supreme, marvellous to relate! where a descendant of Afric's daughters presided." Phillis is also a model of piety. Arthur, Mr. Weston's son, describes her thus: "Her industry, her honesty, her attachment to our family, exceeds everything. . . . Her whole life has been a recommendation of the religion of the Bible." [16]

Not only does it devote more room to portraying slave life than earlier works of Southern domestic fiction had, but Eastman's novel also contains more editorializing on political issues and on the political duties of women than earlier works in the genre. Eastman's novel displays an ideological flexibility on the issue of slavery, mustering both "positive good" and "necessary evil" defenses of the institution. Eastman opens the book by establishing the biblical endorsement of slavery; from the curse of Ham to the historical examples of Egypt and Rome, to Jesus's tacit acceptance of the institution. She also adduces the experience of the Revolutionary forefathers and mothers, who shed their lifeblood to defend the South's social system. She then articulates the "necessary evil" justification — "though an evil, [slavery] is one that cannot be dispensed with; and here they [slaves] have been retained, and will be retained, unless God should manifest his will (which never yet has been done) to the contrary." Her view of slavery is directly inherited from her Revolutionary forefathers, Eastman declares, who "drew the nice line of distinction between an unavoidable evil and a sin." [17]

The only remedy for the evil of slavery was, in Eastman's view, the colonization of ex-slaves in Liberia. Early in the novel Eastman editorializes on behalf of the colonization cause: "If white labor could be substituted for black, better were it that she [the South] should not have this weight upon her. The emancipation of her slaves will never be accomplished by interference or force. Good men assist in colonizing them, and the Creator may thus intend to Christianize benighted Africa. Should this be the Divine will, oh! that from every port, steamers were going forth, bearing our colored people to their natural home!" [18]

Stowe herself advocated colonization in *Uncle Tom's Cabin* — but Eastman's endorsement of the cause had a very different meaning than Stowe's. As we have seen in Chapter 2, by 1852, colonization had ceased to represent a political middle ground for Northerners and Southerners.

Southern colonization societies had become increasingly proslavery in outlook, thereby alienating many of the cause's staunchest female advocates, such as Mary Blackford. Blackford—who was a rare Southern admirer of *Uncle Tom's Cabin*—believed that the slave system was sinful, and saw colonization as a way to dismantle it.[19] In contrast to Stowe and Blackford, Eastman was unwilling to concede that slavery was inherently sinful or that it engendered the widespread abuse of blacks by whites. For Eastman, colonization was not a catalyst to abolition but an alternative to it.

Eastman's characters admit that slavery occasionally produces tragedies such as the separation of slave families, but they argue that such occurrences are "very uncommon." Instead of holding Southerners partially responsible for the deterioration of sectional relations, Eastman lays the blame for the country's fragile condition squarely on the shoulders of abolitionists. She counters Stowe's tales of horror with the story of a poor slave who is seduced away from his master and then mistreated by abolitionists. Such cases occur far more often, Eastman insists, than the "raw-head and bloody-bones" stories of Stowe. Her female characters themselves are not afraid to take on the abolitionists. In one scene, a character named Mrs. Moore holds her own in a political discussion with an abolitionist, criticizing him and his compatriots for not providing suitable jobs and resources for freedpeople.[20]

Throughout the novel, Eastman reminds women of their political duties and influence. It is woman's special duty, she argues, to conserve the values and institutions of the Founding Fathers. She has her characters visit Mount Vernon, and then tells her readers, "Remember this, mothers in America; and imprint upon the fair tablet of your young child's heart, a reverence for the early institutions of their country, and for the patriots who moulded them, that 'God and my country' may be the motto of their lives." Although she counseled Americans to have reverence for the nation's early institutions, Eastman's prescription for sectional harmony was not increased contact between the sections but rather mutual noninterference: "Let the people of the North take care of their poor," she wrote. "Let the people of the South take care of theirs."[21]

That prescription evidently had widespread appeal. *Aunt Phillis's Cabin* sold some 18,000 copies in the space of a few weeks. Eastman's publishers, Lippincott, Grambo and Company of Philadelphia, capitalized on the notion that Eastman was a dispassionate mediator. They advertised her book as follows: "Pledged to no clique or party, and free from the pressure of any and all extraneous influences, she has written her book with a view to its truthfulness; and the public at the North, as

well as at the South, will find . . . not the distorted picture of an interested painter, but the faithful transcript of a Daguerrotypist."²²

Critics in both sections found Eastman's "faithful transcript" to be
to their liking. The *Daily National Intelligencer*, for example, described
Eastman as "the first to stem the torrent which foamed around 'Uncle
Tom,' and, by her true life-like narrative of 'Aunt Phillis's Cabin,' turned
the waters of public feeling into a more natural and healthy channel."
Southern literary journals praised Eastman's "truthfulness." *De Bow's
Review*, published in New Orleans, proclaimed, "Mrs. Eastman has written, perhaps, the very best answer to that gross libel upon the South,
denominated 'Uncle Tom's Cabin.' . . . [She] has furnished many ad-
mirable and truthful pictures, contrasting the slave of the South with
the free laborer of other countries." The *Southern Quarterly Review* of
Charleston agreed that Eastman's work was "truthful, which cannot be
said of Uncle Tom," but lamented that truth was often less seductive
than falsehood. The critical and commercial success of *Aunt Phillis's
Cabin* is a tribute not only to the popularity of the notion that women
should "stem the torrent" of sectionalism but also to Eastman's skill as
a writer. Part of the appeal of the book no doubt lay in its ambiguity—
Eastman declared slavery a "necessary evil" but focused on the harmony
and morality of Southern plantation life. Moreover, unlike other anti-
Tom authors, Eastman refrained from leveling an overall indictment at
the North; instead, she reserved her criticism for the abolitionists.²³

The other anti-Tom novel by a Virginia woman, Martha Haines Butt's
Antifanaticism: A Tale of the South, repeated Eastman's message but
without her skill or ambiguity, and fell far short of the success of *Aunt
Phillis's Cabin*. Butt, a Norfolk native, had been prompted to action by
Uncle Tom's Cabin. "After the perusal of that overdrawn picture," she
wrote, "she really felt it her duty to stand up for her own native place."
Butt defined her position on the peculiar institution in her preface:
"People of the North, who have never visited the South, should not give
heed to stories which are but the figments of a worse than distempered
imagination. Our slaves are infinitely better off than the white servants
of the North. They have kind owners who care for them, and do all in
their power to promote their happiness."²⁴

Butt's novel begins with a familiar device—the visit of Mr. I——,
an abolitionist Northerner, to the Virginia plantation of Mr. and Mrs.
M——. Naturally, the M——s treat their visitor with Southern hospitality, and he leaves the South feeling that he has misjudged slaveowners.
The central black character is the M——s' house servant, Aunt Phebe;
like Aunt Phillis, she is a stern, imposing, and efficient being. Aunt

Phebe was nurse to the M——s' daughter, Medora, the main protagonist of the story. Early in the tale, Medora goes North to be educated at a seminary. Much of the book describes Medora's experience in school. She becomes best friends with a Northern girl, Lydia. Most important, she meets and falls in love with Lydia's brother.[25]

Meanwhile, back at the plantation, Butt informs us, life is good for whites and blacks alike. Her favorite plot conceit is to render slaves as defenders of slavery. The whites in *Antifanaticism* generally concede that freedom is a preferable state to slavery, and repeatedly offer to manumit individual slaves as a reward for faithful service. But the slaves themselves object to emancipation. One slave, Rufus, tells Mr. I—— he prefers not to be free, for if he were, "den nobody would care for Rufus den." Mr. M—— eventually gives the elderly Phebe and her husband Uncle Dick their freedom, despite the fact that they "did not seem very desirous of obtaining it"; he provides the couple with a cottage on his property, so that they can continue to be near their former masters. The novel ends with Medora's graduation and marriage to Lydia's brother. Neither a Northern education nor a Northern husband can challenge Medora's fidelity to the South, though. When Phebe worries about Medora marrying an abolitionist, Mrs. M—— reassures her, "O no, Phebe; she [Medora] will always have her Southern principles." Medora remains untainted by Northern heresy; her Northern husband instead literally comes over to the Southern side. Medora and her Northern husband take up residence at a plantation neighboring Mr. M——'s.[26]

Butt fully subscribed to the comparative defense of slavery—the notion that the Southern slave system compared favorably with Northern capitalism—and her characters endlessly exclaim that slaves are better treated than wage laborers in the North. She specifically allied herself with other Southern domestic novelists, dedicating *Antifanaticism* to anti-Tom author Caroline Lee Hentz, and ending it with a thank-you to Eastman. "If the Northern people have any sympathy to spare, let them give it to their poor white servants," Butt held forth, in a reworking of Eastman's motto, "for our slaves do not stand in need of it at all." But neither critics nor the public thought her in the league of Hentz and Eastman. The *Southern Quarterly Review*, for example, which praised Eastman, said of Butt: "She means well; but the good intentions which are said to pave Hell—it must not be forgotten—make very bad pavements."[27]

The same year that Butt published *Antifanaticism*, another denizen of the Old Dominion, Julia Gardiner Tyler, defended slavery in print. A member of New York's social elite, Julia Gardiner at age twenty-four had married President John Tyler—thirty years her senior—in 1844. After a brief stint in the White House, the couple moved in 1845 to Tyler's homestead, Sherwood Forest, a vast plantation in Charles City County, Virginia, worked by some seventy slaves. Julia Gardiner Tyler seems to have adapted readily to her new home and to the role of plantation mistress. In February of 1853, her essay in defense of slavery, "To the Duchess of Sutherland and Ladies of England," appeared in the *Southern Literary Messenger*. The Duchess and her circle had provoked Tyler's ire by accepting Stowe's portrait of the evils of slavery. Inspired by Stowe, the English ladies held a convention which condemned American slavery and, in an address circulated in American papers, urged the women of America to support abolition.[28]

Tyler began her piece with the disclaimer that American women, generally, restricted themselves to the private sphere. The American woman, she claimed, "knows nothing of political conventions, or conventions of any other sort than such as are held under suitable pastors of the Church, and are wholly directed to the advancement of the Christian religion." While Southern women were content in their sphere, she went on, they were well informed on national issues: "Politics is almost universally the theme of conversation among the men, . . . and the women would be stupid indeed, if they did not gather much information from this abundant source." Southern women understood that the controversy over slavery posed a threat to the Union, Tyler asserted—and they also resented English interference in Southern domestic matters.[29]

As Southern domestic novelists did, Tyler argued that Southerners were trying to do right by their slaves; in her opinion, most slaveowners provided for the religious instruction and the material comfort of the slaves. Furthermore, she noted, Virginia had originated the scheme of African colonization, which Tyler saw not as a prelude to abolition but as the most efficacious means to deal with the growing free-black population. Colonizationists sought to "retribute the wrongs done by England to Africa, by returning civilization for barbarity—Christianity for idolatry." Tyler did not deny that slavery created some "immorality and crime" in the South. For that England was to blame, she asserted, for England had introduced slavery into the Southern colonies. The English had missed their chance to make amends—and now slavery was the business of Southerners. England, she reminded the Duchess, had its own underclass of poor whites to care for. "Leave it to the women of the South to alleviate the sufferings of their own dependents," Tyler told the Duchess, "while you take care of your own."[30]

Tyler's essay, her biographer has written, made her "a national figure and a Southern heroine." Virginia papers hailed her effort; the *Petersburg Gazette* declared that Tyler had "knocked the Duchess's document into next week." One music hall in Richmond featured a song titled "The Duchess," which taunted the English lady with the words, "Mrs. Tyler gave you what was right, But Duchess don't you cry."[31] Tyler had successfully walked a tightrope. She defended slavery without asserting either that the South was perfect or the North irredeemable; she registered her disapproval of the new state of affairs in which women publicly spoke out on slavery, but at the same time defended the necessity and propriety of her own pronouncements.

Neither Eastman nor Butt nor Tyler was a Southern nationalist when she wrote her defense of slavery; not one of them advocated that the South secede from the Union. Eastman remained loyal to the Union during the Civil War. Butt married a Northerner, N. J. Bennett of Connecticut, in 1865, and moved to Hartford, Connecticut, sometime thereafter. Tyler spent most of the Civil War in New York.[32] The three women's antebellum work contributed nonetheless to the nascent cause of Southern literary nationalism, for they advanced principles that Southern nationalists considered central to the case for regional independence—that the North and not the South was to blame for the deterioration of sectional relations, and that peace could be preserved only if the North refrained from interfering in Southern life. While Southern women's literature in the 1830s and 1840s had been optimistic about the prospects of sectional reconciliation, over the course of the 1850s, women's writings on sectional issues became increasingly pessimistic in tone.[33] And pessimism itself, as it turned out, was a kind of fuel for the fire of Southern nationalism.

After 1853, no other Virginia woman directly attacked Harriet Beecher Stowe in fiction or prose. But the decade witnessed the emergence of a new crop of female novelists who defended slavery, condemned Northern radicalism, and quietly argued for the intellectual capabilities of women. In 1854, the woman who would become the most celebrated of Virginia's nineteenth-century authors—Mary Virginia Terhune—burst onto the literary scene. Terhune was born in Amelia County in 1830 to a middle-class family of "mad book-lovers" and educated as if she were a boy preparing for college. Soon after the family relocated to Richmond in 1844, Mary took up writing, publishing short stories in *Godey's Lady's Book* and the temperance journal *Southern Era*. In 1856 she married the Reverend Edward Terhune; the couple resided in Charlotte County for three years, and then moved North, to New Jersey. Not deterred by domestic responsibilities (she bore six children), Mary Terhune would publish novels, biographies, domestic manuals, travel books, magazine and newspaper articles, and a reminiscence of her life during her lengthy and prolific literary career.[34]

Under her pen name, "Marion Harland," Terhune produced four novels in the antebellum period — *Alone* (1854), *The Hidden Path* (1855), *Moss-side* (1857), and *Nemesis* (1860) — to public and critical accolades. *Alone* passed through six printings in its first year of publication, and eventually sold more than 100,000 copies. It received almost as much attention from the *Southern Literary Messenger* as *Uncle Tom's Cabin* had. "It is a Southern production in every sense of the word," the *Messenger* triumphantly proclaimed in June of 1854, referring to the fact that *Alone* had been published as well as written in the South. The influential journal found much to praise in Terhune's other novels, as well.[35]

Terhune's second novel, *The Hidden Path*, is representative of the themes and techniques of her antebellum work: it features a female heroine who by story's end finds true love; it advocates female intellectual development; it offers prescriptions for sectional harmony; and it portrays blacks as inferior beings, content to be dependent on whites. The novel's main protagonist is Bella, the daughter of Mrs. Conway, herself the widowed mistress of a Virginia plantation called "The Grove." As the story opens, Mrs. Conway is married to one Mr. Snowden, much to the distress of Bella, who suspects Snowden to be a man of low character. At her stepfather's insistence, Bella goes north to Philadelphia for her education, and, upon her return to Virginia, finds that the inheritance money left her by her deceased father has mysteriously disappeared. Robbed of her means and determined not to depend on Snowden, she takes up the profession of teaching. Rejecting the frivolity of "fashionable female education," Bella brings seriousness and competence to her various teaching posts. On the romantic front, she is betrayed by a fickle suitor, who chooses to marry a wealthy debutante rather than a poor schoolmarm. But Bella eventually finds true love and marital bliss with her cousin, the honorable Maurice Oakley of Philadelphia. She also, by story's end, uncovers the subterfuge of her stepfather — who was embezzling the family's money — and reclaims her inheritance.[36]

The other female protagonist in the novel is Isabel Oakley, Bella's cousin in Philadelphia. Isabel, a literary woman, may be Terhune herself. After receiving a harsh review from a male critic, Isabel is mortified and begins to feel that she has "transgressed the bounds providence has marked for [women]" by embarking on a writing career. Isabel's brother Maurice counters her doubts, telling her "God never gave a talent which

it would be sinful to improve." He then avers that men only hurt themselves by restricting the mental development of women, who are "the
future guardians of our Republic and Religion." While Maurice defends
women's right to intellectual expression, he simultaneously condemns
the woman's rights movement. "Women like you, my sweet sister," he
tells Isabel, "do more in one year to effect your emancipation, than these
unfeminine ranters will do in a century." [37]

It is into Isabel's mouth that Terhune chooses to place both a commentary on sectional relations and a spirited defense of Virginia. In a
discussion with a Southern visitor to her native city, Isabel proclaims, "It
is a pity that there is not more friendly intercourse between the North
and the South. A mutual understanding of the customs and feelings of
the communities . . . would be a death blow to dissension, or, at least, give
birth to more charity." Isabel loves Virginia, she says, not only because of
its hallowed place in American history but also because it has given her
two of her best friends — Bella and her brother Jamie. The latter, a "fiery
Southerner in principle," is in Isabel's opinion the "soul of chivalry." [38]

In the sections of the novel set in Virginia, Terhune brings forth
the stock elements of plantation fiction. "The Grove" is populated by
stereotypical slaves, who are deeply loyal to their mistress, Mrs. Conway, and openly suspicious of her new husband. A gruff and formidable
cook, Aunt Hagar, and a pompous coachman given to malapropisms,
Ben, head up the cast of slave characters. Terhune's portrayals of slaves
are typified by the following: "The country negro is a nocturnal ani-
mal. Having dozed at the plough handle, and nodded over his hoe all
day, it costs him no trouble to borrow largely from the night, to make
up the complement of waking hours." Terhune remained wedded to
such racist stereotypes; in her reminiscences, published in 1910, she described blacks as "passionate and unreasoning, facile and impulsive."
While Terhune admitted that there was a "dark side" to slavery and was
sympathetic to the colonization cause, she until her last days upheld the
notion advanced by her antebellum writing that "slavery existed in Virginia in its mildest form possible" and that slaveowners were, for the
most part, animated by humane paternalism. Her own family's dozen
servants were, she recalls, "warmly attached to us." [39]

Terhune, like Eastman, Butt, and Tyler, was no Southern nationalist.
A lifelong Whig and avid follower of politics, Terhune was deeply committed to the idea of Union, and indeed remained faithful to the Union
during the Civil War.[40] But her works, in the eyes of Southern critics
and fans, easily became weapons in the cultural contest for sectional su-

premacy. Of *The Hidden Path*, Anna Cora Ritchie, a popular author and actress, declared "let Virginia produce a few more such writers, and the cry that the South has no literature of its own is silenced forever!" Many Virginians, such as Willie and Eliza A. Willson, drew the same conclusion in private. Eliza Willson, an unmarried woman living on a farm in Rockbridge County, was an intellectual mentor to her nephew Willie. While he was away at school in Lexington, Virginia, the pair carried on a lively correspondence on religion, agriculture, literature, and politics. Willie wrote to Eliza in 1858, saying that *The Hidden Path* was well received in the South but not the North: "I suppose it is merely the ebullitions of Northern abolitionistic jealousy lest the South, awakening from the lethargy which has hitherto prevented her accomplishing much in literature, . . . should excel her in literature as well as in everything else, save . . . free-loveism, free-negroism, bloomerism and hatred to the Union." In her response to Willie's letter, Eliza seconded his interpretation: "I am not surprised the Northerners curl their noses when anything good comes out of the South, they are like the ancient Pharisees, disposed to ask if anything good can come out of Nazareth."[41]

Among the other influential literary standard-bearers for Virginia are Margaret Junkin of Lexington and Judith Page Walker Rives of Albemarle County. Born in 1820 in the North, Junkin moved south in 1848 when her father accepted a teaching post at Washington College. She married a Virginia Military Institute professor in 1857 and came to preside over a household of nine children (seven her husband's by a previous marriage) and three slaves. Sharing the secessionist views of her husband, Margaret Junkin Preston put her pen in the service of the South during the Civil War and achieved renown as one of the Confederacy's foremost poets.[42]

Junkin's literary career began before her marriage. In 1856, she anonymously published her only novel, entitled *Silverwood*. It is the story of the widowed Mrs. Irvine and her four daughters—Zilpha, Edith, Josepha, and Eunice—who, having lost their old home to a fire, settle at Silverwood where they struggle to regain a sense of peace and financial stability. Edith Irvine, the principal character, takes up teaching and writing to support the family. A stand-in for Junkin herself, Edith disavows any fondness for the "Amazonian tribe who are fighting for a 'wider sphere'" for women. But she does complain that a lively intellect is a curse to women, for it "puts temptations before her to leave the beaten track—a thing always objectionable for a woman. If she is conscious of these noble strivings, she does feel hampered by the restraints society imposes." Edith, like Junkin, eventually finds true love with a man who accepts her literary career; the Irvine family is rescued from its genteel poverty by a bequest from a relative.[43]

Silverwood features a ringing endorsement of the South's social system and traffics in racist stereotypes. The master of the plantation, before his death, sent to Liberia all the slaves who wanted to go. Among those who preferred to remain were Aunt Rose, a cook/mammy of "elephantine proportions," and the "old negro factotum," Uncle Felix, who was given to "masterly inactivity." Junkin's white characters are kind and respectful to their slaves. In a set piece typical of plantation fiction, the Irvines lovingly fit out one of their slaves, Daphne, on her wedding day. The wedding preparations provide Junkin with an occasion for some commentary on sectional differences: when a Northern visitor says she would never make wreaths for white servants, let alone "darkies," Josepha replies that Southerners try earnestly to win their servants' affection. Northerners had so much trouble with their white servants, Josepha opines, because they took "so little interest in them." Though Junkin was not a skillful novelist, the *Southern Literary Messenger* found her views to be palatable; it called her "a new Virginia claimant for the honors of literary fame," and *Silverwood* "a true story redolent of Virginia."[44]

Judith Page Walker Rives, who, as we have seen, followed politics closely and supported the Whigs in the 1840s, began her literary career in the 1820s while her husband, William, was in the Virginia House of Delegates. She and William traveled widely during his stint as minister to France, and in 1842 Rives published a popular travel account, *Tales and Souvenirs of a Residence in Europe*. In 1857 she brought out *Home and the World*, a sentimental romance that culminates in the wedding of its heroine, Constance Melville, to her suitor, Reginald. Though set mostly in Europe, *Home and the World* begins on a Southern plantation, Avonmore. The estate is presided over by a refined and gentlemanly owner, Mr. Melville. Among his favorite slaves is a "venerable" old man named — not coincidentally, one suspects — Uncle Tom. Uncle Tom has an "air of neatness and comfort" about him and sports a broadbrimmed hat which "Mistis knit for him with her own white hands." When the slave girl Henny, daughter of Avonmore's beloved Mammy, takes sick, Constance and the Melvilles attend to her "with all the care that the best medical aid and ceaseless kindness could provide." Like Butt had before her, Rives has her slave characters reject emancipation and defend slavery. Melville offers Tom his freedom, prompting Tom's wife, Betty, to say, "And what you gwine do then, Tom? . . . I hearn say free people has to wuk all day and wuk all night, and dont' make nothin' at that. . . . If you listen to my racket, you'll let free 'lone." Tom takes his wife's advice and turns down the offer of manumission.[45]

Virginia's leading women writers shared with each other both a fealty to the Southern social system and a profound desire to establish writing as a legitimate calling for women. Those authors who offered up edifying messages — stories of virtuous heroines whose struggles culminate in happy marriages — won acceptance, even if they lacked literary skill. Those who departed from this formula, by contrast, became the objects of harsh criticism. A case in point is Lizzie Petit of Albemarle County. Her first novel, *Light and Darkness* (1855), is the story of a gifted woman who is driven to commit suicide by her good-for-nothing husband; the *Southern Literary Messenger* lambasted the novel for its "spurious morality." Petit's second novel, *Household Mysteries* (1856), hardly fared better. While it had its obligatory complement of slaves who "worshipped" their masters, "their ebony faces shining with content," the novel was a dauntingly convoluted and improbable romance, full of intrigue and deception. The *Messenger* took issue with Petit's story of "guilty love," particularly with a female character, Mrs. St. John, who "is made to conceal for years from her husband, the fact of a previous marriage." The journal could "not accept [*Household Mysteries*] as a truthful picture of 'Southern Society.' "[46]

More dramatically than Petit's, the case of Rebecca Brodnax Hicks reveals that there were limits to what Southern society would tolerate from its female aspirants to literary honors. Hicks, novelist and editor, founded the periodical *Kaleidoscope* in January of 1855. In greater detail than any other Virginia woman in the 1850s, Hicks editorialized on the duties of literary women to the South — and the duties of the South to its literary women. Her ultimate reward was alienation from the society she tried to defend.

Brodnax was born in the village of Lawrenceville, Brunswick County (the heart of the southside blackbelt), in 1823, to a well-to-do, Whiggish, slaveholding family. She was educated at a boarding school in Richmond, and at the age of twenty-one she married Dr. Benjamin Isaac Hicks, a successful middle-class slaveholder, and settled down in Brunswick. After giving birth to three children, Hicks, an admirer of Sarah Josepha Hale, editor of *Godey's Lady's Book*, embarked on a literary career. She published her first novel, *The Lady Killer*, in 1851 and a second, *The Milliner and the Millionaire*, in 1852. Her credits also include poems published in the *Southern Literary Messenger*, and a short serialized novel in *Putnam's Monthly Magazine*. Positive reactions to her early works emboldened Hicks to enter a new field of endeavor. In 1855, she moved to Petersburg and established the *Kaleidoscope*, a weekly publication with the format of a newspaper. Hicks seems to have financed the enterprise with money from her parents' estate. She also seems to have lived in Petersburg alone, with her husband and children remaining in Lawrenceville, about forty miles away. She chose Petersburg because she felt she would be better understood there than in Lawrenceville. The *Kaleidoscope* featured serialized short novels, book reviews, household hints, medical advice, and articles on a wide spectrum of other topics. Hicks penned the lead articles for each issue, and, though she on one occasion claimed that the journal would have "nothing to do with politics," her editorials took on some of the most controversial political issues of the day, including slavery and woman's rights.[47]

Hicks's primary mission was to disseminate "Southern values." "We like to record Southern meetings, Southern speeches, Southern enterprises, and to lend our aid in any way to our Southern friends," she declared. This commitment to the Southern cause initially won her paper the praise of a number of influential editors, a fact of which Hicks frequently reminded her readers. John R. Thompson of the *Southern Literary Messenger* tendered his support, as did editors of newspapers in Richmond and elsewhere. The *American Beacon* of Norfolk, for example, said of the *Kaleidoscope*, "Being a Southern paper, edited by a Southern lady, it . . . should be sustained by our Southern people in preference to the *Post, Saturday Courier* and other abolition sheets." [48]

In her early editorials, Hicks tried to use her pen to combat "fanaticism." Like Hunter, Eastman, Butt, and Tyler, she appealed to Northerners to refrain from their attacks on the South. In an editorial on February 14, 1855, entitled "We Slaveholders," Hicks lashed out at those "isolated, self-loving, self-sustaining Yankee[s]" who slandered well-meaning slaveholders. Northerners had to "check their tauntings, their ridicule, and their brutal mobs" in order for sectional bitterness to subside. "Men overheated in debate, must pause for a time, and reflect," Hicks asserted.[49]

Hicks singled out for condemnation the woman's rights movement. Her first editorial on woman's rights appeared in February of 1855. "That the sole object of a woman's life is *not* fashion, dress, establishments, and matrimony, I sincerely hope the nineteenth century will triumphantly prove," she began. But the likes of Antoinette Brown and Lucy Stone were not the ones to "demonstrate this great oncoming Truth." The leaders of the woman's rights movement, Hicks explained, had wrongly forsaken the one great power of women—the ability to influence men: "There is a *womanly* way to prove our great mission upon earth, which these masculine women will never discover. So long as we are women, we must act as such. . . . I hope I need not remark to the fair readers of the *Kaleidoscope* that it is absolutely necessary that we should *please* the men, before we can ever hope to conquer them. This important truth has been entirely overlooked by the Woman's Rights women." The key to improving relations between the sexes was for women to earn the empathy and intellectual respect of men. And if men were to fulfill their roles as political stewards for women, they had to learn to see things from the women's point of view.[50]

Hicks's notion that women had to "please" men to influence them was seconded by her "Corresponding Editress," Martha Haines Butt, author of *Antifanaticism*. Butt volunteered her services in August 1855. Hicks introduced Butt to her readers with the following praise: "Miss BUTT is, heart and soul, a Southerner. . . . To use her own expressive words, in a recent letter to us, Miss BUTT says, she 'likes to see the South hold on to its rights.' And readers, one of the holiest rights of the South is the *protection of its Literary Women*. . . . They should be holy in the eyes of those who would preserve that beautiful type of South- ern purity and modesty from the fierce invasion of Northern fanatics." Butt weighed in on the "woman question" with an editorial entitled "Woman's Work and Influence." Those in the North who were hold- ing woman's rights conventions were a small and isolated minority of women, Butt declared. The vast majority of women believed, with her, that woman could exert her "most powerful and salutary influence" as a wife and mother in the domestic sphere.[51]

Despite its editors' efforts to establish their allegiance to the South, however, the *Kaleidoscope* soon became the subject of controversy. From the start, Hicks anticipated that some of the members of her commu- nity—those who believed that women should not seek public notori- ety—would oppose her project. In March, the third month of publica- tion, she wrote, "If the public frowns upon us, we shall go on, still on, for frowns and scowls, and all manner of malice and uncharitableness, are just the very things we are accustomed to." By April, the *Kaleido- scope* had received enough criticism that Hicks's husband had to declare that he was not opposed to the paper. The spring and summer issues all included his "Special Notice" countering rumors that his wife was act- ing against his wishes. In the September 1855 issue, Hicks portrayed her paper as a frail bark struggling to stay afloat on an angry sea.[52]

Unfortunately, no records detailing the opposition to Hicks have survived. We do not know exactly which element of the public expressed disapproval—but it is not difficult to surmise what prompted objections. To understand the nature of Hicks's transgressions, it is instructive to compare her to the most influential of the South's political spokeswoman, proslavery/antifeminist essayist Louisa McCord of South Carolina. Historian Elizabeth Fox-Genovese has convincingly mapped out McCord's public identity and accounted for her success. McCord strove for an "objective voice," conceiving of her authorship as an extension of her class position, not personal identity; addressed herself not to women as a group but to the intellectual elite of the South; and defended the social hierarchy, especially the notion that women's most important calling was as mothers.[53] Hicks adopted an entirely different posture. She advocated many of the same principles as McCord, but her tone was indignant rather than objective. Rather than choosing to write anonymously or under a pseudonym (McCord typically signed only her initials), Hicks wrote under her own name, and actively served as her own publicist. Most important, Hicks wrote as a woman for women, and repeatedly and stridently criticized men.

"The man who would deny to woman the cultivation of her intellect ought, for consistency, to shut her up in a harem," Hicks editorialized in defense of women writers, adding, "We are not so anxious to prove that women are capable of any mental effort, as that they *require* mental effort." Other writers made the case for female education, but none directly chastised a community, as Hicks did Petersburg, for failing to provide schooling for its girls. Others placed upon Southern shoulders the responsibility for ameliorating social relations in the region, but none dictated to Southern men their duty to their slaves. The restoration of sectional equilibrium, Hicks asserted, depended not only on a change in Yankee attitudes but a change in the behavior of the Southern master: "He knows the black man. He is his foster brother. He is *obliged* to know what his brother needs, and he should, with that magnanimity which so pre-eminently distinguishes him, above all men on the face of the globe, acknowledge the fact, and do, what he, and he *alone* can do."[54]

Hicks even went so far as to take aim at a powerful man. In April of 1855, she produced an angry editorial directed at the president of Randolph-Macon College, Reverend William A. Smith, who had just given an address in Petersburg on the subject of despotism and civil rights. Smith had apparently defended the despotism of man over woman. Hicks found his comments offensive, and used them as an occasion to attack the notion that men could or should speak for women:

Individual rights are sacred. . . . Let every man, woman or child with a tongue in his head be allowed to speak and say what they want! That is our philosophy.

Will any man dare to say that the Great Economist of a universe, in which every atom has its appointed use, would place a tongue into a woman's mouth that she might *remain silent*? . . . Then, what right has Dr. SMITH, or Dr. Anybody else, to be telling us what we do not want, when we can tell it so much better ourselves?[55]

With her evocation of individual rights and her implication that women had the right to freedom from male despotism, Hicks left McCord and her fellow Southern literary women far behind. For while Southern writers had been quite comfortable invoking woman's *duties* — to promote peace and to defend the values of their communities — woman's rights was a subject none dared touch except to register their criticism.

By November of 1855, with her paper less than a year old, Hicks had become thoroughly disheartened. In a bitter editorial, she accused the South of not living up to its reputation for chivalry, courage, patriotism, and generosity. "*Public opinion* is the tyrant of the South — and public opinion, more than any other institution, keeps down Southern enterprise, and individual talent. Public opinion makes it ungentlemanly to shoulder an axe, or unladylike to use a pen," she asserted. But in the end, Hicks gave in to the tyrant. In February of 1857, publication of the *Kaleidoscope* was discontinued, and Hicks disappeared from the literary scene. Hicks's father died in 1858, his will disowning her; her husband died two years later. In 1862 she moved to Washington, D.C., where she married a Union officer, Captain Hobart E. FitzGerald. Rebecca Hicks died in 1870.[56]

Hicks may have hoped that her paper's motto, "we take no side in religion or politics," would insulate her from criticism. But in fact her independence — her willingness to criticize even her beloved South — made her vulnerable. The female characters who populated the fiction of Terhune et al. experienced moments of frustration with society's conventions, and at times even served as mild critics. But in the end, they always were reconciled to themselves and their communities, through love or faith. Hicks was no stock character, and there was no such happy ending for her.

Hicks's story notwithstanding, Virginia's literary women had, over the course of the 1850s, helped to change the way Virginians conceived of the public role of women.[57] They had intervened in political discourse over slavery and feminism as mediators, specially able to dispel fanaticism by telling the "truth" about the South. They championed the notion that change for the better, for slaves or women, was a matter of evolution not revolution. And they defended the South's right to determine the course of that evolution.

While the notion that women should be sectional mediators co-existed uneasily with Southern partisanship in the writings of Virginia's literary women, it was articulated more forcefully and more consistently in the rhetoric of a new national organization to which many of Virginia's most politically prominent women contributed. That organization, the Mount Vernon Association, united women who were divided on the issue of slavery, by party, and by section. It provided Virginia with a public image of feminine civic virtue that harked back to the past even as it further advanced the notion that women could shape sectional discourse.

Just as the Ladies Association for Erecting a Statue to Henry Clay was the product of a family dialogue between Lucy Barbour and her nieces, so, too, the Mount Vernon Association was conceived by the women of a prominent Southern family. Traveling down the Potomac by boat on a moonlit night in 1853, Louisa Dalton Bird Cunningham, a Virginia-born plantation mistress living in Laurens County, South Carolina, caught a glimpse of Washington's great estate on the shore. The old mansion and its grounds, Cunningham observed, were in a distressingly dilapidated state. The next day Cunningham wrote her daughter, Ann Pamela, at the family plantation in South Carolina, and posed the question: Why couldn't the women of the South join together to restore and preserve Mount Vernon?

Ann Pamela Cunningham, like Lucy Barbour before her, wasted no time in translating a query into a plan of action. Like Barbour, Cunningham chose as her first step an appeal to the press. In a letter of December 2, 1853, to the *Charleston Mercury*, signed "A Southern Matron," Cunningham called on the women of the South to purchase the estate and present it as a gift to the state of Virginia. A few months later, the women of Liberty, South Carolina, met to consider a way to implement Cunningham's suggestion. Their meeting was followed by others around the South. In the summer of 1854, a group of women from Richmond and Manchester, Virginia, met at Metropolitan Hall in Richmond and formed the Mount Vernon Association (MVA). Ann Pamela Cunningham's idea thereby became the business of Virginia.[58]

For the purposes of this study, the significance of the Mount Vernon Association lies less in the fact that it eventually succeeded in preserving

Washington's estate than that it generated a wealth of discourse in Virginia on women's civic duty. Publicized in newspapers such as the *Richmond Enquirer* and *New York Ledger*, in journals like *Godey's Lady's Book* and the *Southern Literary Messenger*, and in hundreds of speeches by dignitaries such as renowned orator Edward Everett of Massachusetts, the MVA was perhaps the most celebrated of all antebellum women's associations. Those who spoke in public on behalf of the movement advanced the idea that women's patriotism differed in kind from men's — it was purer, more self-sacrificing, more enduring. The women of the association saw themselves, and wanted to be seen, as promoters of national unity. That public image was maintained with great difficulty, in the face of internal dissension, public apathy, and even open hostility from men who saw the association as a player in the factional feuds that gripped Virginia's Democratic Party.

In its initial phase, the Mount Vernon project was exclusively a Southern one. Ann Pamela Cunningham's first contact in Virginia was John H. Gilmer, a Whig lawyer from Richmond. While Cunningham remained in South Carolina, Gilmer convened the first meeting of the Virginia Mount Vernon Association on July 12, 1854, in Richmond. The meeting, attended by thirty or so prominent women and men, opened with the appointment of Julia Mayo Cabell as chair, and with the election of officers. The association seems to have been a bipartisan enterprise. Cabell, the president, was a well-known public figure from a Whig family. She was director of the Union Benevolent Society and a contributor to the Clay Association, and had just published a volume of essays and poetry. William McFarland, a prominent Whig who was treasurer of the Clay Association, was named Mount Vernon treasurer, while William F. Ritchie, Democratic editor of the *Richmond Enquirer*, was named secretary.[59]

Gilmer presented a constitution to the women, which they ratified, and also read an address which outlined the purposes of the association. Gilmer noted in the address that although Governor Joseph Johnson of Virginia had recommended that the Commonwealth buy Mount Vernon, "the sons of Virginia [had] passed, unheeded, the calls of patriotic duty." Mount Vernon could only be saved, Gilmer insisted, by the "well-directed effort of the ladies of Virginia." After Gilmer's address, and a brief speech by Governor Johnson himself, the first meeting of the Mount Vernon Association adjourned.[60]

Gilmer's notion that women would heed a call to patriotic duty that men had ignored would find many echoes in the discourse about the association. So, too, would his notion that Virginia women should be the prime movers in the project. For the next half a year, the women of the association encouraged the formation of auxiliaries, while the men took on the task of negotiations with John Augustine Washington, a descendant of George Washington's and the proprietor of Mount Vernon. To Gilmer's request for cooperation, Washington responded that while he appreciated the "pure and disinterested feelings" that inspired the women of Virginia and the South to preserve Mount Vernon, he did not want the estate to pass from his possession unless it went to Virginia or the Union. To let women purchase the estate, he explained, would subject him to "mortification." For while such a sale would illustrate female patriotism, it would also "commemorate the degeneracy of myself and the men of our land."[61]

In a letter of November 1854 to Gilmer, later circulated in Virginia as "An Appeal for Mount Vernon," Cunningham, from her home in South Carolina, responded to Washington's position and called on the ladies of Virginia to take a leading role in what she now conceived of as a national enterprise. She suggested that Virginia women petition the General Assembly to contract for the purchase of Mount Vernon, reserving for Virginia the title to the estate but allowing the "women of America," from "Maine to Texas," to pay for it. Cunningham argued that a direct purchase of the estate by the U.S. Congress would be a rebuff to Virginia's state pride, and make the property a pawn in the national conflict between pro- and antislavery forces.[62]

Cunningham and her colleagues intended Mount Vernon to serve as a monument to civic virtue in an era that had all but forgotten the principles of the Revolutionary generation. In a prescient passage she proclaimed, "If ever in the future period of our national history, the Union should be in serious danger, political storms rocking it to its base, or rending it in twain, there will be such a moral grandeur . . . in the *mere fact* that the tomb of Washington rests secure under the flag of his native state, *enshrined* in the devotional reverence of the wives, mothers and daughters of the Union as will be *felt* over the civilized world, making glad every elevated and patriotic heart!" Like Gilmer and Washington, Cunningham contrasted female patriotism with male. Mount Vernon could only be saved "by *woman's* self-denying generous zeal." At the end of her appeal Cunningham invited the women of Virginia to "unite with us, and form the 'Central Committee of the Union.'"[63]

Unfortunately, Cunningham's instructions on the formation of a "Central Committee" were misinterpreted by the Virginians. Cunningham had meant for the Central Committee to include representatives from all the states. The Virginia contingent, however, simply transformed their state association into the Central Committee. According to the new constitution they drew up, state committees around the country were now to report to the Central Committee in Richmond. This move stirred up a hornet's nest. Cunningham, upset that the Central Committee was not representative enough of the Union or of her authority, immediately repudiated the new constitution. The Virginia women apologized to Cunningham and revised their constitution according to her specifications—a Mount Vernon State Committee of Virginia was formed, distinct from the Central Committee of the Union (to which Cunningham could appoint whom she liked). The State Committee retained Cabell as president, and included a Board of Managers of forty Virginia women. The Central Committee, while it continued to be dominated by Virginians, also included representatives from other states.[64]

The officers and managers of both committees were a distinguished group. Almost all were wives of prominent politicians. The women typically used their husband's names in association reports, presumably to show off their political pedigrees to potential donors. Mrs. John Tyler (Julia Gardiner) and Mrs. William C. Rives (Judith) served as vice presidents on the Central Committee. The State Committee numbered among its managers the wives of John Letcher and Henry Wise (ex-congressmen and future governors), and of Senators R. M. T. Hunter and James M. Mason.[65]

The public rhetoric of the MVA invested this group of women with a profoundly important mission. In 1855, Beverly Wellford Jr. delivered a stirring July 4 address in Richmond on behalf of the association. Wellford's speech, which was reprinted a few months later in the *Southern Literary Messenger*, focused on the civic duty of Virginia women. First he invoked the patriotic example set by Virginia's Revolutionary foremothers. Then he outlined woman's mission: "It is hers to still the angry passions . . . too frequently struggling for the mastery of man." No cause was better suited to woman, Wellford asserted, than "the cause of extinguishing, in our country, sectional feelings and sectional asperities, and reviving those fraternal sentiments which in by gone days constituted us in interest and feeling—in hope and fear one people." By preserving the "Mecca of Republicanism," women could "silence the ravings of a besotted fanaticism."[66]

In 1855, the Mount Vernon Association allied itself with Virginia's burgeoning agricultural reform movement; in that year and the two years that followed, the association solicited contributions during the annual fairs of the Virginia Agricultural Society. Formed in 1852, the

Virginia Agricultural Society (VAS) promoted the idea of agricultural diversity and development. The VAS included among its advocates both political moderates like William Rives and George Summers, who saw agricultural reform as a national cause behind which Southerners and Northerners could rally, and Southern nationalists, such as Willoughby Newton and Edmund Ruffin, who wanted to promote the economic independence and solidarity of the South.[67]

The VAS sponsored yearly fairs which were highly publicized and massively attended. The society's first fair, in November 1853, drew tens of thousands of visitors—including an estimated 3,000 women—to Richmond. Women displayed their handiwork, such as fabrics, flowers, and other products, and in return they had their names printed in the newspapers that covered the proceedings. The high point of each fair was the keynote address, given by one of the officers of the VAS. These speeches typically tied agricultural reform to sectional politics. For example, in 1853 featured speaker John Edmunds argued that "in the development of [Virginia's] material power, fanaticism shall find an impassable barrier, and our peculiar institutions shall find not only security, but a cessation from disturbance." According to the *Virginia Gazette*, women as well as men took in Edmunds's message: "A multitude of ladies and gentlemen [listened to his speech] with the profoundest attention and most intense interest."[68]

At the 1855 annual fair of the VAS, a male advocate (identified in the papers only as "L.V.") for the Mount Vernon project made a stirring appeal to the men and women of Virginia. Reminding his audience of agriculturalists that "Washington was a farmer," L.V. connected the Mount Vernon project with the Revolutionary mothers' support for Washington's Continental Army: "In the town of Alexandria alone, were collected by women, under the lead of 'Lady Washington,' about seventy-five thousand eight hundred dollars. In our sister town of Fredericksburg, sixteen hundred pounds were subscribed by women for the use of the army. Oh! if such were the deeds of the *mothers*, shall the *daughters* refuse to perform the simple, pious act of honoring their tombs, and *his tomb* of all others?" L.V. urged the women of Virginia to "struggle against the heavy fetters of Mammon" and give generously to the cause.[69]

The MVA did not rely exclusively on male orators to raise funds; instead, Virginia State Committee vice president Susan Pellet and Central Committee vice president Anna Cora Mowatt Ritchie literally went door to door in Richmond, soliciting contributions. Nor did the women shy away from using partisanship to their advantage in their quest for allies.

Ritchie, a nationally famous actress who originally hailed from New York, was the wife of William Foushee Ritchie, editor of the Democratic *Richmond Enquirer*. "Mrs. Pellet made capital out of my name (*Ritchie* I mean)," she reported to Cunningham, "whenever we found ourselves amongst democrats." Raising subscription money was, however, only half the battle. In January of 1856 the women of the MVA began their efforts to win support from the Virginia General Assembly. They drafted a bill asking for incorporation and authorizing the sale of the estate to the Commonwealth. The female officers of the MVA proved themselves shrewd negotiators in their dealings with legislators. Ritchie wrote to Cunningham in February that she had been busy "electioneering." She instructed her husband to invite as many legislators as he could to an evening party at the Ritchies'. As the ladies began to retire after dinner, she and Pellet took former Governor John Buchanan Floyd aside and convinced him to support their bill. The leaders of the MVA kept up the pressure on Floyd and on Representative O. Langfitt, their principal ally in the House of Delegates, during the winter session of the Virginia General Assembly.[70]

Finally, on the morning of March 17, 1856, as the session was drawing to a close, the MVA's bill was voted upon. The association's managers went en masse to the capitol to witness the proceedings. They created quite a stir — some men mumbled that it was "outrageous" for women to be taking up the General Assembly's valuable time — but their bill passed the House and then the Senate. The bill incorporated the MVA and authorized it to purchase 200 acres of the estate, for the price of $200,000. The MVA, according to the bill's provisions, would hold the estate in perpetuity; if the association ever ceased to exist, the estate would revert to the Commonwealth of Virginia. Julia Mayo Cabell, president of the Virginia committee, wrote to Cunningham of the passage of the bill: "I never worked harder in my life to accomplish a purpose than I did for *that*."[71]

The MVA's victory brought it further praise and new allies. In May of 1856, a poem on patriotism by John Thompson, editor of the *Southern Literary Messenger*, appeared in that journal, holding up the MVA as the very embodiment of civic virtue: "This is True Patriotism — this the spirit / Which all earth's real Patriots inherit." An appeal in the *Richmond Enquirer* the same month described the MVA's efforts as a "means of awakening a glow of patriotism in hearts too frequently untouched by such emotions." The man who would prove to be the most influential supporter to the cause signed on in 1856. Edward Everett, a former U.S. senator from Massachusetts, was a nationally famous orator who was also the nation's foremost authority on the life of George Washington. Everett met Cunningham in Richmond in 1856, and she enlisted his services. He would lecture on Washington's life 129 times in the next three years; he also wrote a series of 53 weekly articles for the *New York Ledger* on behalf of the MVA. Not only did Everett add to the MVA's national prestige, he also filled its coffers, raising a sum of $69,024—one-third of the total price of Mount Vernon—through his efforts. Another influential supporter was Sarah Hale, editor of *Godey's Lady's Book*. Through her journal, Hale regularly publicized the MVA's affairs; like her Southern counterparts, Hale believed the goal of the MVA was nothing less than the preservation of the Union.[72]

Unfortunately, the 1856 victory did not guarantee the success of the enterprise. An unexpected obstacle arose in the form of John Augustine Washington's renewed opposition. In 1856 he wrote to William Ritchie, MVA corresponding secretary, that he was disappointed by the "languid mismanagement of the Association," and that he doubted the ability of the women to maintain the estate. He would only sell to the state or federal government. Washington's charge of mismanagement was not without merit. Julia Cabell herself admitted to Cunningham that the business of collecting donations was slow. "Tis a melancholy truth Alas!," she reported, "that there is not here, the enthusiasm that *ought* to exist in such a cause." An appeal by the editors of the *Richmond Whig* criticized the apathy of Richmond women. "Even among her ladies, only a choice few have taken part," it announced; the central and state committees together numbered no more than fifty women. Official reports, in the *Southern Literary Messenger*, sounded a similarly despondent note. An August 1857 report by Susan Pellet, who had recently resigned from the Virginia State Committee to take up the role of corresponding secretary for the Central Committee, declared that the State Committee had collected only $2,324.83, "a meagre sum for the patriotism of Virginia." Pellet urged Virginia not to be "a laggard in this race of honour"; upon her devolved "the duty of leading the enterprise."[73]

The MVA's biggest problem was that the cause was increasingly becoming a victim of the fierce partisan wars in Virginia. The MVA lost an important ally in the legislature when Representative Langfitt lost his 1857 bid for reelection. Pellet explained the matter to Cunningham in December: "None but *pure* democrats can have a seat in the Va. legislature. Mr. L. *was* a Know Nothing."[74] More important, the MVA was dragged into the battle between the two principal factions of the Democratic Party in Virginia, one led by Governor Henry A. Wise and the other by Senator R. M. T. Hunter. At issue between Wise and Hunter was sectionalism itself—at this stage in their long rivalry, each man wanted to prove himself a more steadfast defender of Southern rights and values than the other. Wise was the acknowledged leader of the Commonwealth's Democratic Party throughout the 1850s. Eager to identify himself with the statesmanship exemplified by George Washington and to restore Virginia's reputation as the "mother of all states," Wise embraced the cause of the MVA as his own. Hunter, an aristocratic planter and self-proclaimed champion of states' rights, took on Wise and his pet project. William and Anna Ritchie and John A. Washington were in the Wise camp, and therefore became the political enemies of the Hunter clique.[75]

The prospects of the MVA looked bleak in 1858. Hunter supporters, Pellet informed Cunningham from Richmond, were trying to turn William Ritchie out of the office of public printer because he stood by Wise. Worse yet, Roger Pryor, editor of the pro-Hunter newspaper *The South*, took it upon himself to launch an attack on Wise, Everett, and the MVA itself. The focus of Pryor's attack was a new charter that the MVA submitted to the legislature in 1858. The charter provided for the appropriation of state funds: the MVA was asking the state to pay John Washington the purchase price of $200,000, which the association would repay in a series of installments. Since the MVA was asking for public funds, Pryor explained in a January 1858 editorial, he was absolved from "obligations of chivalric forebearance"—he would expose the "Mount Vernon humbug" for what it was. The association was "supposed to be animated by [the] noble aspiration" of preserving Washington's estate; instead, he charged, the women and John Washington were really interested in turning a profit. Pryor singled out Edward Everett for special criticism. Everett was, Pryor charged, in league with the fanatical abolitionists of the North, and deserved to be execrated by the South.[76]

Pryor was not alone in his attacks on the MVA. Edmund Ruffin, Virginia's most influential Southern nationalist, viewed the Mount Vernon project as a "great fraud." He wrote to the *South* under the name of "CALX," arguing that state guardianship of Washington's home set a dangerous precedent; the state, after all, could not be asked to pay for the homes of all of its illustrious statesmen. He also noted, incorrectly, that "not one Virginian woman or man has yet occupied one of the most prominent positions as a patron or promoter of this scheme. All such who have been most conspicuous, in office or action, in Virginia, and in the effort to instruct Virginians how they should venerate WASHINGTON, are by birth or residence, or both, foreigners to Virginia and the Southern States."[77]

The women of the MVA did not take Pryor's criticism lightly. In February of 1858 Pellet wrote to John Washington telling him that the ladies were busy combating the prejudice excited by "Mr. Pryor's malicious misrepresentation, and exertions to defeat our Bill." Pellet reminded him that the MVA had "powerful and influential friends in the Legislature." To counter the bad press generated by Pryor, the MVA invited Andrew H. H. Dawson of Savannah to Richmond, to deliver his "Oration on the Origin, Purposes and Claims of the Ladies' Mt. Vernon Association." Dawson, who had given the speech in towns around the South, spoke in Richmond on February 13, and in other towns in Virginia during the ensuing weeks. He sounded the familiar theme of the superiority of female patriotism: "Woman's patriotism is love of country; man's patriotism is love of self, of party, and he has no uses for a party that does not appreciate him. . . . But it is left for woman to adore virtue . . . [and] to love her country better even than life itself." In his opinion, the Mount Vernon project contained the germ of the nation's salvation. Dawson's assertions were reiterated at the inauguration on February 22 of the equestrian statue of Washington in Richmond. Colonel George Munford delivered yet another stirring tribute to female patriotism. "[T]here are mutterings between the sections, that ought to be hushed," he proclaimed. Fortunately, the women of the MVA were weaving delicate links between the sections, "constituting a bond of affection that ought not to be broke, and that ought to bind them indissolubly together forever."[78]

Meanwhile, Cunningham worked behind the scenes to convince Washington that he and she were on the same side, both victims of unfair attacks. In her correspondence with Washington, Cunningham excoriated the Virginia legislature. "The bitter & intrigued party *spirit*, between Wise & Hunter men, is almost inconceivable & threatens to draw into its whirlpool *all State business*—," she lamented. A few days later she added,

> . . . Mr. Pryor's *personal animosity* to Mr & Mrs. Ritchie . . . and *now to me* for having got the better of him in our recent passage of arms— has induced him to use the power he possesses as a warm *Hunter Man*, over a *Hunter* Legislature to mix our affairs up with the *fierce party strife* now raging here, and we have to play a most skillful game to extricate ourselves from *party* clutches, and fight the battle on high patriotic ground—not an easy matter in *Virginia* where *party* is more than food and clothes!

In March, Cunningham's efforts with Washington paid off. On the twenty-third of that month, 1858, the new Mount Vernon charter finally passed the Virginia legislature. Washington, no doubt eager to extricate himself from the whole controversy, accepted Cunningham's terms. On April 6, 1858, he signed a contract of sale to the MVA.[79]

Ironically, the sale brought to the fore sectional tensions within the MVA that had lain dormant. Cunningham immediately dissolved the Virginia-dominated Central Committee and set about appointing a vice regent for each state of the Union. The vice regent she picked for Virginia was Anna Ritchie. In an April 1858 letter to Samuel Ruggles, an association ally in New York, Cunningham stated that the MVA owed more to New York, because it was Ritchie's native state, than to any other (save her own South Carolina).[80]

Virginia women were stung by Cunningham's actions. In May Eliza Semmes, a former officer of the Central Committee, wrote an angry letter to Cunningham. She felt betrayed by the dissolution of the Central Committee and the appointment of Ritchie—a Northerner by birth—as the Old Dominion's regent; she would have preferred a native Virginian to be regent. Semmes was also worried that the Virginia State Committee had not received due recognition of its contributions to the cause. Semmes and her sympathizers, moreover, may have been alienated by the fact that, as one Northern vice regent put it, "the Republicans [were the] warmest and most liberal supporters" of the MVA in the North. Cunningham herself conceded that while she only wanted as vice regents ladies "who will rise above party prejudices," some of her regents were Republicans.[81]

Semmes was not the only Southerner loath to let Northerners seize undue credit for Mount Vernon. In September of 1858 the *Southern Literary Messenger* printed a July commencement address by the Reverend C. W. Howard before the Cassville Female College in Georgia. Howard's tribute to the MVA is noteworthy for its sectional tone. The MVA, he declared, "shall rebuke those insane men, who with worse than Ephesian fury, under cover of liberty, would fire the temple of liberty. It shall tell them that he who was 'first in war, first in peace and first in the hearts of his countrymen,' was an 'accursed slaveholder.' It shall remind them that they cannot malign their brethren of the South, without one in the same breath, parricides as they are, reviling the memory of the illustrious dead." By 1859, for more than a few Southerners, Mount Vernon was not a symbol of national unity, but rather a rebuke to the North.[82]

Miraculously, however, neither sectional antipathy nor war itself undermined the accomplishments of the MVA. Notwithstanding the disappointment of Semmes and her allies, the MVA made great progress in enlisting supporters and "lady managers" in Virginia in 1858. As the year came to a close, the leaders of the MVA, such as Susan Pellet, still believed that the association was "a conservative power for good, . . . the bond which shall link together and fraternize in *one* brotherhood North, South, East and West, whose aim shall be the preservation of the union now and forever!" Indeed, what had begun as a Southern enterprise had grown into a national one: substantial contributions toward the purchase price of Washington's estate came from Massachusetts, New York, California, and Pennsylvania. At the end of December 1859, a few months after John Brown's raid on Harpers Ferry, Everett wrote to Cunningham, congratulating her on skillfully guiding the association "amidst the rocks and quicksands of sectionalism." [83]

Cunningham's skill was manifest during the war—despite the fact that she remained in the South during the conflict, loyal to her region, she stayed on as head of the MVA, and corresponded with her Northern colleagues. Mount Vernon was occupied during the war by two people—Sarah Tracy, a secretary to the MVA from New York, and Upton Herbert, the estate's superintendent, a Virginian. Tracy skillfully extracted assurances from the armies of both sides that they would not station soldiers on the estate. Mount Vernon remained neutral territory during the war, a literal "middle ground," left behind by partisans of both sections, but not obliterated, not forgotten. After the war, Northern and Southern women resumed the work of refurbishing the estate. In 1872, in an ending befitting a domestic novel, Sarah Tracy and Upton Herbert, Northerner and Southerner, were married.[84]

Long after the Civil War, the MVA represented for Virginians not only the values of the founding fathers but also the political influence of women in the antebellum period. Two women on different sides of the Civil War, for example, both fondly remember the MVA in their memoirs. Mary Virginia Terhune, who remained committed to the Union, was impressed by the status of the MVA when she attended a meeting of the association at the governor's mansion in 1856. Lucy Parke Chamberlayne, an ardent Confederate, remembering the 1858 Washington's birthday celebration in Richmond, wrote of the MVA—"Great enthusiasm pervaded the U.S. & especially were the women & they raised 200,000 [dollars]—*without* being able to vote." [85]

The MVA, like the Clay Association, dealt not in votes but in political symbols. For each group, a great man symbolized sectional peace, patriotism, and fidelity to the values of the Revolutionary generation. Each group implied that women were drawn to these leaders less by choice than by nature; feminine nature itself dictated that women support the champions of harmony. Yet each group discovered that even the act of memorializing political virtue could create conflict. Along with the literary women who defended the South against the likes of Harriet Beecher Stowe, the Virginia women of the MVA sought to fulfill a dual political mandate: to stem the tide of sectionalism and to promote pride in the culture and values of their native state and region. But as sectional tensions mounted, those goals proved to be less and less compatible. Literary women, in their "true" stories of sectional life, were increasingly hostile to the North, pessimistic about reconciliation and unwilling to admit that the South needed reform. Their works were appropriated by advocates of Southern literary nationalism as proof of the South's cultural superiority to and independence from the North.

Lest we think that by the mid-1850s pessimism had won the battle with optimism and sectional antipathy the battle with sympathy in Virginia, the MVA is an important reminder of the resilience of the notion that harmonious relations between the North and South could and should be restored. Through the MVA's national publicity campaign in newspapers, journals, and speeches, the idea that women were specially suited to promote sectional reconciliation reached a wide audience — at least as wide an audience, it would seem, as the more ambivalent messages of Virginia's female novelists and essayists did. Indeed, pessimism and optimism about North-South relations were not only competing rhetorical themes in the public discourse of Virginia but also competing tendencies in the hearts and minds of individuals. Three of Virginia's literary defenders — Julia Gardiner Tyler, Judith Rives, and Mary Virginia Terhune — were also staunch supporters of the MVA.

It is only when we look behind the MVA's public rhetoric that we can see the toll sectionalism took on the unity of the association. Despite their efforts to serve as representatives of disinterested patriotism, the Virginia women of the MVA became enmeshed in both partisan and sectional controversies. First in their squabbles with Ann Pamela Cunningham over whether the association should be primarily a Virginian one or a national one; then in their feud with the Hunter wing of the Democratic Party; and finally in their alienation from the Northern wing of the MVA on the eve of secession, the Virginia women of the MVA proved every bit as partisan as their fellow "mediators" in the field of literature.

The rhetoric of the Mount Vernon Association argued explicitly what women's literature on sectionalism only implied — that it was women's duty to serve as mediators because they were by nature more patriotic than men. In the wake of the MVA's successful purchase of Mount Vernon in 1858, the public discourse on female civic duty would undergo a radical change. The notion that women were more patriotic than men would prove to be enduring; the notion that women should serve as sectional mediators would not.

'Tis Now Liberty or Death

THE SECESSION CRISIS

> Throughout the war, from its commencement to its close, the
> women of the Confederacy, although its greatest sufferers, were
> the truest of the true. In all the trials and vicissitudes of the war,
> it was their unfailing constancy that nerved the arms and
> strengthened the hearts of their fathers, husbands, sons and
> brothers. . . . It is due to the truth of history to say that the
> women of the Confederacy made the men of the Confederacy
> what they were.[1]

So wrote John Goode of Virginia, some fifty-five years after he
served as a delegate to his native state's 1861 secession convention.
Goode's words are an archetypal expression of what historians have
called "Confederate womanhood," or "Spartan motherhood." A new
ideal of women's civic duty which emerged in 1861, Confederate womanhood held that Southern women were patriotic exemplars, ready to offer
up their menfolk for the cause of Southern independence. Although it
began as a prescription for appropriate behavior by women, Confederate womanhood survived the Civil War intact as the dominant narrative
of how white Southern women had actually experienced the war. For
more than a century that narrative held captive the historical imagination — monuments to Southern women, literature, and historical writing on the "Cause" all repeated, as Goode's memoirs did, the story of
women's unwavering loyalty to the Confederacy.[2]

In the past few years this narrative of women's loyalty has been radi-
cally revised by historians. In a recent highly acclaimed book, Drew
Gilpin Faust argues that while women may have fulfilled the ideal of
feminine self-sacrifice during the early part of the war, they soon found it
restrictive and burdensome. Focusing on women's own accounts of the
war in their diaries, memoirs, and letters to Confederate officials, Faust
discerns a pattern of waning loyalty to the Cause over the course of the
war. Women's expressions of disillusionment ranged from letters urging
men to desert the army to public protests against Confederate policies.[3]

Rather than examining the wartime implications of Confederate womanhood, this chapter attempts to trace the ideology's emergence during the secession crisis. Confederate womanhood marks not only a beginning point but an end point in Southern women's political history, the end of a long and complicated transition from partisanship to sectionalism to Southern nationalism as the dominant theme of political life. As late as 1858, the reigning ideal of female civic duty in Virginia held that women should, because of their superior patriotism, promote sectional harmony. Southern nationalists, who took issue with this view of female duty, were still in the political minority. By 1861, the public discourse on women had been dramatically transformed, as a result of changes in the political balance of power. In the years 1859 to 1861, a series of developments — John Brown's raid, Lincoln's election, the Deep South's secession, and the firing on Fort Sumter, to name the most important — undermined the cause of Unionism in Virginia and strengthened the hand of Southern "fire-eaters," as ardent secessionists were called. As the political philosophy of Unionism lost popularity, so, too, did the idea that women should serve as sectional mediators. As Southern nationalism gained popularity, a new ideal of female civic duty began to take shape — that women were purer *Southern* patriots than men, and that they should lead the way not in the struggle to preserve the Union but in the battle to defend the South.

On October 16, 1859, John Brown, already infamous in Virginia for his exploits in "bleeding Kansas," led a small band of followers to Harpers Ferry, Virginia, where they seized the federal arsenal there in the hope of enlisting the slaves in the surrounding countryside to rise up against their masters. Rumors of the raid spread like wildfire, and soon the governor of Virginia, Henry Wise, directed local militias to restore order. The militias proved ineffectual, and on October 18, the U.S. Marines, led by Colonel Robert E. Lee, arrived at the scene and captured Brown. Brown was tried in a county court in Charlestown, Virginia, and sentenced to death. On December 2, he was hanged.[4]

"The attack of John Brown upon Harper's Ferry came upon Virginia like a clap of thunder out of a clear sky," John S. Wise, Henry's son, wrote in his reminiscences some forty-one years after the fateful events of 1859. According to the younger Wise, Brown's raid effected a "great change of feeling in Virginia towards the people of the North" — it made Virginians "look upon the people of the North as hating them." Historians have affirmed the notion that the Harpers Ferry raid was a major turning point in the sectional crisis. Douglas Southall Freeman, Henry T. Shanks, and others have concluded that the Brown raid did more than any other single event to reconcile Virginians to the possibility of secession. The consolidation of the free-soil movement and the rise of the Republican Party intensified fears, which had haunted white Virginians ever since the Nat Turner Rebellion of 1831, about the possibility of an abolitionist-inspired slave rebellion. Those fears were stoked by the news that Brown had been backed by prominent Northern abolitionists. To make matters worse, Brown quickly became a martyred hero in the North, the subject of laudatory legislative resolutions, editorials, prayers, poems, and public meetings. Southern-rights politicians in Virginia such as Governor Wise and Senator James Mason, and newspapers such as the *Richmond Enquirer*, seized on Brown's martyrdom as proof that the Northern people could no longer be reasoned with.[5]

Elaborating on the notion that the Harpers Ferry raid was a turning point, George C. Rable's study of Southern women and the Civil War has argued that Brown's "thunder clap" effected, among other things, a political awakening of white Southern women. He writes that after Brown's raid, women's "relative indifference to politics suddenly seemed a foolish and dangerous luxury."[6] The Virginia sources bear out neither Rable's characterization of antebellum women as politically indifferent nor his interpretation of the raid's significance. Brown's raid did not precipitate a political awakening of women; rather, it accelerated an ongoing process of political reorientation, in which women cast off old political allegiances and came to embrace the cause of Southern nationalism.

Brown's raid elicited a wide range of responses, private and public, from Virginia women. By far the most common response was condemnation of Brown and his co-conspirators. Eliza A. Willson of Rockbridge County, for example, hotly debated the meaning of the raid, as she did most political developments, in correspondence with her brothers and nephew. Eliza condemned both Brown and his Northern supporters. Her nephew Willie, who tended to share Eliza's political opinions, likewise excoriated the abolitionists; he wrote his aunt that "Gerrit Smith & Giddings & some others deserve hanging almost as much as Brown and his confederates." Eliza's brother William, a physician in Ohio, was a Republican, and, while he disapproved of Brown's actions, he expressed his hope that they would further the Republican Party's aim of limiting the extension of slavery. He persistently tried to get Eliza to "see the Republican party in the right light," but she never came around. A year after the raid she condemned Lincoln for having been "chairman of the meeting in Boston to sympathize with Old John Brown."[7]

While before 1859, expressions of sectional antipathy by Virginia women had been largely restricted to critiques of the abolitionists, after the raid, some Virginia women began to express hostility to the Northern people in general. Amanda Virginia Edmonds, a young woman of twenty who lived on a substantial estate in Fauquier County, wrote a detailed account of the Harpers Ferry incident—one that seethes with rage—in her diary. On the question of how to punish Brown and his men, Edmonds averred, "I would see the fire kindled and those who did it singed and burnt until the last drop of blood was dried within them and every bone smouldered to ashes. Ah! but couldn't I! I don't think my heart could harbor feelings of sympathy for heartless, ungrateful wretches." Brown's execution she described as "an awfully sublime, glorious, charmed scene." Noting that a rumored rescue attempt for Brown never materialized, she concluded that "all the North are afraid to meet the men of our Southern State." Julia Gardiner Tyler wrote to her mother a few days before the execution that Brown "will reap the miserable consequence of his shameful outrage." "If there is not an *important demonstration* of good feeling on the part of the North towards the South," she added six days after Brown was hung, "I think disunion will be the consequence."[8]

Even Southern critics of slavery conceded that Brown's raid had caused a sea change in public opinion. Elizabeth Van Lew, daughter of a prominent Richmond merchant and Philadelphia-born mother, was a rare Tidewater Republican. She regarded the rise of pro-secession sentiment among her fellow Virginians with horror. "There is no denying the fact that our people were in a palpable state of war from the time of the John Brown raid," Van Lew wrote disapprovingly in her journal. "Henry A. Wise was Governor of Virginia [in 1859]," she continued, "and did everything to keep up excitement, thinking, perhaps, to use his zeal as a stepping stone to popularity and the presidential chair. . . . Our people required blood, the blood of all who were of the Brown party."[9]

Van Lew's assessment of Wise has some merit—he did take full advantage of the Harpers Ferry incident to consolidate his new position as leader of the Southern-rights faction of the Democratic Party in Virginia. But in the task of "keeping up excitement," Wise had many allies, including women. The most prominent of those was Margaretta Mason of King George County, wife of Virginia senator James Mason. In the winter of 1859, she and Wise carried on a highly publicized dialogue with abolitionist Lydia Maria Child on the issue of Brown's raid. The dialogue began on October 26, 1859, with Child's letter to Wise requesting him to forward a missive to John Brown in prison and to permit her to visit "the brave and suffering man." Wise responded a few days later, granting Child permission to see Brown but also laying the responsibility for the raid at her feet. Brown's action was "a natural consequence of your sympathy, and the errors of that sympathy ought to make you doubt its virtue," he wrote. Child shot back with a denunciation of slavery, declaring that "because slaveholders so recklessly sowed the wind in Kansas, they reaped a whirlwind at Harper's Ferry." [10]

The correspondence appeared in a host of newspapers, North and South, including the *New York Tribune* and the *Richmond Enquirer*. As Stowe's novel had, Child's letter drew fire from Virginians of both sexes. A female correspondent wrote to the *Alexandria Gazette* pointing out a few grammatical errors in Child's letter and urging her to mind her own business—"If our Northern sisters would . . . work willingly *with their hands* for the poor around them, as Southern ladies do for their servants," the correspondent argued, "they would have no time to 'sow discord among brethren,' and thus place themselves in the category with those whom the Lord hates." [11]

A similar argument was made by Mason, who interjected herself directly into the Child-Wise correspondence with a letter of November 11, 1859, to Child. Mason began by asking, "Do you read your Bible, Mrs. Child?" and rehearsing some of the biblical justifications for slavery. She then made the familiar case that Southern masters and mistresses were compassionate to their slaves, more compassionate than the abolitionists. "Would *you* stand by the bedside of an old negro, dying of a hopeless disease, to alleviate his sufferings as far as human aid could?" she queried. "*We* do these [things] and more for our servants . . . ," she continued, "because we endeavor *to do our duty in the state of life it has pleased God to place us.*" She urged Northerners to direct their philanthropy to their own people: "If the stories read in the public prints be true, of the sufferings of the poor of the North, you need not go far for objects of charity." Mason ended the letter by calling on like-minded women to boycott Child's writings—"no Southerner ought, after your letter to Governor Wise and to Brown, to read a line of your composition, or to touch a magazine which bears your name in its list of contributors; and in this we hope for the 'sympathy,' at least of those of the North who deserve the name of woman." In the last installment of the correspondence, Child responded to Mason by charging that Mason and other Southern-rights advocates "will not even allow your own citizens a chance to examine this important subject [slavery]." Child defended the philanthropy of Northern women with the kind of phrase likely to infuriate Southerners: "after we have helped the mothers [among the Northern poor], *we do not sell the babies.*" [12]

As Julia Gardiner Tyler's letter to the Duchess of Sutherland had been in 1853, Mason's missive was widely publicized, both in newspapers and in a pamphlet published in 1860 by the American Anti-Slavery Society; the pamphlet sold some 300,000 copies.[13] In some respects, Mason's defense of slavery echoes Tyler's. Mason's central point—that the North should mind its own business—had been advanced by Tyler, and by other Virginia women, such as Mary H. Eastman and Martha Haines Butt, as well. Mason's letter was, however, noticeably different in some respects from previous commentaries on slavery by Virginia women. Mason was decidedly unapologetic—she did not concede that slavery even occasionally produced injustices; she did not hide behind fictional characters; she did not suggest that it was unusual or inappropriate for a woman to speak out on politics.

While Mason's letter is one index of changes in the political roles and attitudes of women, women's part in the new boycott movement is another, more revealing one. By mid-November, newspapers in Richmond and elsewhere were advancing the idea that Southerners should boycott Northern goods. As the agricultural reform movement had, the boycott movement called on Southern men and women to display their industry, and invested the most mundane activities, such as making cloth or food, with patriotic significance. Like agricultural reform, the boycott appealed both to those who wanted to pressure the North into compromise and to those who suspected that the time for compromise had passed. "Men and women, old and young, the most moderate and conservative, as well as the most fiery and determined," an editor of the Richmond *Daily Dispatch* argued, were in favor of the boycott.[14]

Unlike previous movements for economic development, however, the boycott was plainly punitive in spirit—meant to punish the Northern people for the transgressions of the radicals among them. While the rhetoric of agricultural reform stressed that economic development was a means to restore sectional equilibrium, the rhetoric of the boycott movement advocated not only Southern economic equality but independence. "The movement towards Southern independence is progressing steadily," proclaimed an editor of the *Richmond Whig* in an article on the boycott, adding that the "people of Virginia are in dead earnest about this matter."[15]

Perhaps the most significant difference between the boycott movement and prior efforts to foster Southern economic independence is that women were leaders as well as followers in the boycott. In early December, an article circulated in Virginia papers announcing some Richmond women's plans to hold a meeting in Mechanics' Hall in order to encourage home manufactures and thereby to "ensure the independence of Virginia, and her safety from Northern aggression." On December 17, 1859, women in Richmond held their meeting, resolving not to wear anything that came from the North. Soon similar "Homespun Clubs" were formed in Norfolk, Alexandria, and other cities and towns. Female advocates of the boycott provided some spirited and sometimes humorous statements to the newspapers, such as a letter from a "Daughter of Virginia" to the *Daily Dispatch* declaring that although women were willing to "purchase no more from *Yankee land*," she hoped that hoop skirts, which she considered a necessity, could be furnished from England. Another woman suggested that each farmer's wife in Virginia give the proceeds of one pot of "Southern Rights Butter" to the state for the purpose of promoting direct trade with Europe.[16]

Men invested women's part in the movement with great political significance. In the rhetoric of the boycott campaign, women became exemplars not of fidelity to the Union but of fidelity to the South. Under the heading "A Homespun Party," the *Richmond Whig* declared that the "ladies were far ahead of the gentlemen" in the homespun movement, adding, "When our mothers, our wives, daughters, sisters, sweethearts, lead the way, who can refuse to follow?" The paper proudly reported that news of the Virginia women's initiative made its way as far South as Montgomery, Alabama, where the local paper praised the "patriotic resolutions adopted by the ladies of Richmond." Recasting the familiar argument that women were purer patriots than men, an article in the *Daily Dispatch* asserted that women were truer to the South than men were: women are "even more patriotic than the men, and if they once determine not to encourage Northern manufactures, the Yankee trade with the South will instantly cease."[17]

In addition to promoting the boycott, women took advantage of other popularly approved means to express their political opinions. John Brown's raid sparked the formation and reorganization of volunteer companies and militias all over the state. Women supported these companies by providing them with uniforms and other goods and supplies. The *Daily Dispatch* declared that such efforts "show that the right spirit is alive in both sexes." Women in Madison County, the *Alexandria Gazette* noted, presented a "handsome banner" to the volunteer company in that county; in other communities as well, women participated in militia rituals by presenting uniforms, banners, or flags to volunteers.[18]

Echoing Lucy Barbour's 1844 letter proposing a tribute to Henry Clay, "one of the most intelligent and estimable ladies" in Virginia wrote a letter to the *Daily Dispatch* in December of 1859 suggesting that women raise subscriptions to buy a "service of plate" for Governor Wise, to commemorate the manner in which he "met the wicked and atrocious raid of the 'miscreant BROWN.'" Just as the Clay tribute was meant to demonstrate the Whig dictum that "the ladies are all Whigs," the Wise tribute, too, was intended to demonstrate female solidarity. "There is but one heart and one voice among the daughters of the Old Dominion," the woman who proposed the tribute declared in her letter.[19]

Although John Brown's raid did much to deepen sectional antipathy, the notion that Southern women were of "one heart and one voice" was far from accurate in 1859. While most Virginia women condemned Brown, great differences of opinion persisted on the question of which political course — reconciliation or secession — Virginia should ultimately choose. The boycott societies faded in importance as Virginians geared up for the presidential election campaign of 1860. In that campaign the emerging image of women as exemplary Southern patriots would compete with the idea that women were, by nature, "all for the Union."

John Brown's raid had a profound impact on Virginia's party politics, for it dashed the hopes of former Whigs who wanted to forge an alliance with conservative Republicans, and it increased the clout of the Southern-rights extremists within the Democratic Party. In January of 1860, former Whigs and Know-Nothings united under the banner of the "Constitutional Union" Party, which pledged that its candidates, John Bell of Tennessee and Edward Everett of Massachusetts, would uphold the principles of the Compromise of 1850 and safeguard both slavery and the Union. The Republican Party, which had a small following in the northwestern region of the state (present-day West Virginia), played down the slavery issue in Virginia and played up the longstanding resentment of western Virginians against the politically dominant easterners. The Democrats for their part split into Douglas and Breckenridge factions. Douglasites favored congressional control of slavery in the territories, and, like Constitutional Unionists, portrayed themselves as the party of sectional harmony. The Breckenridge wing of the Democratic Party was dominated by Southern-rights advocates, including Governor Wise and his rival, Senator Hunter of Virginia, whose priority was to ensure the safety of slavery and to promote Southern unity in preparation for the possible secession of the South.[20]

More so than in any previous campaign, the rhetoric of the 1860 contest focused on women. The Constitutional Union Party made a conscious effort to evoke the "spirit of 1840" and to outdo its opponents in its appeals to women. One correspondent to the *Richmond Daily Whig* said of a meeting in Portsmouth that "the immense assemblage of ladies in the Hall . . . signified by their presence and their smiles the lively interest they took in promoting the success of the good cause of 1860, as their mothers and kindred did before them in that of 1840." Women made their standard contributions to the campaign. The Union ladies of Alexandria, for example, presented a Union flag to the Central Bell Club in that town, and on a later occasion threw bouquets — "every leaf of which sends up a prayer for the preservation of the Union" — to men marching in a Bell procession. The *Staunton Spectator* reported that young ladies at the Wesleyan Female Institute had planted a banner on the porch of the school reading "The Institute for Bell and Everett," and added that the cheering of students at the Virginia Female Institute for a Bell procession proved that "that 'Institute' was also for Bell and Everett."[21]

In the tradition of earlier campaigns, Bell newspapers attached great significance to women's activities. Speaking in Petersburg, John Minor Botts made an "eloquent appeal to the ladies present to use all their influence with husbands, brothers and sons, in behalf of the Union." One correspondent to the *Richmond Daily Whig* from Culpeper went so far as to say of the women who were out in large numbers at a meeting there, "Pity they are not allowed to vote." As its Whig forebears had routinely done, the Constitutional Union Party claimed that it had not merely some female supporters but most and even all the women in the state. Transmuting the old rallying cry that the "ladies are all Whigs," the *Lynchburg Virginian* declared in September that "the ladies are all for *Union*; and they can manifest their laudable desires in that respect by cooperating with the gallant sons of Campbell [County]" in supporting Bell.[22]

Not only male commentators but female ones as well gave voice to the idea that the women were all for Union. A few days before the election, a correspondent with the pen name "Virginia" sent an appeal to the pro-Bell *Alexandria Gazette*, imploring the women of America to use their influence on behalf of the Union cause. Her missive began with a not-so-subtle critique of men: "Would that men would take a proper stand point and calmly view the consequences, so far as may be seen, of so horrible a deed as the sundering of the ties of common brotherhood which have so long, so sweetly bound us together." While she thought it just that women were prevented from voting in elections, she believed it women's duty to "plead for deliverance from the impending ruin."[23]

The Constitutional Union Party tried to capitalize on the popularity among Virginia women of vice presidential candidate Edward Everett, who had been the greatest male advocate of the Mount Vernon Association. The *Richmond Daily Whig* reprinted an article from a Massachusetts paper which noted that "Mr. Everett, by his disinterested conduct in furthering the views of the ladies of America, in the purchase of the grave of Washington, has placed the ladies under obligations to him of a very sacred character," obligations they could fulfill by becoming members of Bell and Everett clubs. Women themselves attested to their admiration for Everett. A female correspondent to the *Whig* penned a campaign song which praised Everett for his role in preserving Mount Vernon. Mary Virginia Terhune supported the Bell ticket in part because of her "fondness for Mr. Everett," whom she had seen speak on behalf of Mount Vernon; so, too, did Elizabeth Lindsay Lomax, who had long admired Everett but knew Bell only "through the press." [24]

Many women took the Constitutional Union Party's rhetoric to heart, and worked in private as well as in public on behalf of the Bell ticket. Lucy Wood of Charlottesville, for example, had a suitor, Waddy Butler, who leaned toward Breckenridge. In October of 1860 she wrote to him that "I am very much interested in Mr. Bell; and as the ladies have been exhorted to exert their influence with the Gentlemen for him, you must excuse me for attempting it in an indirect manner, by trying to silence so formidable an opponent as yourself." Mary Virginia Terhune prevailed upon her husband not to vote for Lincoln but for Bell. "I have never interfered with your political opinions, as you know, and I don't care to vote, myself," she told him, "but if I had a vote, I should be in no doubt where to cast it. Lovers of peace and concord should unite upon Bell and Everett." [25]

Eliza A. Willson tried to influence her two nephews, Willie and Frank. A few days before the election, she told Willie, "Don't fail to kill your Uncle Will's vote [for Lincoln]. Vote for Bell and Everett." To Frank, then too young to vote, she wrote:

> Next Tuesday will be one of the most important days that the people of the United States ever saw. The results of that day will bind the bands of a common brotherhood closer and firmer; or give cause to unprincipled and designing men to try and let loose all the horror of civil and servile war. . . . You will have a word to say about who is to be our next ruler, but before that time comes, you ought to be informing yourself in the questions that are most important to us as a people, and I beg you not to study how we shall divide in the most

easy and most practicable manner, but what will add to our prosperity as an undivided people.[26]

The comments of Wood, Terhune, and Willson testify to the resilience of the notion that women, by nature "lovers of peace and concord," should be sectional mediators. Unwilling to concede the mantle of Unionism or the support of women to Bell, each wing of the Democratic Party asserted that it could preserve the Union, and each appealed to women. The less popular of the two factions, the Douglas Democrats, attracted the support of traditionally Democratic citizens who thought Stephen Douglas the candidate best qualified to engineer a sectional compromise. Women turned out at Douglas rallies such as an October event of which the local paper said: "The Ladies (God bless them!) caught the inspiration . . . [and] gave evidence by their presence that Douglas and the National Democracy were RIGHT, for where WOMAN smiles and approves, *who* can do wrong." The *Wellsburg Herald* told the story of a heated discussion between a Douglas lady and a Breckenridge one; the Douglas lady was, naturally, "too sharp for the Breckenridge lady," who was "taken down at every turn."[27]

The election campaign made a strong impression on some of Douglas's female followers. In her memoirs, Margaret Muse Pennybacker of Mount Jackson remembers "so well the excitement during the campaign of 1860, and how anxious we were for the election of Stephen A. Douglas." Martha Buxton Porter Brent recalls in her reminiscences that as a young girl she saw Douglas speak in Portsmouth. "I little thought at what a prominent man I was gazing," she recalls, but she nevertheless had a strong opinion of the Republican Party in 1860: "The new Abolition party came into being, and we Southern children thought it meant an incarnation of all the wickedness and hatred to our people that could be imagined."[28]

Even the Breckenridge Democrats argued that they were committed to the Union—but one in which slavery and Southern rights were protected and the likes of the Republicans were powerless. When, in October, state contests in the North made it clear that Lincoln was guaranteed victory, the differences between the three principal contenders in Virginia were thrown into relief. The Bell and Douglas parties did not believe a Lincoln victory was a justification for disunion, while the extremists who ran the Breckenridge Democrats contended that Lincoln's victory would not only justify but necessitate secession. Radical papers like the *Richmond Enquirer* in the fall of 1860 advanced the idea that should Lincoln's victory precipitate the secession of the lower South states, Virginia should follow them out of the Union.[29]

Like their opponents, the Breckenridge Democrats called on women to support the party, but more so than other parties they stressed the physical danger in which a Lincoln victory would put the South and its women. A poem entitled "The 'Irrepressible Conflict' Clouding the 'Southern Matron's Home,'" printed by the *Enquirer*, gave voice to Democratic fears. The Republicans, the poem read, were "lighting 'Abolition' fires around the Southern Matron's Home"; only a Breckenridge victory could protect the South from Northern fanaticism. Throughout the campaign, women turned out in great numbers to hear leading Breckenridge Democrats intone Southern-rights arguments. In Covington, Alleghany County, women presented a bouquet to a Breckenridge speaker who had just asked them to "rally under the old Democratic banner of the states rights school." When fire-eater William Lowndes Yancey of Alabama spoke in Abingdon, women listened in, "not from idle curiousity, but because they felt a lively interest in the affairs of the nation, as the undivided attention they paid the speaker plainly manifested." A large crowd of women heard secessionist Roger Pryor speak at a barbecue in Charlotte, while four hundred women attended a speech by Governor Wise in Princess Anne County. A Winchester paper bragged that a thousand ladies turned out at a Breckenridge mass meeting in that town.[30]

The beleaguered Virginia Republicans, who had the support of less than 1 percent of the Old Dominion's voters, could not plausibly claim that the ladies were for Lincoln, but they nonetheless made the most of women's partisanship. The Republican organ, the *Wheeling Daily Intelligencer*, featured frequent reports on women's contributions to the party. The paper carried a series of articles, for example, on a September 1, 1860, Republican rally in Martinsville. Thirty-three young ladies, sixteen dressed in white, sixteen in black, and one in red, representing "bleeding Kansas," presented a flag to the local Lincoln club. The flag presentation was accompanied by a speech by Miss Louisa Griffith. "Though not allowed the privilege of being called voters," Griffith declared, "yet we enter with all spirit in the campaign you're engaged in. We represent to you our Union. . . . We shout aloud the name of Lincoln." The pro-Breckenridge *Wheeling Union* saw a pernicious message in the Martinsville ceremony. The thirty-two women dressed in black and white, the *Union* charged, represented racial amalgamation. The *Intelligencer* shot back that the color of the women's dresses had no significance whatsoever, and that contrary to the *Union*'s claims, the flag presentation "had not been a fizzle."[31]

The 1860 election itself proved to be a Pyrrhic victory for the Constitutional Union Party. With the Democratic vote split between two candidates, the Bell ticket won Virginia by a small plurality. But to the dismay of Unionists, Lincoln's election only gave added momentum to the burgeoning secessionist movement. Secessionists such as Edmund Ruffin, Henry Wise, Muscoe Garnett, and James Seddon championed disunion in the press and on the streets in the winter of 1860, arguing that Lincoln's election was itself a "revolution," for it represented the North's complete abandonment of the principles on which the Union had been founded. The rapid secession of seven lower South states in the aftermath of Lincoln's election only strengthened the secessionists' hand — disunion was no longer an abstract possibility but a reality, and Virginia's fate lay, so the "fire-eaters" argued, with her sister states to the South. The prospects for reconciliation dimmed further as compromise measures failed in Congress and as Northern legislatures denied the right of secession and expressed their willingness to "coerce" the seceded states back into the Union.[32]

When the Virginia General Assembly convened in January, it passed resolutions condemning Northern "coercion" and vowing that if further attempts at compromise failed, Virginia would join the South. Its most important act was to pass a "Convention Bill," which provided for the election of delegates to a special state secession convention to be held in February. The results of that election illustrate how complicated political lines had become in Virginia. The election seemed to be a resounding victory for Unionists: approximately 50 of the 152 elected delegates were Unionists, about 30 were secessionists, and 70 were moderates, not firmly in either camp. But, as Henry T. Shanks has explained, the results of the election were misleading, for most moderates were closer in their views to secessionists than to Unionists — moderates believed that Virginia had the right to secede and should do so, if compromise proved impossible, while Unionists denied the right of secession. Moreover, secessionists had, since the time of Lincoln's election, won a large following among voters in the region of the state east of the Blue Ridge, where slavery was deeply entrenched. Numerous counties in this region held pro-secession meetings intended to influence the course of the convention; these meetings, like the ones political parties convened to choose delegates to conventions and to design party platforms, were generally "men only" affairs.[33]

Since they did not vote, serve as delegates, or attend these early secession meetings, it is difficult to gauge political opinion among women,
but diaries and letters suggest that on the eve of the secession convention, moderates and Unionists greatly outnumbered secessionists
among women. In the analysis that follows, the term "conservative" will
be used to refer to both moderates and Unionists, and to distinguish
both groups from the "radical" secessionists, following Shanks's usage.

Support for the Union ran deepest in those northwestern counties
of the state that would go on to spearhead the West Virginia statehood
movement in the aftermath of secession. Northwestern counties had
more in common economically and socially with neighboring regions
in Ohio and Pennsylvania than they did with slaveholding regions of
Virginia, and had long resented the political dominance of the eastern
planter-elite. Alarmed by the rapid rise of secessionism in the wake of
Lincoln's election, northwesterners held Union mass meetings throughout January, in preparation for the election of delegates to the secession
convention. These meetings often prominently featured female participants. On the 26th of January, for example, Unionists in Kingwood,
Preston County, held a meeting at the courthouse, during which the
Union women of the town presented a flag and address to the crowd.
"The ladies of Kingwood are influenced by circumstances heretofore
unknown to American history, to give some suitable expression of their
abiding love for their Country," the address started. It expressed the
women's hope that "no rash act may deprive our Country of her glory,
so dearly won and fondly cherished." [34]

Judging by the extant sources, conservatism prevailed — albeit by a
smaller and ever-shrinking margin — among women in the Tidewater
and Valley as well as in the western counties. Conservative women clung
to the view that extremists in the North and South shared the blame
for the Union's troubles. Judith Rives, whose husband, William, was a
leader among the Unionist delegates, summed up the conservative position when she wrote to her son during the January legislative session
that Virginia was in the unenviable position of having to steer between
"scylla and charibdis [sic]" — the "dogmatical rule of the secessionists"
on the one hand and the "pragmatical intermeddling of the abolitionists" on the other. Other women as well singled out the South's political
leaders for criticism. Mary Louisa Dabney Carrington wrote to her sister Betty on January 31, 1861, that if more "honorable" men — namely
Unionists — had been in public service, "we would never have gotten
into this *fix*." She also disparaged the Washington correspondent of the

Richmond *Daily Dispatch*, who, in her mind, did everything he could to "inflame the public mind, and prevent any attempt at an adjustment—which hope, is faint enough anyway." [35]

In her correspondence with her nephew, Eliza A. Willson indicted Southern leaders for a lack of vision. She feared that advocates of disunion had not counted the costs, she wrote, adding her own retrospective prescription for the South's ills: "The South has never acted to please me, when the difficulties first began she talked too much of what she was going to do, without doing anything to make herself independent, she ought to have had her own manufactorys [*sic*] of shoes hats clothes all ready for her own people and have not spent her breath talking." The same forces that were breaking up the Union—ambition and greed— would prove the undoing of the South. "The idea of a great Southern Republic is but a chimera," Willson observed. "What is to prevent its being broken up into sections? nothing; the passion of designing politicians will be brought into play then as now." [36]

Willson's nephew Willie, whom she tried so hard to influence, indeed shared her views on secession. Not all conservative women, however, were so fortunate. Private papers reveal that many women disagreed with their men about the prospect of secession. For example, Lucy Wood's suitor Waddy Butler advocated disunion well before she did. By January 21, Wood, a former Bell supporter, had inched closer to the secessionist camp. But, as she explained to Waddy, she was yet not ready to give her full support to the idea of a Southern republic. Her objection to joining with the lower South was a common one among Virginians. "As soon as it is in the power of the South the slave trade will be reopened," she predicted, adding that such a move was not only morally repugnant but would also have dreadful consequences for the South. Lucy reassured Waddy that if Virginia did secede, she would "do everything in my power consistent with the character of a southern lady for the sake of my Country. . . . I shall learn what part I ought to play, and I shall perform it, let the dangers be what they may." [37]

Maria Louisa Wacker Fleet, mistress of a vast plantation in King and Queen County, remained true to the Union long after her son Fred had embraced secession; she blamed ruthless politicians in both sections for sowing discord. Mary Blackford's family had maintained a tenuous Unionism until 1860, but in the wake of Lincoln's election, the tide of secession sentiment swept her sons and husband away. To Blackford, her family's secessionism signified her failure to do her patriotic duty. "To see my sons arrayed against one part of their country, our own 'Star

Spangled Banner,' and in such a cause, is a sorrow that makes me feel the grave is the only place for me," she wrote her brother in January of 1861. "You did not know, my dear John, the pains I took to train my five sons in the sentiments of patriotism." In closing she requested, "Pray don't show my letter, you know it is treason in the eyes of many to hold the sentiments I do—and I do not want to injure my husband and children." [38]

Blackford's reference to "treason" is one marker of the "revolution in sentiment" that, according to Shanks, took place between Lincoln's election and the opening of the secession convention. During that time, secessionists, though a numerical minority, succeeded in putting conservatives on the defensive by waging a relentless publicity campaign aimed at convincing the populace that Unionism represented treason.[39] Interestingly, anecdotal evidence suggests that, on the eve of the convention, secessionism had made greater inroads among young women (those in their teens and twenties) than among older ones (those over thirty), who had experienced the political developments of the 1840s and 1850s as adults. That many women of Mary Blackford's generation were slow to accept the secessionist viewpoint may reflect their attachment to the argument that it was woman's nature and her duty to love the Union and curb men's passions. Young women, less thoroughly steeped in the philosophy that women should be political mediators and less aware of the horrors of war than older ones, were more easily swept away in the excitement of secession.[40]

Louisa H. A. Minor of Charlottesville, twenty-eight years old in 1861, wrote in her diary on January 27 that she was upset at "Old Virginia's slowness in this contest for our rights." She concluded a diatribe against Northern aggression with the observation, "It is easy to conceive now what our forefathers felt when Old England wanted to make them drink tea." Some of the strongest expressions of secession sentiment on the eve of the convention came from teenagers. Mary Evelyn Hill, a student at the Rappahannock Female Institute, wrote her friend Belle on January 29, 1861, that "the South has borne with the North until forebearance ceases to be a virtue." "It is really a sin & shame that those meddling abolitionists should have spoiled our glorious Union," she averred, and wished that Virginia had "a little more South Carolinian fire." [41]

Elizabeth Randolph Preston Allan of Lexington, stepdaughter of Margaret Junkin Preston, was exposed to "South Carolinian fire" in person. Allan, who was thirteen years old in 1860, was secure in her support for the Union until, during the Christmas holidays of that year, she met a handsome and persuasive secessionist cousin from the Palmetto state.

His eloquence captivated her, and from then on she considered Lincoln nothing less than a "monster." Allan believed that age was a factor in determining political loyalties. "Many of the young people in the town were beginning to wear the blue cockade, the Confederate badge," she remembers, looking back on the first months of 1861, while "the older people, with but few exceptions, hoped to preserve the Union."[42]

Kate Virginia Cox Logan was another Virginia girl who caught secession fever. Logan, whose father would serve as a Unionist delegate at the secession convention, was no stranger to politics in 1861. "I had been fed on political questions since early childhood, so felt fully prepared to assume my own attitude" toward secession, she wrote in her memoirs. She was a committed Unionist until the winter of 1860, when she paid a visit to relatives in Macon, Georgia, where she soon adopted a new point of view, since she was "surrounded on all sides by secessionists of the extreme sort." Logan seems to have kept her secessionist leanings to herself until April of 1861, when her father came over to the Confederate side.[43]

A few women served in public as recruiters for the secessionist cause, through the medium of the newspapers. One such woman wrote an appeal to the "Women of Virginia" and sent it to the *Lynchburg Republican* a few weeks after the 1860 presidential election. The appeal, which was reprinted in the *Daily Richmond Enquirer*, called for a revival of the boycott movement, and leveled a stinging attack not only at the "Black Republicans" but also at Virginia's leaders: "How long has South Carolina surpassed us . . . ? Can she see coming disasters one whole year before us? . . . Heretofore I have been proud to say, 'I am from Virginia,' hereafter, I fear I must hang my head in shame when the question of my nativity is asked."[44]

In the months between Lincoln's election and the start of the secession convention, however, such public expressions of secession sentiment by women were rare. As of February 1861, male secessionists in Virginia had made little effort since the presidential election campaign to solicit contributions from women or to include women in their public rituals. But that would soon change — the months of the secession convention (February through April 1861) would witness a sea change in the political images and sentiments of Virginia women, a change brought about not only by dramatic events outside of Virginia's borders but also by a change in tactics by Virginia secessionists, men and women alike. By April of 1861, Mary Evelyn Hill, the student who wished Virginia had a little more "South Carolinian fire," was in the political majority, for Judith Rives, Mary Carrington, Eliza Willson, Lucy Wood, and Mary

Blackford, along with scores of other conservative women, had come over to her side.

"Every woman was to some extent a politician," Sallie A. (Brock) Putnam of Richmond wrote in her memoirs in 1867, looking back on the secession convention of 1861. The hall where the convention met became women's "favorite place of resort," she remembers, and "every prominent delegate had his partisans among the fair sex." According to Putnam, an ardent secessionist who went on to serve the Confederacy as a nurse, there was no doubt about where Virginia women's loyalty lay during the secession crisis: "The fact was, that long before the ordinance of secession was passed by the Convention, almost every woman in Richmond had in her possession a Confederate flag—ready, at any moment, to run it out her window." [45]

Each of Putnam's assertions—that women were on hand in large numbers at the convention and that the majority of Virginia women supported the Confederacy long before the Commonwealth seceded from the Union—was advanced at the time of the convention and has been repeated by modern-day historians.[46] It can be confirmed beyond doubt that women attended the secession convention, but the question of women's loyalty is more complicated than Putnam lets on. Putnam viewed secession through the prism of Confederate womanhood, an ideology that stipulated the political unity of Southern women. That ideology itself took shape during the months of the secession convention.

The secession convention was played out in three acts. The first act, lasting from February 13 to March 9, has been characterized by Shanks as a period of delay, during which the Unionists and moderates who dominated the convention bided their time, looking to Washington, D.C., for signs that compromise was still possible; it culminated with the failure of a Peace Conference in the capitol and with Lincoln's inaugural address. During the second act, or period of agitation, lasting until April 4, the conservative coalition of Unionists and moderates unraveled as hopes for compromise faded, and secessionists gained the upper hand in the convention. The final act, which closed with Virginia's secession on April 17, was dominated by the Fort Sumter crisis; Lincoln's handling of that crisis was the straw that broke the back of Unionism in Virginia.[47]

The secession convention pitted three political factions against each other—Unionists, moderates, and secessionists—each of which included women in its fold. Each successive act in the convention was characterized by changes not only in the actions and attitudes of Virginia men but of women as well. During the first act of the convention, women played a relatively passive but nonetheless significant role in the secession debate—as spectators, as symbols and images in the rhetoric of the delegates, and as commentators who recorded in their private papers illuminating interpretations of political developments. During the second act, women took a far more active part in the debate, as public partisans of secession, or, to a lesser extent, of Unionism. In the month of March, secessionist men and women began to elaborate the ideal of Confederate womanhood, and actively campaigned to win over the hearts and minds of the Old Dominion's women. That campaign culminated during the third act of the convention in a resounding victory for the secessionists, and in the establishment of Confederate womanhood as the dominant ideal of female civic duty in Virginia.

From its opening day, the secession convention in Richmond was packed with throngs of spectators, male and female; the official proceedings of the convention note that "one gallery was reserved exclusively for ladies, a large number of whom were present during the session of the Convention." The crowd was so large that the delegates immediately voted to relocate their proceedings from the Hall of Delegates in the capitol to the larger Mechanics' Hall, which had often before been the scene of political mass meetings. In the new venue, wherein one gallery was again reserved for women, the noise and jostling of the spectators proved so distracting to the delegates that one of them moved to have the galleries cleared of all onlookers. In a chivalrous nod to women's superior restraint, another delegate moved that the ladies should be permitted to remain on hand. After the crowd complied with a request to "refrain from loud displays," the motion to disperse them was withdrawn. The public, men and women together, would witness every day of the proceedings until the convention retired into a secret session on April 16.[48]

In the ladies' gallery were women of every political stripe: Unionists such as Judith Rives and Elizabeth Van Lew; secessionists like Sally Lyons Taliaferro and Lucy Parke Chamberlayne; and women who were still undecided, including Lucy Wood and Ellen Mordecai. Some women went with their families and others with their female friends; some attended only one day of the debates while others, like Chamberlayne, went daily to hear the delegates' speeches. The ladies' gallery was usually filled by 8:00 in the morning, two and a half hours before each day's session began; some women knitted to help pass the time.[49]

Women were present in the convention not only as spectators in the galleries but also as images and symbols in the discourse of the delegates. Historian Nina Silber has elucidated the ways in which the political discourse of Reconstruction was gendered. Northerners, she argues, attributed to the defeated South an effeminacy which they contrasted with the manliness of the victorious North; ultimately, the image of a "feminized South" served as a vehicle of reconciliation—the political reunion of North and South was symbolized by the metaphor of marital reunion between Northern men and Southern women.[50] A close look at the debates of the Virginia convention reveals that the political discourse of the secession debate was heavily gendered. Delegates' speeches were suffused with discussions of manhood and womanhood and with metaphors of marriage, divorce, and family.

During the first act of the debate, Unionists and moderates evoked the long-popular image of Virginia as the "mother of all states," who must act, in the words of J. W. Sheffey, as the "great mediator and pacificator of this family strife." They also paid homage to the notion that real women were natural mediators. Moderate W. L. Goggin declared that he loved the Union "because its fair daughters . . . have bedewed with their tears the shrine of the Father of his country at Mount Vernon . . . and sent up their aspirations together to the Home of the Most High for the welfare and protection of this great people." Not only the Mount Vernon Association but the Clay Association, too, received a nod—Unionist Waitman Willey told his fellow delegates how his patriotism had been stirred as he passed the statue of Henry Clay on the way to the hall.[51]

Not content to be on the defensive, the secessionists, led by visiting delegates from the seceded states of South Carolina, Georgia, and Mississippi, used gendered images in their attack on what they characterized as the "submissionist" position. Along with attributing passivity and weakness to conservatives, secessionists portrayed the Union as a marriage gone bad, from which the South must withdraw. As they had during the 1860 election campaign, secessionists played on men's fears, telling delegates that only by allying with the Confederacy could they protect their women and children from the specter of a Northern invasion. But interestingly, secessionists did not consistently equate feminine images with weakness. They frequently described the Confederacy as a sisterhood; Virginia, one delegate proclaimed, must serve as the "living barrier behind which her Southern sisters may rally."[52] The presence of negative and positive images of women in the rhetoric of delegates across the political spectrum speaks to the duality in the prevailing public images of women—as weak and submissive on the one hand, and as virtuous and stoic on the other. The dissonance between these negative and positive images became even more striking as the debate wore on.

Secessionist arguments that the North was unwilling to compromise were seemingly vindicated by the failure of the Peace Conference in late February and by Lincoln's inaugural address on the 4th of March. The Peace Conference, which was attended by delegates from fewer than half the states in the Union (all of the seceded states were absent), proved to be ineffectual; its recommendations for compromise were summarily rejected by the Republican Congress. Lincoln's speech was an even greater blow to conservatives. Far less conciliatory than Unionists and moderates had hoped, the speech was widely interpreted by Virginians as a declaration that Lincoln would use "coercion" to restore the Union and to enforce the fugitive slave law. Secessionist papers proclaimed that Lincoln's speech inaugurated Civil War, while conservatives, despairing of the possibility of reconciliation with the North, held out hopes for a border-state conference.[53]

These developments occasioned a great deal of written commentary by women, both those who attended the convention and those who followed it from afar. A deep pessimism took hold of many conservatives. Mary Custis Lee, wife of Robert E. Lee, believed that if Lincoln had been a "distinterested patriot" he would have resigned before taking office. By February 19, she was convinced that "the prospects before us are sad indeed"; she maintained her belief that "both parties are in the wrong in this fratricidal war." Noting that the Peace Conference had failed, Samuella (Hart) Curd, daughter of a prosperous landowner and merchant in Albemarle County, wrote in her diary that she feared compromise was no longer possible in the convention, and predicted that "the record of 1861, will be one of unprecedented sorrow, should this glorious Republic be broken down." Angelina Selden Edrington of Stafford County, along with many others, viewed Lincoln's inauguration with dread. "To morrow is the 4 of March the Enaugurel [sic] of Mr Lincoln," she wrote on March 3, adding "oh my God . . . let harmony prevail through this land again forbid it God that war should ravage this country." Judith Carter (Lewis) McGuire confided her fears to her daughter, writing on the eve of the inauguration, "I think Lincoln's administration are acting over the reign of Terror in France and they would establish the Guillotine if they dared—but I trust a righteous God will frustrate their designs."[54]

Chastened but not yet beaten, conservative delegates in the convention endorsed the report of the Federal Relations Committee, which had been appointed to make a study of the South's grievances and make recommendations to the convention. The report, which opened the second act of the secession convention drama, condemned the use of "coercion" by the federal government, recognized the right of a state to withdraw from the Union, and recommended that the convention continue to press the federal government for a compromise. Conservatives wanted the convention to approve the report, adjourn, and prepare for a border state convention. Secessionists, who preferred not to close the debate but rather to buy time as secession sentiment grew, countered by making long pro-Confederate speeches and by presenting to the Convention a series of pro-secession resolutions that came from around the state.[55]

"*The Ladies* still continue to throng the Convention Hall, daily, and in some instances encroach upon the consecrated domain of the members, who don't appear to like it much," declared the *Richmond Daily Dispatch* in March. Women were more prominent in the discourse of the second phase of the secession debate than they had been in the first, both as negative referents and as positive ones. Delegates, conservatives and extremists alike, made harangues against the abolitionists; some of these singled out Northern women for opprobrium. Ironically, the more radical a delegate was, the more power he attributed to the abolitionists. In his comments on the origins of the crisis, John Baldwin, a Unionist, said that abolitionism "first took possession of the harebrained men and old maids of the North—the material of fanaticism everywhere," but concluded that abolitionists had ultimately failed to win over the North. Moderate delegate George Bruce, by contrast, conjured up the image of Lowell Mill girls in Massachusetts, who during their free time "turn[ed] over the gilded leaves of some Abolition author, and in a short time they became indoctrinated in abolitionism." These women, Bruce averred, inculcated in their own children "hatred to the South and its inhabitants."[56]

The anxieties about women's political loyalties that were implicit in some of the delegates' speeches were made explicit in the secessionists' response to an incident that took place in the convention hall on March 23. On that day a group of Richmond women asked the convention if they could pay "a compliment to a member of the Convention," namely Unionist John Baldwin, by presenting him with a poem, a wreath, and some roses in the convention hall, after the day's proceedings were over. The poem, which was read aloud by one of the delegates and published in the *Richmond Whig*, evoked the theme of woman's superior patriotism. Woman deemed "*Union* right," and it was "*Man's duty—to support her!*," the poet proclaimed. Baldwin's speech of thanks to the ladies was also published; it declared that "the approving smile, the approving word of the just, the good and the true" gave him a "joy unspeakable." Secessionists took a very different view of the proceedings, denying that a pro-Union testimonial could have originated among Richmond women. "We are credibly informed," the *Daily Richmond Enquirer* contended, "that the contribution for the purchase of the wreath and arrangement for its presentation were instigated and mainly achieved by *Northern ladies, and the verses were written by a lady from New England.*"[57]

The Baldwin tribute was objectionable to the *Enquirer* because it flew in the face of secessionist claims that women were exemplars of Southern patriotism. In the aftermath of Lincoln's inauguration, the secessionist press in Virginia carried on a relentless campaign on behalf of disunion; one of the primary goals of that campaign was to win the allegiance of women. Secessionist papers began to call on women to attend political meetings. Seats were reserved for the ladies, for example, at a mass meeting to be held at First African Church in Richmond "in regard to the immediate secession of the State of Virginia from Black Republican rule." The newspapers described women's participation in secession meetings in language that mimicked the rhetoric of partisan elections. At a flag raising in Richmond, "The ladies too joined in with a zest that wreathed their fair faces with sweet smiles . . . [and] exultant pride and approval," declared the *Enquirer*.[58]

Women not only participated in rallies organized by men but took their own initiatives. Louisa H. A. Minor and her friends raised a flag over her hometown of Charlottesville on March 23; the flag was a Confederate facsimile with the addition of a black star for "*poor old Virginia.*" Likening secession to the American Revolution, Minor wrote in her diary, "We fix upon Patrick Henry's favorite words for our motto — '*If this be Treason make the most of it.*'" Women also submitted pro-secession appeals to the newspapers. The Richmond *Daily Dispatch* printed a poem from a Bedford County woman urging Virginia to get on the "Dissolution wagon." The *Staunton Vindicator* featured a pro-secession letter from a Virginia woman living in South Carolina. The author of the letter presented herself as a paragon of Confederate patriotism. "I have three sons," she wrote, "whom God knows I would bid farewell and cheer on to the field of battle" to defend the South.[59]

Female commentators enthusiastically advanced the notion that women's special moral perspective on politics made them superior

patriots. In another piece in the *Dispatch*, entitled "The Ladies Secessionists," a female correspondent suggested that women advocated secession because "they are not politicians, but go for the good of the
country, without reference to party." The *Democratic Mirror* of Leesburg reported on April 3 that a group of pro-Confederate women had
recently met in Essex County. They resolved, in yet another tribute to
woman's superior patriotism, to "show the world that however weakly
the fire of noble pride is flickering in the bosoms of Virginia's sons, it yet
glows with its pristine vigor in the hearts of our daughters." They vowed
to use every means in their power to imbue their countrymen with the
"spirit of immediate secession." [60]

Male secessionists made the most of these manifestations of Confederate sentiment, interpreting them as proof that the majority of Virginia
women favored disunion. Remarking on the letter from South Carolina quoted above, the *Staunton Vindicator* claimed that "the ladies are
always quicker in their apprehension than the men, and hence all of
them nearly are in favor of Virginia uniting with the South." Not content
simply to lay claim to a female majority, a correspondent from Petersburg noted that women "discuss eagerly and familiarly political affairs"
and asserted that "they have *all* abandoned the Union, and raised the
cry of secession." An editorial in the *Daily Dispatch* similarly asserted
that women as a group supported "the Cause," and offered the following explanation: "The instincts of woman lead her to detect the slightest
taint in the moral atmosphere, and . . . she proudly withdraws from such
a companionship as black republicanism proposes." [61]

The secessionist campaign for women's support that took place in
the press and in the streets was carried over into the convention hall
itself, much to the dismay of conservatives. Moderate delegate John
Nelson acknowledged the secessionists' success in winning female support when, on March 26, he addressed the women of the secession convention audience directly. He began by noting that "gentlemen on this
floor have intimated that even the ladies of Virginia are far ahead of
the Union party of this body in their zeal for war; and I have heard it
stated, that in one county the ladies had held a meeting and resolved,
that they would come here and teach 'our hands to war and our fingers
to fight.'" Nelson went on to explicitly invoke Spartan motherhood,
urging "secesh" women to think about the consequences of their Confederate zeal: "Mothers, wives, sisters of Virginia! I doubt not that when
your sons, your husbands, and your brothers are called to battle, like
the Spartan mother you will tell them 'to return *with* their shields or to
return *on* them.' But when they are brought back to you in the cold em-

brace of death, will it assuage your grief that you have urged them on to an unnecessary contest in a deadly civil war?" [62]

Nelson's premise — that the women of Virginia were far ahead of the Union Party — was, strictly speaking, untrue. Women were no more unified behind secession than men were. Many women remained undecided as to the course Virginia should pursue, and many others clung to the Union. Ellen Mordecai of Richmond, for example, stayed on the fence, observing that "speakers on opposite sides use strong arguments which if they have no other effect keep *lady politicians* in a state of indecision." After watching back-to-back speeches by Unionist and secessionist delegates, she concluded, "I trust that they all speak from honest principles and that an overruling Providence may decide the all important result." [63]

Mary Virginia Terhune, visiting Richmond from her home in New York, was unmoved by secessionist arguments. "To my apprehension, so much that we heard was sheer gasconade," she later recalled, "amusing for a time from its very unreason and illogical conclusions, and often indicative of such blatant ignorance of the spirit and the resources of the Federal government." Judith Rives, another Unionist, concurred. On April 4, the convention defeated a preliminary ordinance of secession by a vote of 88 to 45, bringing to a close the debate's second phase. Three days later, Rives wrote her son a long letter on the state of affairs in Richmond. "A grand fuss seems to be going on among the secessionists, who are getting very impatient to push our old state out of the Union whether she will or not," she observed. Richmond "looked more like revolutionary France than a sober American city. Groups of men were standing about in busy idleness, talking and gesticulating. Bands of music going round, serenading secession orators — blackies rambling about . . . school boys, and worse, school girls, raising secession flags." [64]

That Rives was especially appalled at the specter of school girls raising secession flags is not surprising, for it signified the eclipse of a particular construction of female civic duty — women as sectional mediators — which Rives had done much to bring about and to exemplify, in her capacity as an officer of the Clay and Mount Vernon Associations. Secessionist women may not have yet outnumbered conservative ones, but they certainly outdid them in their public zeal. Rives knew that while secessionists did not yet control the convention, they did control the streets and the press — and the public discourse on women's civic duty.

From April 4 on, the debates inside the convention hall and outside it were dominated by the Fort Sumter issue. The fort, which lay in

Charleston Harbor, was occupied by a small federal garrison, a thorn in the side of the Confederacy. Throughout March, Lincoln reassured the South that he would not reinforce the fort, but in the latter part of the month he decided to replenish the fort's supplies. As early as April 3, rumors of the resupply effort were rife in Virginia; on April 8, they were officially confirmed. The reply of the Confederacy was swift and decisive. On April 12, 1861, Confederate military officials began the bombardment of Fort Sumter. Three days later, Lincoln issued a proclamation calling on the states of the Union, Virginia included, to furnish 75,000 troops to "coerce" the seceded states back into the Union.[65]

Contemporary commentators and historians alike have identified Lincoln's proclamation as the great turning point in Virginia's debate over secession. With war a reality, Virginia had to choose sides, and the great majority of men were unable to countenance taking up arms against the citizens of their fellow slave states. Delegate John Goode wrote in his reminiscences that Lincoln's call for troops "destroyed all hope of a peaceful settlement." Historian Shanks agrees. "After Lincoln's proclamation," he asserts, "moderates as well as secessionists, outside of the Convention, were ready for independent state action, for they felt the 'end was at hand.' "[66]

Female commentators, too, identified Lincoln's call for troops as the turning point in Virginia's deliberations. Cloe Tyler Whittle of Norfolk thought that the proclamation brought about a "radical change in the opinions of the people." "The effect was magical!" she wrote in her diary on April 15. "I have read & I have heard, repeatedly, of the fluctuations of public opinion but never realized it as much as now. . . . 'Secession! Immediate Secession!,' is the universal cry!" "When Lincoln's proclamation, calling on Virginia to contribute [toward the] quota of 75,000 men [was issued]," Cornelia McDonald of Winchester wrote in her reminiscences, "what a change!" Sara Pryor believed that the fate of Virginia was decided on "April 15, when President Lincoln demanded troops for the subjugation of the seceding states of the South." Elizabeth Randolph Preston Allan went one step further. "When Lincoln demanded that Virginia furnish troops to coerce her sister States," her memoirs declare, "no loyal Virginian had any further hesitation."[67]

Not surprisingly, Unionists found the public spectacle surrounding the firing on Sumter to be disturbing and even terrifying. Mary Virginia Terhune's memoirs include a detailed account of the atmosphere in Richmond on April 14. "The living stream poured toward the Capitol Square, and it swept us with it. The grounds were filled with a tumultuous crowd," she remembers. In the same place, three years before, Terhune had seen the inauguration of Richmond's celebrated equestrian statue of George Washington. "Was it all a farce, even then, this talk of brotherhood and patriotism?" she poignantly asked. Terhune sadly conceded that Sumter "decide[d] the question for Virginia." Unionist Samuella Curd likewise saw the furor over Sumter as ominous: "News came this evening that Fort Sumpter had been taken by the South Carolinians, greatest excitement, amounting almost to a mob, to night pulled down the Stars & Stripes off the Capitol, & raised the Secession flag, had a torch light procession & truly evil days have fallen on us, none can say what the future will be for us. The people seem most mad." [68]

On April 16, the day after the convention received word of Lincoln's call for troops, the galleries of the convention hall were cleared and the delegates went into secret session. A revolutionary spirit gripped the state capital. Not far from the legal convention, an extra-legal "Spontaneous Southern Rights Convention" met and called for immediate secession. As popular pressure on the delegates mounted, a slim secessionist majority turned into a decisive one. On April 17, the convention passed an ordinance of secession, by a vote of 88 to 55. Although the ordinance was to be presented to the voters for ratification on May 23, "for all practical purposes," historian James M. McPherson has written, "Virginia joined the Confederacy on April 17." The convention quickly took measures to muster an army, to exercise the powers of a sovereign state, and to conclude a treaty with the Confederate government. Virginia formally entered the Confederacy on May 7; the Confederacy agreed to adopt Richmond as its new capital on May 21. [69]

"Farewell to Whigs and Democrats, Secessionists and Submissionists, and political characters of every variety of here heretofore," wrote a female correspondent from Louisa County to the Richmond *Daily Dispatch* on April 18, the day after Virginia seceded. "Farewell, forever!" she continued. "'Tis now North or South, Liberty or Slavery, Life or Death. . . . Mothers, wives and daughters, buckle on the armor for the loved ones; bid them, with Roman firmness advance, and never return until victory perches on their banners." [70] This "Woman's Appeal" can and should be read two ways—as the product of two decades of political activity and discourse by women, and as a statement inaugurating a new stage in the sectional conflict in Virginia. By 1861, women had long served as recruits and recruiters in Virginia politics; the Confederate women of 1861 had first been, to paraphrase the Louisa correspondent, Whigs and Democrats, secessionists and Unionists. Moreover, inherent in Confederate womanhood are assumptions that had been part of the public discourse on female civic duty since the 1840s: that women, because of their superior moral virtue, possessed a greater love of country than men, and that they played an indispensable public role in the creation of political consensus. Both assumptions underlay the hyperbolic claims (women were all for the Whigs, or the Union, or disunion) that contending political forces made in the antebellum period.

The image of women offered up by the Louisa correspondent—that of impassioned patriots whose job it was to stoke men's desire for combat—soon dominated the public discourse. Secessionist newspapers praised women's ability to "nerve the most timid" men. The *Richmond Daily Whig* (which had been purchased by secessionists in late March) printed a "passionate appeal," signed by a hundred women of Gloucester County, urging men to stand up and fight; "no woman ever trusted a coward," the appeal read. Newspapers also gave credit to individual women such as Mary Roberts of Suffolk, who accompanied her six sons to the local depot "and bid them God speed in defending their country." While commentators occasionally referred to Confederate women as "Spartan mothers," an even more popular reference point was the example of the "Revolutionary foremothers." The notion that Southern secession was analogous to the American Revolution had long been a favorite theme of secessionists; after secession, the Revolutionary metaphor appeared again and again in the rhetoric on women's duties. For example, a correspondent to the *Daily Richmond Enquirer* declared that the ladies showed "the spirit of '76." "One of the first in the county . . . said to me yesterday, with great feeling, that if she had ten sons, she would gladly send them to the war. With such spirit animating men, women and boys, and God and truth on our side, we may surely defeat Lincoln."[71]

Although the antebellum political world, which had given rise to the dual image of women as both partisans and mediators, was presumed dead by Confederate ideology, the construction of women's civic duty in the new Confederacy continued to be paradoxical. The image of women as mediators was not completely banished; rather, it was faintly echoed in Confederate rhetoric on women's relief work. In the immediate aftermath of secession, Virginia women quickly established a host of Confederate relief associations, which made food, clothing, tents, and other necessities for the soldiers. Women's wartime relief work was praised by newspapers as a new manifestation of an old phenomenon, namely female benevolence. "The ladies, ever foremost in every benevolent work," wrote a Petersburg correspondent, invoking a familiar phrase, "have contributed large quantities of bandages and lint for the use of our troops."[72]

"Distinterested" insofar as it involved providing for strangers as well as family, relief work was seen by some as a way for women to promote unity within the Confederacy and to counteract the damage wrought by the passions of war. In an article entitled the "Patriotism of the Ladies," the *Alexandria Gazette* praised women's efforts to make uniforms for the soldiers: "It is a fit office for woman to ameliorate by her gentle and beneficent ministrations the evils which flow from the present excited condition of affairs." A similar article declared that women, "as ministering angels, are pouring oil on the troubled waters, and doing their utmost in assistance to bring about an honorable peace, by rendering the soldier comfortable." Such a view of woman's duty was occasionally reflected in private papers. In May 1861, shortly after joining a relief society, Lucy Wood wrote that, "our needles are now our weapons. . . . we women have mighty work to perform . . . it is ours to calm the fierce feelings of hatred and revenge, to be with and minister to the dying and the wounded."[73]

Confederate ideology in Virginia, then, posited the existence of a unified South, one which women, as patriotic exhorters and ministering angels, helped to hold together. Even in the opening stage of the war, however, before the first major battle, at Manassas/Bull Run in July of 1861, Confederate womanhood was a poor reflection of the actual experiences of women. Secession did not eliminate, even temporarily, political divisions among Virginia women.[74]

A significant minority refused to support secession even after it was a fait accompli. The greatest concentrations of Unionists were, of course, located in the northwestern counties of the state, in present-day West Virginia. Just as Confederate women served as recruiters and relief workers for the newly formed Confederate army, so, too, did Union women in northwestern Virginia perform those tasks for the federal army. Women in Preston County, for example, presented a flag to Union recruits there, with the injunction " 'quit yourselves like men,' and when the sound of victory is heard over the tented field, let that flag be found still waving; and only with the fall of your entire company, let it be your winding sheet." Julia Augusta Pierpont, wife of Unionist governor Francis Pierpont, worked for the Union cause by providing supplies to federal soldiers. So, too, did Laura Ann Jackson Arnold, the sister and lifelong confidante of Thomas "Stonewall" Jackson. Up until 1861, she kept a steady and intimate correspondence with her beloved brother Thomas. But after secession, Laura became estranged from her brother and husband alike, for while they supported the Confederacy, she refused to abandon her Union principles. She eventually divorced her husband on the grounds that his Confederate sympathies made it impossible for the couple to coexist peacefully.[75]

Unionist women who lived in the solidly Confederate regions of present-day Virginia were faced with a painful choice in the wake of secession — to leave the state or to make themselves vulnerable to ostracism and persecution. Mary Virginia Terhune, who returned home with her husband to New York immediately after Virginia left the Union, believed that public pressure was too much for many former Unionists to bear: "I do not attempt to estimate what proportion of men, who would have remained loyal to flag and government if they could, were coerced, or cajoled, into bearing arms under a government they abhorred."[76]

Unionist Elizabeth Van Lew, by contrast, chose to stay in Richmond and work clandestinely for the Union cause. With the help of former servant Mary Elizabeth Bowser, she went on to run the most celebrated federal spy ring of the war. Van Lew's Unionism was grounded in a deep hatred of slavery. In her journal, Van Lew offered up her own explanation of the origin of secession. "Shallow thinking, violent men — negro traders — false teaching — false preaching — corrupt press," were all to blame for the conflict. But Van Lew singled out women for special condemnation, for they had, "unknowing and unreflecting," become secession's "strongest advocates." According to Van Lew, Richmond's women were overjoyed at the news of secession. The torchlight procession that was held in Richmond on the evening after secession she described in dark and ominous terms: "Such a sight! The transparencies with their ... wicked and blasphemous mottoes — the carriages with ladies — the women on foot — the multitude of the mob — the whooping — the tin-pan music and the fierceness of a surging, swelling revolution this I witnessed. I thought of France, and as the procession passed I fell upon my knees under the angry heavens, clasped my hands and prayed, 'Father, forgive them, for they know not what they do!' "[77]

The personal papers of Confederate women reveal that, contrary to Van Lew's characterizations, they were neither unknowing nor unreflecting. Among conservatives (those Confederate women who had formerly opposed secession) and even among longstanding disunionists, reactions to secession varied greatly. Many conservatives enacted what has come to be seen as a quintessentially Virginian part in the drama of the birth of the Confederacy. Like the most famous of their contemporaries, Robert E. Lee, they held out hope for compromise until secession was a fact; when faced with a choice between loyalty to the Union or to their native state, they embraced the latter, and adopted the Confederate cause in short order.[78]

In the minds of these women, Virginia had played the noble and tragic role of scorned mediator in the sectional drama. Two days before the secession ordinance was ratified, Judith W. McGuire, wife of a high school principal in Alexandria, confided to her diary her interpretation of the recent course of events: "I am thankful that [Virginia] . . . set an example of patience and long-suffering, and made an earnest effort to maintain peace; but as all her efforts have been rejected with scorn . . . I trust that she may now speak decidedly." McGuire found that the camaraderie of relief work shored up her faith in the cause. Of women's efforts to equip the soldiers she wrote, "The fires of our enthusiasm and patriotism were burning all the while to a degree which might have been consuming, but that our tongues served as safety valves. Oh, how we worked and talked, and excited each other! One common sentiment animated us all; no doubts, no fears were felt."[79]

For every conservative woman who came to embrace Confederate womanhood, there was another who, although she supported the South, was unable to banish fear and doubt. Sidney Sophia Carter Gore, the daughter of a Unionist delegate to the secession convention, had been "deeply imbued with the Gospel of Peace," and "dreaded the idea of war." On the day of ratification, she wrote in her journal a poignant lament: "Can it be that our beloved country is indeed just trembling on the verge of ruin? . . . I turn with loathing from the drilling of the Volunteers, and mentally exclaim: Oh! My God, is our world . . . this world which was once the abode of purity, become *so sinful* as to cause a 'Needs be' to exist, to *teach men to fight*?"[80]

Conservative women who had adult sons found themselves in a particularly unenviable position, for they were asked to sacrifice their sons to a cause about which they felt ambivalent. Maria Louisa Wacker Fleet was one such woman. Fleet wrote her son Fred at the end of April that she was unwilling that he go to war "until there is greater necessity for it than there is at present." A month later, she realized her former position was untenable. "Of course you cannot sit idly by when our country expects every one of her sons to be up and doing," she told Fred, adding, "I can't think of this *awful war* with any composure, it haunts me waking and sleeping." Mary Blackford was another reluctant Spartan mother. On May 26, 1861, she wrote to her brother, "I have five sons in this dreadful civil war. . . . I have heard of mothers saying they are glad to have their sons go; they wish they had a hundred to send. I am not one of those heroines. I regard it as a dire necessity only."[81]

Secessionist women, like conservative ones, responded to the fateful decision of April 17 in a bewildering variety of ways. "Even those most anxious for the event could not unmoved break the ties which bound them to the dear old Union," Emma Mordecai of Richmond wrote in her own firsthand account of the secession convention. But according to Emma, the news of secession united and galvanized both her city and her family. Describing a torchlight procession which took place a few days after secession, she observed, "Richmond was never in such a state of deep intense excitement as at present and for the last week. . . . The streets were thronged Friday night as many women as men all apparently of the best classes constituted the crowd — the order and decorum were wonderful." She explained that her sister Caroline, who had been less sure of disunion than Emma, had become "a strong warm southern rights woman" and seemed "born anew." By April 25, Emma and Caroline were busy making bandages for the soldiers, with the latter "practising [sic] the Marseillaise" all the while.[82]

Even those deeply committed to the "Cause" struggled with an emotion that Confederate ideology did not countenance, namely a profound sense of foreboding. Sally Lyons Taliaferro thought that secession was "glorious news" but was plagued by visions "of the *fiery trial* which is before us," while Cornelia McDonald "had a constant sense of coming evil." When, on April 23, 1861, the women of her neighborhood presented a flag to soldiers there, Amanda Virginia Edmonds of Fauquier County wrote in her diary, "A never to be forgotten day, though I cannot say that it was pleasant." Almost two months before the first major battle of the war was fought in nearby Manassas, Edmonds seemed to know exactly what kind of fate awaited the Old Dominion. "Peace will never inhabit our happy land till years and years shall have passed away," she wrote in her diary. "Our own dear Virginia, [is] destined to be the battleground."[83]

EPILOGUE *The War and Beyond*

Once war broke out, expressions of dissatisfaction with the gender prescriptions of Confederate womanhood proliferated among Southern women. "I wish I were a man!" became a common refrain in women's diaries and letters.[1] Such laments span the entire war, from the firing on Fort Sumter to the last desperate battles of 1865. In the days after Sumter, Cloe Tyler Whittle, as committed a secessionist as one could find in Virginia, experienced not only anticipation but also a gnawing frustration that bordered on self-loathing—for she was barred, by virtue of her sex, from taking part in the "action," namely in the male work of fighting. To celebrate the bombardment of the fort, Whittle put on her "Secession Dress," but felt shame that all women could do was "to put a few brass buttons up the front of their dresses!" "When I see young men wasting their time and talents I can scarcely help the thought arising, 'Why hast thou made me thus?'" she wrote in her diary in April of 1861. Her curse, as she construed it, was to have been given male qualities without male opportunities: she lamented that "Ambition to excess, & Perseverance [*sic*] indefatigable should be given to me & still the thraldom of Womanhood thrown around me, making these qualities which would so advance my cause were I a man, turn almost to indwelling fiends to torment & mock me by continually showing me my incapacity for action!"[2]

Two years later, in August of 1863, Lucy Breckenridge of Grove Hill expressed similar frustration. "I wish the women could fight," she confessed to her diary, "and I do think they might be allowed to do so. . . . Their lives are not more precious than the men's." Two years later still, on the eve of Confederate defeat, Caroline Davis wrote, "I sometimes wish I was a man that I might take my place among the gallant defenders of our rights instead of being contented to work in the sphere in which Providence has placed me."[3]

For Whittle, Breckenridge, and Davis and others like them, such laments were acts of fantasy; only an infinitesimal fraction of women actually took up arms during the war.[4] When looked at in the context of their antebellum political experiences, however, women's wartime fantasies take on a new significance. In some sense, the women who lived through the secession crisis and war had, of course, long been barred from taking a full part in the "action"—they could neither vote nor hold office. But the comment "I wish I were a man" is never found in ante-bellum writings by Virginia women. The absence of such complaints speaks to the effectiveness of public discourse in defining and valorizing women's political roles. Virginians of both sexes argued that by standing at a slight remove from direct participation in electoral conflict, women occupied a privileged position—they were able to exert an influence over political affairs without being corrupted by them.

Confederate womanhood attempted to adapt this argument to new circumstances. Women were asked to keep up their roles as guardians of the public morals, at a safe remove from the worst corruptions of war. The kinds of political action defined as appropriate by Confederate womanhood reflected women's antebellum political functions. On behalf of political parties, Virginia women had exhorted men to do their duty; in their benevolent societies, women had played the role of "ministering angels." The problem for the likes of Cloe Tyler Whittle was that such contributions to political life no longer seemed significant or purposeful at a time when the stakes of political conflict were not simply electoral victory and defeat but life and death.

Not content to express their dissatisfaction in private, countless Confederate women found public ways to challenge the gender prescriptions of Confederate womanhood. Some used familiar political tools: hundreds petitioned Confederate officials, registering their opposition to policies such as conscription. Some, leaving behind the familiar territory of voluntary relief work, wandered into the uncharted realm of paid war work, as nurses or clerks in the Confederate government, only to meet with ambivalence and even hostility from men. Public protests against the government's management of the war took on myriad forms, from working-class women's dramatic bread riots of 1863 to elite women's indulgence in what one observer called "reckless revelry" in the Confederacy's final hours.[5]

Historians agree that the Civil War revolutionized the lives of white Southern women, and that it precipitated a widespread reconsideration of gender conventions. But they disagree about its long-term legacy. Anne Firor Scott argued in 1970 that the war undermined the Southern patriarchy and made possible the emergence of a "new woman" in the South, one who played a much more prominent role in the region's public life than the antebellum "lady" had. Suzanne Lebsock and George C. Rable countered Scott's thesis in the 1980s, contending that the postwar decades should be seen as a time of losses rather than gains for women. In an atmosphere of structural devastation and ideological reaction, most of the economic and political opportunities to which the war gave rise quickly evaporated; women were too caught up in the struggle for survival to focus on extending their sphere. Drew Gilpin Faust has recently adopted an intermediate position in the debate, finding that women in the postwar South sought both to rehabilitate patriarchy and to transcend their traditional dependence on men. She sees in the simultaneous emergence of the conservative United Daughters of the Confederacy and a Southern suffrage movement evidence of the paradoxical legacy of the war.[6]

Without denying the profound impact the war had on women, I argue for the existence of significant continuities between the prewar and postwar eras — continuities brought into focus by my reinterpretation of the antebellum period. To a greater degree than scholars have acknowledged, white Southern women's postbellum political roles and activities were extensions of their antebellum ones. In Virginia, sources from the 1870s, 1880s, and 1890s suggest, elite and middle-class white women relied on time-tested vehicles — benevolent societies, memorial associations, literary appeals, and partisan campaigns — to express their political opinions. And they continued to wrestle with a mandate to be both partisans and mediators in the public sphere.

Women's organizational energies, channeled into relief work during the war, were rechanneled into benevolent activities afterward. Some institutions, such as the Richmond Female Humane Association and Lynchburg Dorcas Society, had survived the war intact, while others, such as Richmond's Retreat for the Sick (1877), were built from the ground up. Religious organizations — women's missionary societies especially — proliferated in Virginia as they did elsewhere in the nation, giving rise to a new generation of civic leaders. Lottie Moon of Albemarle County, for example, a pioneering Baptist missionary to China, was influential in the founding of the Woman's Missionary Union (1888) of the Southern Baptist Convention. Local, male-run temperance associations enlisted female supporters in the 1870s; with the establishment in 1882 of the Richmond chapter of the Woman's Christian Temperance Union, Virginia women both reaffiliated with the national crusade and embarked on a new journey of autonomous organizing.[7]

As in the antebellum period, charitable, evangelical, and moral-reform societies were linked together by ideas and by individuals. Such organizations were predicated on the doctrine of female moral superiority and sought a suprapolitical status. They drew on a committed cadre of middle-class and elite women, many of whom followed the path from church work into reform activism. And women's efforts met with much approbation from men. Joel Chandler Harris, one of the South's most influential writers, noted approvingly in 1890 that, while the typical Southern woman preferred domesticity to politics, she was "an earnest and untiring temperance worker." Echoing the rhetoric of Thomas Dew, John Holt Rice, Ralph Gurley, and others, he concluded, "There is no question and no movement of real importance in which she is not interested."[8]

The work of memorialization took on new significance after the war. Societies honoring the Confederate dead, such as the Ladies' Lee Monument Association (1870), can be seen as heirs to the legacy of the Clay and Mount Vernon Associations. The memorial societies of the immediate postwar decades and the United Daughters of the Confederacy (1894) alike offered homage to male heroism and leadership even as they advanced the view of women as arbiters of civic worth in men and as architects of public opinion. They simultaneously promoted sectional reconciliation and Southern pride. Women, the UDC in particular argued, were specially suited to tell the "true" story of the war, one on which patriots in both sections could agree. As in the late antebellum period, however, the "truths" Virginians advanced were self-serving ones — they sought in their educational programs and other propaganda to justify the system of slavery and deny that it had been the central cause of the war.[9]

The war strengthened the consensus that literature was an appropriate outlet for women, and made household names of Southerners such as Margaret Junkin Preston of Virginia and Augusta Evans of Alabama. After the demise of the Confederacy, Virginia authors participated, historian Jane Turner Censer has demonstrated, in the production of novels of sectional reconciliation; such works typically featured romances between Southern ladies and Northern men. Reviving the notion of women as sectional mediators, postwar novelists were, by the 1880s, more willing than their predecessors had been to serve as social critics. Virginians such as Julia Magruder and Mary Greenway McClelland took aim at Southern gender conventions by comparing Southern men unfavorably with Northern ones. But they ultimately proved just as sectionally partisan as the likes of Eastman, Butt, and Terhune. Censer finds that in the 1890s, as white Southerners committed themselves to the glorification of the past and grew increasingly intolerant of criticism, female authors retreated from the theme of sectional reunion and positioned themselves as defenders of Southern culture.[10]

As they had before the war, political parties exercised an important influence on women's roles. The era of Radical Reconstruction witnessed dramatic departures from antebellum gender conventions: the incorporation of African American women into the Republican Party; the appointment of Elizabeth Van Lew to a prominent office in the Republican hierarchy; and the formation of a fledgling woman's suffrage movement. Each of these developments proved ill-fated. The demise of the Republicans and resurgence of the Democrats in Virginia signaled a reversion to the antebellum script, in which white women were cast as supporting players in the drama of electoral politics, and black women were excluded altogether.

Historian Elsa Barkley Brown's pathbreaking work on postwar Richmond has charted the trajectory of black women's partisanship. After emancipation, black women assumed a prominent role in building a network of benevolent and political organizations — secret societies that had been established before the war could now go public, and they were joined by hundreds of new organizations dedicated to the causes of religion, education, temperance, and poor relief. Once black men gained the ballot, African American women were active participants in Republican election campaigns, "educating the community on the issues, raising funds for candidates, and getting out the vote"; not only did they turn out at Republican meetings, they founded explicitly partisan organizations such as the Rising Daughters of Liberty. Brown argues persuasively that black women's political activism was not grounded in the white discourse on female moral superiority but rather in traditions indigenous to the black community — in an "ethos of mutuality" which made men and women partners in the struggle for their rights. African Americans saw the ballot as "collectively owned" by families and communities rather than as the exclusive property of voters. Brown describes how whites used violence and intimidation to undermine black voting rights, a tragic process culminating in Virginia's 1901–2 constitutional convention, which disfranchised black men.[11]

One of the very few white women in Virginia who publicly defended black civil rights in the 1870s — Elizabeth Van Lew — also fought a losing battle to widen the sphere of white women. In 1869, President U. S. Grant, recognizing her service as a Union spy, appointed Van Lew postmistress of Richmond. The office was a key position in the Old Dominion's Republican hierarchy, as postmasters controlled resources and jobs that could be dispensed to the party faithful. Although control of the state soon passed from Radical Republicans to the Conservative Party (a coalition of former Whigs, Democrats, and moderate Republicans), bringing an end to Virginia's brief Reconstruction, Van Lew stayed in office for eight controversial years. The *Richmond Enquirer and Examiner* considered her presence there "a deliberate insult to our people," as she symbolized the power of Grant's administration. In keeping with expectations, Van Lew used her office as a bully pulpit to advance her political views. In October of 1876, at the height of that year's presidential campaign, she published a newspaper appeal to Northern Democrats, urging them to repudiate the Democrats of the South. She told of the campaign of terror that the latter were carrying out against African Americans. Not only were black men "crowded into the penitentiary, for small offences," but the "lash was used even upon the women." Not surprisingly, such actions infuriated Virginia Democrats, who launched a vitriolic campaign against Van Lew's reappointment. In 1877, President Rutherford B. Hayes, eager to demonstrate his commitment to Southern self-rule, replaced Van Lew with an ex-Confederate officer.[12]

Van Lew believed that her downfall as a politician lay in the disabilities of her gender. She thought herself an "active and earnest Republican so far as a woman can be," and was able, thanks in part to the legacy of Lucy Barbour, to "subscribe freely to party purposes — get up torch light processions — tell men what to say at meetings." But such exercises of female influence were unavailing in the world of postwar politics. Lacking the full rights of citizenship, Van Lew had been unable to build a following of loyal partisans; she felt herself to be the victim not only of Democratic attacks but of a "conspiracy" of men in her own party, who thought a woman not fit for such a coveted office. Her experience strengthened her conviction that if women were truly to wield political power, they needed to lift up their voices and ask for their due — the right to vote.[13]

A small but determined cadre of Virginians agreed with Van Lew, and set out with her on the long march toward the enfranchisement of women. In May of 1870, after hearing New Yorker Matilda Joslyn Gage of the National Woman Suffrage Association deliver a lecture, Anna Whitehead Bodeker and a group of Richmond women founded the Virginia State Woman Suffrage Association (VSWSA), the first such organization in the Old Dominion. Some of its supporters, such as Maria Underwood of Richmond and Orra Langhorne of Lynchburg, had long been political dissenters, opposing slavery and the Confederacy and supporting the Republican Party. But other suffragists possessed more mainstream credentials. Bodeker herself was the wife of a prominent pro-Confederate businessman who after the war served as a Conservative legislator. Among Bodeker's first suffrage recruits was Susan L. Pellet, former secretary of the Mount Vernon Association and headmistress of one of the city's elite girls' schools. The VSWSA included as a vice president none other than Martha Haines (Butt) Bennett, defender of slavery and author of anti–woman's rights editorials for the *Kaleido-scope* in the 1850s.[14]

The suffrage movement did not have a substantial following in Virginia until the first decade of the twentieth century, however. Their diverse backgrounds notwithstanding, the first generation of suffragists were labeled as radicals, associated in the public mind with the policies of the Republican Party. The timeworn counterargument to the call for suffrage—that women could make meaningful contributions to electoral politics without the vote—proved extremely resilient. Newspapers such as the *Richmond Whig* and *Richmond Enquirer* regularly featured women in their election coverage, trying to conjure up the spirit, as the *Whig* put it, of the "old-time campaigns of 1840 and '44." Party rhetoric was replete with references to "ladies" whose "countenances" showed the "deep interest" they felt in political affairs.[15]

Just as political parties in the Old South, especially by the 1850s, had served as vehicles through which white women expressed their commitment to the institution of slavery, they served in the postwar decades as vehicles for women's commitment to white supremacy. When Conservative candidate James Lawson Kemper defeated Radical Republican Colonel R. W. Hughes in the gubernatorial contest of 1873, women in Harrisonburg illuminated their houses in approval, "showing how deep an interest [they] felt," the *Richmond Whig* reported, "in the success of white man's supremacy over the negro equality hordes who desired to . . . compel both sexes to drink deep of the degrading cup of social equality." In the 1876 presidential campaign, Virginia women were encouraged to join Democratic Tilden and Hendricks clubs, to unite with men in bringing an end to the federal presence in the South. By the mid-1880s, the resurgent Democratic Party had absorbed the Conservatives, ended the four-year reign of the reform-minded Readjuster Party, and established what would be a lasting dominance over state politics. Republicans in the North and West were finding new ways to win female allegiance—by including African American women in their campaigns; featuring candidates' wives prominently in their rhetoric; encouraging the formation of Republican women's associations and even of public speaking by women. But Southern Democrats hewed to the prewar model of female partisanship. With its homages to the moral virtue and influence of the "ladies," and its message of white supremacy and states' rights, the Democratic Party commanded the support of white women in the Commonwealth.[16]

In sum, Virginia women's political activities after the Civil War resembled those in antebellum times, and so did much of the public discussion of those activities. The postwar period recalls the antebellum in this respect not only because women's place in Southern politics was circumscribed in the late nineteenth century, but also because the part women had taken in Virginia's antebellum politics was more substantial—and in some ways more like that played by the women in the North—than historians have realized.

To be sure, Southern attitudes toward women's participation in politics did change after the Civil War. That the number of politically active women and of female associations—particularly those dedicated to missionary work and temperance—increased markedly in the postwar decades suggests that Southern women's wartime mobilization had strengthened their claim to a role in politics.[17] And now, with the women's suffrage movement working to make inroads into the South, public discourse on the nature of that role took on a new dissonance. The longstanding gap between the rhetoric about women's civic duty and the reality of their political activities became even wider than it had been in the antebellum period, for critiques of "politicized" females proliferated as more and more women spoke out publicly on the issue of enfranchisement.

The very same Southern newspapers that encouraged women to support the Conservative and Democratic political parties portrayed suffragists as irrational, passionate, and fractious beings, given, as the *Daily Dispatch* put it, to "hissing and brow-beating and tongue-lashing" all who did not agree with their views. Indeed, with leaders of the suffrage crusade arguing that women could purify the political process by casting ballots, the time-honored axiom that women were more disinterested than men came under attack in the South. An article in the *Southern Magazine* in 1871 by Robert Lewis Dabney, a prominent Virginian, answered the rhetorical question "Will women's entrance into politics purify it?" with a resounding "No." Political excitements would corrupt women "ten times more than men," Dabney contended, because women were "naturally more emotional and less calculating." A "Daughter of Virginia," in a letter to the *Richmond Whig*, made a similar case. By entering the "arena of political strife," she wrote, women would "cast aside all that is beautiful and excellent in the female character." Since the suffrage movement threatened the "overthrow of our political fabric," she argued—as Hicks, Butt, and others had in the 1850s— Southern women should reject it "*en masse*."[18]

The irony of a woman like the "Daughter of Virginia" repudiating politics even as she publicly and vociferously weighed in on one of the most controversial issues of the day seems to have escaped the letter's author. In 1871, however, the *Richmond Whig* evinced a sharper sense of irony in an article entitled "The True Woman Against the Woman's Righters." The piece told of the efforts of a group of Southern women to petition Congress against women's enfranchisement. The *Whig* was sure that this "counter-movement" represented the majority opinion among women. Or almost sure: "It may come to this," the paper declared, "that the polls will have to be opened throughout the whole country to ascertain the sense of women on the question of female suffrage. What a day that would be!"[19]

Notes

ABBREVIATIONS

APCL   Ann Pamela Cunningham Library, Mount Vernon Ladies'
        Association, Mount Vernon, Va.
LC   Library of Congress, Washington, D.C.
LV   Library of Virginia, Richmond, Va.
UNC   Southern Historical Collection, University of North Carolina,
        Chapel Hill, N.C.
UVA   Manuscripts Department, Alderman Library, University of Virginia,
        Charlottesville, Va.
VHS   Virginia Historical Society, Richmond, Va.
WM   Manuscripts and Rare Books, Early Gregg Swem Memorial Library,
        College of William and Mary, Williamsburg, Va.
YU   Manuscripts and Archives, Sterling Memorial Library,
        Yale University, New Haven, Conn.

INTRODUCTION

1. On plantation mistresses, see Catherine Clinton, *The Plantation Mistress: Woman's World in the Old South* (New York: Pantheon Books, 1982); Jane Turner Censer, *North Carolina Planters and Their Children, 1800–1860* (Baton Rouge: Louisiana State University Press, 1984); Jean Friedman, *The Enclosed Garden: Women and Community in the Evangelical South, 1830–1900* (Chapel Hill: University of North Carolina Press, 1985); Elizabeth Fox-Genovese, *Within the Plantation Household: Black and White Women of the Old South* (Chapel Hill: University of North Carolina Press, 1988); and Joan E. Cashin, *A Family Venture: Men and Women on the Southern Frontier* (New York: Oxford University Press, 1991). On urban women, see Suzanne Lebsock, *The Free Women of Petersburg: Status and Culture in a Southern Town, 1784–1860* (New York: W. W. Norton, 1984); Jane H. Pease and William H. Pease, *Ladies, Women, and Wenches: Choice and Constraint in Antebellum Charleston and Boston* (Chapel Hill: University of North Carolina Press, 1990); and Barbara L. Bellows, *Benevolence among Slaveholders: Assisting the Poor in Charleston, 1670–1860* (Baton Rouge: Louisiana State University Press, 1993). On farmers' wives and poor women, see Victoria E. Bynum, *Unruly Women: The Politics of Social and Sexual Control in the Old South* (Chapel Hill: University of North Carolina Press, 1992); Stephanie McCurry, *Masters of Small Worlds: Yeoman Households, Gender Relations, and the Political Culture of the Antebellum South Carolina Low Country* (New York: Oxford University Press, 1995); and Brenda E. Stevenson, *Life in Black and White: Family and Community in the Slave South* (New York: Oxford University Press, 1996).

2. On women's supposed exclusion from politics, see Clinton, *Plantation Mistress*, pp. 181–82; Fox-Genovese, *Within the Plantation Household*, p. 195; Leb-

sock, *Free Women of Petersburg*, p. 224; McCurry, *Masters of Small Worlds*, pp. 215–17; Stevenson, *Life in Black and White*, pp. 42–43; and Drew Gilpin Faust, *Mothers of Invention: Women of the Slaveholding South in the American Civil War* (Chapel Hill: University of North Carolina Press, 1996), pp. 5–6. See also George Fitzhugh, *Sociology for the South: Or the Failure of Free Society* (Richmond, Va.: A. Morris, 1854), pp. 214–15.

3. Until 1830, only landowners (approximately one-fourth of all white men) could vote. The constitutional convention of that year extended the franchise to male leaseholders and taxpaying heads of household, meaning that half of the state's white freemen could now cast ballots. The 1850–51 constitutional convention extended the franchise to all free white men over the age of twenty-one. Julian A. C. Chandler, *The History of Suffrage in Virginia* (Baltimore, Md.: Johns Hopkins University Press, 1901), pp. 22, 36–40, 51.

4. For insights into the definition of politics and the public sphere, all of which inform my interpretation, see Glenna Matthews, *The Rise of Public Woman: Woman's Power and Woman's Place in the United States, 1630–1970* (New York: Oxford University Press, 1992), pp. 3–10; Mary P. Ryan, *Women in Public: Between Banners and Ballots, 1825–1880* (Baltimore: Johns Hopkins University Press, 1990), pp. 3–18, 131; and Jürgen Habermas, *The Structural Transformation of the Public Sphere: An Inquiry into a Category of Bourgeois Society*, trans. Thomas Burger (1962; reprint, Cambridge: MIT Press, 1994), pp. 43–67.

5. Anne Firor Scott, *The Southern Lady: From Pedestal to Politics, 1830–1930* (Chicago: University of Chicago Press, 1970), esp. pp. 4–21.

6. James Oakes, *The Ruling Race: A History of American Slaveholders* (New York: Vintage Books, 1982), pp. 38–39, 52, 57–65; Charles Lowery, *James Barbour, A Jeffersonian Republican* (University, Ala.: University of Alabama Press, 1984); Evelyn Pugh, "Women and Slavery: Julia Gardiner Tyler and the Duchess of Sutherland," *Virginia Magazine of History and Biography* 88 (April 1980): 186–202; and L. Minor Blackford, *Mine Eyes Have Seen the Glory: The Story of a Virginia Lady, Mary Berkeley Minor Blackford, 1802–1896, Who Taught Her Sons to Hate Slavery and to Love the Union* (Cambridge: Harvard University Press, 1954). On Hicks, see Barbara H. Browder, "Our Remarkable Kinswoman" (unpublished typescript, 1988), LV.

7. John H. Moore, "Judith Rives of Castle Hill," *Virginia Cavalcade* 13 (Spring 1964): 30–35; E. Lee Shepard, "The Hunter Family of Fonthill," *An Occasional Bulletin: The Virginia Historical Society* 59 (December 1987): 4–6.

8. Moore, "Judith Rives," p. 31; Browder, "Our Remarkable Kinswoman," p. 4. In 1860, approximately 15 percent of the women and 11 percent of the men in the South were illiterate; illiteracy rates were higher in rural than in urban settings. Catherine Hobbs, ed., *Nineteenth-Century Women Learn to Write* (Charlottesville: University Press of Virginia, 1995), p. 11; Lee Soltow and Edward Stevens, *The Rise of Literacy and the Common Schools in the United States: A Socioeconomic Analysis to 1870* (Chicago: University of Chicago Press, 1981), pp. 159–62, 184–92. On the connections between literacy and female partisanship in the North, see Ronald J. Zboray and Mary Saracino Zboray, "Political News

and Female Readership in Antebellum Boston and Its Region," *Journalism History* 22 (Spring 1996): 2–14.

9. McCurry, *Masters of Small Worlds*, pp. 47–48, 76; D. Harland Hagler, "The Ideal Woman in the Antebellum South: Lady or Farmwife?," *Journal of Southern History* 46 (August 1980): 405–18; Keith L. Bryant, "The Role and Status of the Female Yeomanry in the Antebellum South: The Literary View," *The Southern Quarterly* 18 (Winter 1980): 73–88. On the agricultural reform movement, see Charles W. Turner, *Virginia's Green Revolution* (Waynesboro, Va.: Humphries Press, 1986), pp. 13–15, 30–33; on the boycott movement, *Alexandria Gazette*, November 17, 1859; *Richmond Whig and Public Advertiser* (semiweekly; hereafter *Richmond Whig*), December 16, 1859.

10. On the 1831–32 laws, see June Purcell Guild, *Black Laws of Virginia: A Summary of the Legislative Acts of Virginia Concerning Negroes from the Earliest Times to the Present* (Richmond: Whittet & Shepperson, 1936), pp. 106–8, 175–76.

11. On black benevolence in antebellum Virginia, see First African Baptist Church, Richmond, Va., Minute Books, 1841–1930, December 4, 1848, p. 138, LV; John T. O'Brien, "Factory, Church, and Community: Blacks in Antebellum Richmond," *Journal of Southern History* 64 (November 1978): 530–31; Philip Morgan, ed., *"Don't Grieve After Me": The Black Experience in Virginia, 1619–1986* (Hampton, Va.: Hampton University, 1986), p. 45; Marie Tyler-McGraw and Gregg Kimball, *In Bondage and Freedom: Antebellum Black Life in Richmond, Va.* (Richmond, Va.: Valentine Museum, 1988), pp. 35–41; and Tommy L. Bogger, *Free Blacks in Norfolk, Virginia, 1790–1860: The Darker Side of Freedom* (Charlottesville: University Press of Virginia, 1997), p. 153.

12. Elsa Barkley Brown, "Uncle Ned's Children: Negotiating Community and Freedom in Postemancipation Richmond, Virginia" (Ph.D. diss., Kent State University, 1994), pp. 302, 309–10, 345–60; Deborah Gray White, *Ar'n't I a Woman? Female Slaves in the Plantation South* (New York: Oxford University Press, 1985); Jacqueline Jones, *Labor of Love, Labor of Sorrow: Black Women, Work, and the Family from Slavery to the Present* (New York: Oxford University Press, 1985); Lebsock, *Free Women of Petersburg*, pp. 87–111; Fox-Genovese, *Within the Plantation Household*, pp. 290–333; Stevenson, *Life in Black and White*.

13. Alison Goodyear Freehling, *Drift Toward Dissolution: The Virginia Slavery Debate of 1831–1832* (Baton Rouge: Louisiana State University Press, 1988), pp. 11–35, 87–116; Edward L. Ayers, "Introduction: The Edge of the South," in Edward L. Ayers and John C. Willis, eds., *The Edge of the South: Life in Nineteenth-Century Virginia* (Charlottesville: University Press of Virginia, 1991), pp. 1–8; David R. Goldfield, *Urban Growth in the Age of Sectionalism: Virginia, 1847–1861* (Baton Rouge: Louisiana State University Press, 1977), p. xxix; Fox-Genovese, *Within the Plantation Household*, p. 78.

14. The most extensive treatment of Southern women's public activism is Guion Griffis Johnson's underappreciated classic *Ante-bellum North Carolina: A Social History* (Chapel Hill: University of North Carolina Press, 1937); for

background on Johnson and other pioneers in the field of Southern women's history, see Anne Firor Scott, ed., *Unheard Voices: The First Historians of Southern Women* (Charlottesville: University Press of Virginia, 1993). For more recent works on the upper South, see Janet L. Coryell, *Neither Heroine nor Fool: Anna Ella Carroll of Maryland* (Kent: Ohio University Press, 1990) and Jayne Crumpler DeFiore, "COME, and Bring the Ladies: Tennessee Women and the Politics of Opportunity during the Presidential Campaigns of 1840 and 1844," *Tennessee Historical Quarterly* 51 (Winter 1992): 197–212. For evidence that women were integral to evangelical benevolent societies in the Deep South, see Frederick A. Bode, "A Common Sphere: White Evangelicals and Gender in Antebellum Georgia," *Georgia Historical Quarterly* 79 (Winter 1995): 775–809, and John W. Quist, "Slaveholding Operatives of the Benevolent Empire: Bible, Tract, and Sunday School Societies in Antebellum Tuscaloosa County, Alabama," *Journal of Southern History* 57 (August 1996): 481–526. On women and partisan and sectional politics in the lower South, see Elizabeth Moss, *Domestic Novelists in the Old South: Defenders of Southern Culture* (Baton Rouge: Louisiana State University Press, 1992) and Christopher J. Olsen, " 'Molly Pitcher' of the Mississippi Whigs: The Editorial Career of Mrs. Harriet N. Prewett," *Journal of Mississippi History* 58 (Fall 1996): 237–54.

15. Gerda Lerner, "Placing Women in History: Definitions and Challenges," *Feminist Studies* 3 (Fall 1975): 5–14; Gerda Lerner, editor's introduction to Jane Jerome Camhi, *Women Against Women: American Anti-Suffragism, 1880–1920* (Brooklyn, N.Y.: Carlson Publishing, Inc., 1994); Elna C. Green, *Southern Strategies: Southern Women and the Woman Suffrage Question* (Chapel Hill: University of North Carolina Press, 1997).

CHAPTER ONE

1. Chapter title from speech by Robert J. Taylor in William S. White, *Total Abstinence from Intoxicating Drinks as a Beverage Expedient: Being the Substance of an Address before Lexington Division No. 45, Sons of Temperance* (Richmond, Va.: Samuel Gillock, 1849), p. 18. Speech written by Mary Virginia Early while she was a student at the Buckingham Female Collegiate Institute, June 13, 1842, Mary Early to Elizabeth Early, c. 1838–39, and Mary Virginia (Early) Brown Diary, March 7, 1853, Early Family Papers, VHS; Legislative Petitions, Lynchburg, Va., January 2, 1846, LV.

2. There are two schools of thought on the subject of Southern women's benevolence. The first, represented by Lebsock, Scott, Bode, and Quist, holds that female-run voluntary associations flourished in Southern cities, towns, and rural settings and that, like Northern female societies, Southern ones gave elite white women an outlet for exercising moral authority, promoting gender solidarity (among whites), and wielding public influence. Scholars in the second, such as Fox-Genovese, Friedman, Bellows, McCurry, and Murray, see fundamental differences between Southern and Northern benevolence. They argue that Southern societies were paternalistic in nature—they did not push at gender boundaries or institute civic reforms but rather reinforced the social hierarchy and the class prerogatives of elite women. These same scholars have

also debated whether the doctrine of domesticity (or separate spheres) — which posited female moral superiority and therefore served as the ideological pretext for female benevolence — had wide currency in the South. Lebsock offers the most potent case in favor of domesticity's influence in the South; Fox-Genovese the most potent case against it. In arguing that the ideology of female moral superiority undergirded an extensive network of women's associations in Virginia, this book lends support to the Lebsock/Scott camp. Suzanne Lebsock, *The Free Women of Petersburg: Status and Culture in a Southern Town, 1784–1860* (New York: W. W. Norton, 1984), pp. 143–44, 194–236; Suzanne Lebsock, "A Share of Honour": *Virginia Women, 1600–1945* (Richmond, Va.: Virginia Women's Cultural History Project, 1984), pp. 55, 60–63; Anne Firor Scott, *Natural Allies: Women's Associations in American History* (Urbana: University of Illinois Press, 1991), pp. 19–20, 195; Frederick A. Bode, "A Common Sphere: White Evangelicals and Gender in Antebellum Georgia," *Georgia Historical Quarterly* 79 (Winter 1995): 775–809; and John W. Quist, "Slaveholding Operatives of the Benevolent Empire: Bible, Tract, and Sunday School Societies in Antebellum Tuscaloosa County, Alabama," *Journal of Southern History* 57 (August 1996): 481–526. Elizabeth Fox-Genovese, *Within the Plantation Household: Black and White Women of the Old South* (Chapel Hill: University of North Carolina Press, 1988), pp. 61–66, 232–35; Jean E. Friedman, *The Enclosed Garden: Women and Community in the Evangelical South, 1830–1900* (Chapel Hill: University of North Carolina Press, 1985); Barbara L. Bellows, *Benevolence Among Slaveholders: Assisting the Poor in Charleston, 1670–1860* (Baton Rouge: Louisiana State University Press, 1993); Stephanie McCurry, *Masters of Small Worlds: Yeoman Households, Gender Relations, and the Political Culture of the Antebellum South Carolina Low Country* (New York: Oxford University Press, 1995), pp. 188–89; and Gail S. Murray, "Charity Within the Bounds of Race and Class: Female Benevolence in the Old South," *South Carolina Historical Magazine* 96 (January 1995): 54–70. On Northern women's benevolence, see, for example, Mary P. Ryan, *Cradle of the Middle Class: The Family in Oneida County, New York, 1790–1865* (New York: Cambridge University Press, 1981); Nancy A. Hewitt, *Women's Activism and Social Change: Rochester, New York, 1822–1872* (Ithaca, N.Y.: Cornell University Press, 1984); and Lori D. Ginzberg, *Women and the Work of Benevolence: Morality, Politics, and Class in the Nineteenth-Century United States* (New Haven, Conn.: Yale University Press, 1990).

3. Norfolk women organized a female orphan asylum in 1804, Richmond women in 1805, Petersburg women in 1811, and Alexandria women in 1812; Lebsock, "Share of Honour," pp. 60–63; *Constitution and By-Laws of the Female Humane Association of the City of Richmond* (Richmond, Va.: Shepherd and Colin, 1843), pp. 6–7.

4. On Lucy Minor, see L. Minor Blackford, *Mine Eyes Have Seen the Glory: The Story of a Virginia Lady, Mary Berkeley Minor Blackford, 1802–1896, Who Taught Her Sons to Hate Slavery and to Love the Union* (Cambridge: Harvard University Press, 1954), pp. 3–5; Legislative Petitions, Fredericksburg, Va., December 21, 1803, LV. On Taylor, see Lebsock, *Free Women of Petersburg*, p. 206; on Wood, see Legislative Petitions, Richmond, Va., December 13, 1810, LV, and

obituary reprinted in William Maxwell, *A Memoir of the Rev. John H. Rice, D.D.: First Professor of Christian Theology in Union Theological Seminary, Virginia* (Philadelphia: J. Whetham, 1835), p. 176.

5. Legislative Petitions, Fredericksburg, Va., December 21, 1803, LV. The 1803 petitioners included members of the most prominent families in Fredericksburg—the Chews, Wellfords, Crumps, Carters, Pages, Lomaxes, and Mercers. For background on some of these families, see, for example, John T. Goolrick, *Historic Fredericksburg: The Story of an Old Town* (Richmond, Va.: Whittet and Shepperson, 1922), pp. 145, 184, and S. J. Quinn, *The History of the City of Fredericksburg, Virginia* (Richmond, Va.: Hermitage Press, 1908), pp. 132, 139, 150. As of 1803, the state of Virginia was not in the practice of funding primary or secondary schools. It was common for schools that wanted to raise money to ask the legislature to grant them permission to hold a lottery. Cornelius J. Heatwole, *A History of Education in Virginia* (New York: Macmillan, 1916), pp. 127–28.

6. Legislative Petitions, Fredericksburg, Va., December 21, 1803, LV. On republican motherhood, see Linda K. Kerber, *Women of the Republic: Intellect and Ideology in Revolutionary America* (New York: W. W. Norton, 1980). On the format and function of petitions, see Robert Bailey, *Popular Influence upon Public Policy: Petitioning in Eighteenth-Century Virginia* (Westport, Conn.: Greenwood Press, 1979), pp. 9–19, 27–32.

7. Legislative Petitions, Richmond, Va., December 13, 1810, LV; Ginzberg, *Women and the Work of Benevolence*, pp. 48–52; Lebsock, *Free Women of Petersburg*, pp. 195–236; Legislative Petitions, Fredericksburg, Va., December 24, 1807, LV; H. W. Burton, *The History of Norfolk* (Norfolk, Va.: Norfolk Virginian Job Print, 1877), p. 223.

8. *Political Arena* (Fredericksburg), November 22, 1831; John H. Rice, "Short Discourses for Families [To Young Women.]," *Virginia Evangelical and Literary Magazine* 2 (April 1819): 173; John H. Rice, "Extract from Camelford's Letter No. V," *Virginia Evangelical and Literary Magazine* 3 (February 1820): 91.

9. Lori D. Ginzberg, who employs the term "benevolent femininity" in her penetrating study of the North, elucidates how reformers there made distinctions between the "moral" and the "political." Ginzberg, *Women and the Work of Benevolence*, pp. 1–10, 13–15, 65–67.

10. James M. Garnett, *Lectures on Female Education, Comprising the First and Second Series of a Course Delivered to Mrs. Garnett's Pupils, at Elm-Wood, Essex County, Virginia* (Richmond, Va.: T. W. White, 1825), pp. 7–15, 111, 336, 340, 347–48.

11. Thomas Dew, "Dissertation on the Characteristic Differences Between the Sexes, and on the Position and Influence of Woman in Society," *Southern Literary Messenger* 1 (May–August 1835): 496–98, 504–5, 630–32.

12. Virginia Cary, *Letters on Female Character, Addressed to a Young Lady, on the Death of Her Mother*, 2d ed. (Richmond: A. Works, 1830).

13. Ibid., pp. 22, 31–40.

14. Legislative Petitions, Richmond, Va., January 31, 1834, LV; June Purcell Guild, *Black Laws of Virginia: A Summary of the Legislative Acts Concerning Negroes from the Earliest Times to the Present* (Richmond, Va.: Whittet & Shep-

person, 1936). According to Ira Berlin, the General Assembly received so many petitions for exemptions to the removal law that in 1815 it gave county courts jurisdiction over such cases; certain judges and courts were surprisingly sympathetic to black petitioners and readily granted exemptions. When local courts proved hostile to freemen, they "armed themselves with letters of recommendation attesting to their good character, and petitioned the General Assembly." Ira Berlin, *Slaves Without Masters: The Free Negro in the Antebellum South* (New York: New Press, 1974), pp. 146–48. Such appeals were generally unavailing. Clara Robinson of Richmond, for example, asked the legislature for permission to remain after being manumitted, on the grounds that she had served the community well as a midwife; despite a testimonial signed by "a large number of the medical faculty of Richmond" who had consulted her, Robinson's petition was rejected. Legislative Petitions, Richmond, Va., December 20, 1848, LV.

15. Legislative Petitions, Richmond, Va., January 31, 1834, LV. The legislature was perhaps influenced by the fact that Caswell had a free wife and children in Richmond. Guild, *Black Laws of Virginia*, p. 110.

16. Eliza Carrington owned two slaves over the age of twelve in 1835. Richmond City Personal Property Tax Lists, 1835, LV.

17. Lebsock, *Free Women of Petersburg*, pp. 211–12; Marie Tyler-McGraw and Gregg D. Kimball, *In Bondage and Freedom: Antebellum Black Life in Richmond, Virginia* (Richmond, Va.: Valentine Museum, 1988), pp. 35–41. The Orphan Asylum of Norfolk made a policy of "excluding coloured servants from the Institution"; the reasons for that policy are not spelled out in the asylum's records. Norfolk Female Orphan Asylum Minute Book, October 1, 1848, UVA. On the Poor Saints Committee, see First African Baptist Church, Richmond, Va., Minute Books, 1841–1930, December 4, 1848, p. 138, LV.

18. On the founding of the Union Benevolent Society, see *Watchman of the South* (Richmond), November 16, 1837. Other new charities included the Alexandria Orphan Asylum and Female Free School Society, founded in 1832; Richmond's Saint Joseph's Orphan Asylum and Free School, established in 1834 by the Catholic Sisters of Charity; and Lynchburg's female orphan asylum, set up in 1846. Legislative Petitions, Alexandria, Va., February 13, 1847, LV; Mary Agnes Yeakel, *The Nineteenth Century Educational Contribution of the Sisters of Charity of Saint Vincent De Paul in Virginia* (Baltimore, Md.: Johns Hopkins University Press, 1939), pp. 39, 57; Legislative Petitions, Lynchburg, Va., January 2, 1846, LV.

19. *Watchman of the South* (Richmond), November 16, 1837.

20. Ibid., December 29, 1838; *Richmond Whig*, November 12, 1850; *Daily Dispatch* (Richmond), November 17, 1859.

21. Julia Cabell, *An Odd Volume of Facts and Fictions: In Prose and Verse* (Richmond, Va.: Nash and Woodhouse, 1852), pp. 3–13.

22. Female Orphan Society of Norfolk Minute Book, January 2, 1845, UVA; *Lynchburg Virginian*, January 23, 1845.

23. On disbursements of city councils to female charities, see *Constitution and By-Laws of the Female Humane Association*, p. 1; Female Orphan Society of Norfolk Account Book, 1850, UVA; Legislative Petitions, Alexandria, Va., February 19, 1847, LV; *Lynchburg Virginian*, August 20, 1852. On the administration

of the Literary Fund, see A. J. Morrison, *The Beginnings of Public Education in Virginia, 1776–1860* (Richmond, Va.: Davis Bottom, 1917), pp. 10, 29, 48; Heatwole, *A History of Education in Virginia*, pp. 106–7.

24. Legislative Petitions, Fredericksburg, Va., December 5, 1833, LV.

25. Ibid.; Legislative Petitions, Spotsylvania County, December 19, 1835, January 17, 1835, and December 6, 1836, LV; Catherine Lomax to Martha Fenton Hunter, November 23, 1837, Hunter Family Papers, VHS. On Lomax, see Anne J. Carter, *Recollections of the Early History of the Presbyterian Church of Fredericksburg, Va.* (Fredericksburg, Va.: R. A. Kishpaugh, 1906), pp. 9–10.

26. Lomax to Hunter, November 23, 1837, VHS.

27. Legislative Petitions, Spotsylvania County, January 31, 1838, LV. One more female petition, appealing to the "Paternal regard of the Legislature," was essayed in vain in 1839; ibid., February 5, 1839, LV.

28. Legislative Petitions, Spotsylvania County, January 8, 1840; *Journal of the House of Delegates of Virginia, Session 1839–40* (Richmond, Va.: Samuel Shepherd, 1840), pp. 127, 160, 206, 211, 222, 240.

29. "Extracts from the Reports of School Commissioners Relating to the Progress and State of the Primary Schools under Their Direction in the Year 1838," pp. 20–35, LV. Meanwhile, the cause of higher education for females was flourishing. In the period from 1840 to 1860, Virginians established 48 female academies, more than three times the number that had been founded in the previous two decades. Only 40 new male academies were established in 1840–60, compared with 33 in 1820–40. Heatwole, *A History of Education in Virginia*, p. 127.

30. Legislative Petitions, Alexandria, Va., February 13, 1847, LV. The Alexandria Orphan Asylum was assisted in its work by a second concern, the Ladies Benevolent Society, which, like Richmond's Union Benevolent Society, divided up the city into districts and provided wood, food, and clothing to the poor. *Alexandria Gazette*, November 3, 1855.

31. *The Mission and the Destiny of Woman; An Address Delivered at the First Annual Commencement of the Petersburg Female College, July 18, 1855, by Rev. David S. Doggett, D.D.* (Petersburg: Lewellen and Marks, Printers, 1855), p. 7; Maria, "The Ladies of Richmond," *The Family Christian Album* 1 (April 1855): 113–15.

32. Lebsock, *Free Women of Petersburg*, pp. 227–30; *Daily Richmond Enquirer*, November 20, 1844; Eugene Ferslew, comp., *First Annual Directory for the City of Richmond* (Richmond, Va.: Geo. M. West, 1859), p. 244; *Richmond Whig*, November 12, 1850; *Daily Richmond Enquirer*, November 9, 1857; David R. Goldfield, *Urban Growth in the Age of Sectionalism: Virginia, 1847–1861* (Baton Rouge: Louisiana State University Press, 1977), pp. 161–63; H. W. Burton, *The History of Norfolk, Virginia* (Norfolk: Norfolk Virginian, 1877), p. 223.

33. Lebsock, *Free Women of Petersburg*, pp. 227–34.

34. John Kuykendall, *Southern Enterprize: The Work of the National Evangelical Societies in the Antebellum South* (Westport, Conn.: Greenwood Press, 1982), pp. 4–5, 13–18. The AES was founded in 1815 and based in Boston; the ABS

in 1816 and based in New York; the ASSU in 1824 and based in Philadelphia; the ATS in 1825 in Boston; and the AHMS in 1826 in New York.

35. Garnett Ryland, *The Baptists of Virginia, 1699–1926* (Richmond: Virginia Baptist Board of Missions and Education, 1955), pp. 183–213; Mrs. Charles F. Cole, "History of Woman's Work in East Hanover Presbytery" (unpublished typescript), Tyler Family Papers, Women of Virginia Project, WM, p. 23; *American Beacon* (Norfolk), October 11, 1816; "Sunday Schools," *Virginia Evangelical and Literary Magazine* 1 (September 1819): 431. On women's religious benevolence elsewhere in the South, see Bode, "A Common Sphere," pp. 775–809; Quist, "Slaveholding Operatives of the Benevolent Empire," pp. 521–23; and Richard Rankin, *Ambivalent Churchmen and Evangelical Churchwomen: The Religion of the Episcopal Elite in North Carolina, 1800–1860* (Columbia: University of South Carolina Press, 1993), pp. 47–48, 89–91. On the North, see Carolyn Lawes, "Public Women, Public Lives: Women in Worcester, Massachusetts, 1818–1860" (Ph.D. diss., University of California, Davis, 1992).

36. Geo. D. Fisher, *History and Reminiscences of the Monumental Church, Richmond, Va., from 1814 to 1878* (Richmond, Va.: Whittet and Shepperson, 1880), p. 223; William S. Forrest, *Historical and Descriptive Sketches of Norfolk and Vicinity, Including Portsmouth and the Adjacent Counties, During a Period of Two Hundred Years* (Philadelphia: Lindsay and Blakiston, 1853), pp. 150, 227; Fannie E. S. Heck, *In Royal Service: The Mission Work of Southern Baptist Women* (Richmond, Va.: Educational Department, Foreign Mission Board, Southern Baptist Convention, 1913), p. 45; *Southern Religious Telegraph* (Richmond), May 8 and June 19, 1830; *Religious Herald* (Richmond), December 20, 1832.

37. Sadie Bell, *The Church, the State, and Education in Virginia* (Philadelphia: University of Pennsylvania Press, 1930), pp. 244–46; *Twenty-Fourth Annual Report of the Bible Society of Virginia* (Richmond, Va.: Office of the Southern Churchman, 1837), pp. 11–12; *Thirty-Fourth Annual Report of the Bible Society of Virginia* (Richmond, Va.: Advocate Office—C. H. Wynne, 1847), pp. 12–14; "Seventh Anniversary of the Bible Society of Virginia," *Virginia Evangelical and Literary Magazine* 1 (February 1818): 94; *Third Annual Report of the Virginia Tract Society, With the Proceedings of the Annual Meeting, Held in the City of Richmond, April 7, 1837* (Richmond, Va.: William MacFarlane, Printer, 1837), p. 20; *Watchman of the South* (Richmond), November 17, 1837; Anne Boylan, *Sunday School: The Formation of an American Institution, 1790–1880* (New Haven, Conn.: Yale University Press, 1988), p. 31. For an example of a female Sunday schoolteacher who received material from the ASSU, see Cynthia A. Kierner, "Woman's Piety Within Patriarchy: The Religious Life of Martha Hancock Wheat of Bedford County," *Virginia Magazine of History and Biography* 100 (January 1992): 79–98.

38. Marie Tyler-McGraw, "I Believe: Evangelicalism in Southern Urban Culture" (unpublished typescript lent to author), pp. 9–10; Theodosius, "Review of the Cultivation of the Female Intellect in the United States," *Literary and Evangelical Magazine* (June 1827): 307; "Religious Intelligence: Benevolent Societies," *Literary and Evangelical Magazine* 10 (October 1827): 550–51; Rev. David S.

Doggett, "The Proper Ornament of Woman," *The Patriarch: Or Family Library* 1 (November 1841): 212–13; H. Keeling, *Hints on the Best Method of Originating and Conducting Sunday Schools* (Richmond: H. K. Ellyson, 1847): 23.

39. Ryland, *The Baptists of Virginia*, pp. 230–61; William Cabell Bruce, *John Randolph of Roanoke, 1773–1833* (Putnam: New York, 1922), 2:363.

40. Bessie Rowland James, *Anne Royall's U.S.A.* (New Brunswick, N.J.: Rutgers University Press, 1972).

41. Anne Royall, *The Black Book: Or, a Continuation of Travels, in the United States* (Washington, D.C.: Published for the author, 1828), pp. 152–57; Anne Royall, *Mrs. Royall's Southern Tour: Or Second Series of the Black Book* (Washington, D.C.: Published for the author, 1830), pp. 44, 60–61, 98.

42. Royall describes Virginians' negative reactions to her and her work in *Mrs. Royall's Southern Tour*, pp. 33, 39–40, 110; see also W. Asbury Christian, *Lynchburg and Its People* (Lynchburg, Va.: J. P. Bell, 1900), pp. 103–4. For general background on anti-missionism, see Bertram Wyatt-Brown, "The Anti-Mission Movement in the Jacksonian South: A Study in Regional Folk Culture," *Journal of Southern History* 36 (November 1970): 517–20.

43. Kuykendall, *Southern Enterprize*, pp. 77–79; Anne C. Loveland, *Southern Evangelicals and the Social Order, 1800–1860* (Baton Rouge: Louisiana State University Press, 1980), pp. 224–25; Tyler-McGraw, "I Believe," p. 10; Thomas L. Webber, *Deep Like the Rivers: Education in the Slave Quarter Community, 1831–65* (New York: W. W. Norton, 1978), pp. 43–45; Janet Duitsman Cornelius, *"When I Can Read My Title Clear": Literacy, Slavery, and Religion in the Antebellum South* (Columbia, S.C.: University of South Carolina Press, 1991), pp. 109–16; John Holt Rice, "On Affording Religious Instruction to Slaves," *Evangelical and Literary Magazine* 5 (February 1822): 70; William Meade, Preface to *Sketches of Old Virginia Family Servants* (Philadelphia: Isaac Ashmead, 1847), pp. 5–6.

44. Cornelius, *"When I Can Read My Title Clear"*, pp. 105–8; Luther Porter Jackson, "Religious Development of the Negro in Virginia from 1760 to 1860," *Journal of Negro History* 16 (April 1931): 202; Ruth Coder Fitzgerald, *A Different Story: A Black History of Fredericksburg, Stafford and Spotsylvania, Virginia* (Greensboro, N.C.: Unicorn, 1979), p. 73; Kuykendall, *Southern Enterprize*, p. 76; C. W. Andrews, *Memoir of Mrs. Ann R. Page* (New York: Protestant Episcopal Society for the Promotion of Evangelical Knowledge, 1856), pp. 24–27, 36, 45–46; Louis Gimelli, "Louisa Maxwell Holmes Cocke: An Evangelical Plantation Mistress in the Antebellum South," *Journal of the Early Republic* 9 (Spring 1989): 39, 62; Donald G. Mathews, *Religion in the Old South* (Chicago: University of Chicago Press, 1977), pp. 116–19.

45. Guild, *Black Laws of Virginia*, pp. 106–7, 174–75; C. G. Woodson, *The Education of the Negro Prior to 1861: A History of the Education of the Colored People of the United States from the Beginning of Slavery to the Civil War* (New York: G. P. Putnam's Sons, 1915), pp. 179–204; Kuykendall, *Southern Enterprize*, pp. 76–77. For an example of a "colored Sunday school" that offered only oral instruction, see the records of the Trinity Episcopal Church Sunday School in Staunton. White teachers — seventeen of them women and three men — taught

black students to memorize the Lord's Prayer, the Ten Commandments, and assorted hymns and scriptural passages. Reports, 1839–40, of J. W. Smith, Superintendent, concerning the Sunday school at Trinity Episcopal Church, Staunton, Va., in the Frederick Deane Goodwin Papers, VHS.

46. Moncure Conway, *Autobiography, Memories and Experiences of Moncure Conway*, 2 vols. (Boston: Houghton Mifflin, 1904), 1:21; Willard B. Gatewood, Jr., ed., *Free Man of Color: The Autobiography of Willis Augustus Hodges* (Knoxville: University of Tennessee Press, 1982), pp. 8, 24–26.

47. Interviews with Mrs. Julia Frazier and Levi Pollard, in Charles L. Perdue et al., eds., *Weevils in the Wheat: Interviews with Virginia Ex-Slaves* (Charlottesville: University Press of Virginia, 1976), pp. 97, 229–30.

48. On clandestine instruction, see Woodson, *The Education of the Negro*, pp. 205–28; Berlin, *Slaves Without Masters*, pp. 305–6; Marilyn Dell Brady, "Mary Smith Kelsey Peake," in *Black Women in America: An Historical Encyclopedia*, ed. Darlene Clark Hine (Brooklyn: Carlson Publishing Inc., 1993), 2:914; Robert Francis Engs, *Freedom's First Generation: Black Hampton, Virginia, 1861–1890* (Philadelphia: University of Pennsylvania Press, 1979), pp. 12–13, 205; Fitzgerald, *A Different Story*, p. 74 (quotation).

49. Mary Blackford, "Notes Illustrative of the Wrongs of Slavery," February 20, 1836, p. 16, Blackford Family Papers, UVA; Mary Blackford to Ralph Gurley, February 23, 1835, American Colonization Society Papers, LC; Guild, *Black Laws of Virginia*, pp. 178–79; *Richmond Daily Dispatch*, October 25, 1855.

50. Phillip Foner and Phillip Pacheo, *Three Who Dared: Prudence Crandall, Margaret Douglass, Myrtilla Miner—Champions of Antebellum Black Education* (Westport, Conn.: Greenwood Press, 1984), pp. 58–67; Margaret Douglass, *Educational Laws of Virginia: The Personal Narrative of Margaret Douglass* (Boston: John P. Jewett, 1854), pp. 29–33.

51. Foner and Pacheo, *Three Who Dared*, pp. 65–69, 72–83; Douglass, *Educational Laws*, pp. 63–68.

52. The American Education Society and American Home Missionary Society both eventually went under in the South. The Education Society encountered resistance on the grounds that it sought to "usurp the prerogative of the denomination" in training men for the ministry. By the 1840s, the AHMS had made a policy of withholding assistance from any minister who owned slaves; this stance thoroughly alienated its Southern supporters. The ABS, ASSU, and ATS fared better, but in 1857 the American Tract Society split into abolitionist and conservative factions. The Tract Society's association with abolitionists prompted some Virginians to renounce it. See Kuykendall, *Southern Enterprize*, pp. 103–4, 109–10, 138–39, 163–69; Clifford S. Griffin, *Their Brothers' Keepers: Moral Stewardship in the United States, 1800–1865* (New Brunswick, N.J.: Rutgers University Press, 1960), pp. 191–97; *Richmond Daily Dispatch*, November 19, 1850; *The South* (Richmond), May 18, 1857.

53. *Daily Southern Argus* (Norfolk), February 9, 1854. Abolitionist papers, by contrast, hailed Douglass as a heroine. The *Liberator* in Boston, noting that a Quaker woman in Norfolk had delivered a sermon on Douglass's behalf while

Douglass was in jail, went so far as to claim that "the women are a great trouble to our Norfolk neighbors. If they want peace, they must expel all Christian women . . . from the city." Foner and Pacheo, *Three Who Dared*, p. 91.

54. C. C. Pearson and J. Edwin Hendricks, *Liquor and Anti-Liquor in Virginia, 1619–1919* (Durham, N.C.: Duke University Press, 1967), pp. 41–53, 56–59; Ian R. Tyrrell, "Drink and Temperance in the Antebellum South: An Overview and Interpretation," *Journal of Southern History* 48 (November 1982): 495–510; Ryland, *The Baptists of Virginia*, p. 26; *Norfolk and Portsmouth Herald*, March 9, 1831; *Christian Sentinel* (Richmond), January 31, 1834.

55. *Political Arena* (Fredericksburg), August 26, 1831; *Christian Sentinel* (Richmond), April 19, June 28, August 2 and 9, and September 6, 1833, January 31 and May 9, 1834; *Norfolk and Portsmouth Herald*, March 9, 1831; Extract from the Proceeding of the Semiannual Meeting of the Tinkling Spring and Waynesboro Temperance Society held July 18, 1833, VHS. The two foremost historians of temperance in antebellum Virginia virtually ignore women, who, they claim, "never held office or took conspicuous part in public proceedings" of the movement. Pearson and Hendricks, *Liquor and Anti-Liquor*, p. 62.

56. *An Address on Intemperance, Delivered at the Meeting of a Temperance Society in Louisa County on the 4th of July, 1830* (Fredericksburg, Va.: Arena Printing Office, 1830); *Southern Religious Telegraph* (Richmond), October 9, 1830; N. R., "The Temperance Reform," *Virginia Historical Register* 3 (January 1850): 105; Pearson and Hendricks, *Liquor and Anti-Liquor*, pp. 59–62. In 1831, Virginia ranked eighth in the nation in temperance membership. Tyrrell, "Drink and Temperance," p. 486.

57. Jane Chancellor (Payne) Payne Diary, August 15, 1835, April 5, 1843, VHS.

58. Tyler-McGraw, "I Believe," p. 15; on Rutherfoord, see *Richmond Portraits: In an Exhibition of Makers of Richmond, 1737–1860* (Richmond, Va.: Valentine Museum, 1949), p. 180; Gimelli, "Louisa Maxwell Holmes Cocke," pp. 63–64; Martin Boyd Coyner Jr., "John Hartwell Cocke of Bremo: Agriculture and Slavery in the Ante-Bellum South" (Ph.D. diss., University of Virginia, 1961), pp. 334–40; Pearson and Hendricks, *Liquor and Anti-Liquor*, p. 63. For evidence of black temperance activism, see the reference to the Richmond African Temperance Society in the *Religious Herald* (Richmond), September 17, 1830, and to temperance lectures in the Minutes of the First African Baptist Church, January 14, 1844, p. 60, LV.

59. Pearson and Hendricks, *Liquor and Anti-Liquor*, pp. 62, 69, 98–99; Tyrrell, "Drink and Temperance," p. 490; Lucian Minor, "The Temperance Reformation in Virginia," *Southern Literary Messenger* 16 (July 1850): 430.

60. *Reasons for Not Joining the Temperance Society, By a Clergymen* (Richmond, Va.: Published by Request, 1836), pp. 25, 33.

61. Pearson and Hendricks, *Liquor and Anti-Liquor*, pp. 80–90; *Christian Sentinel* (Richmond), March 7, 1834; Benevolent Temperance Society of Salem, Va., Papers, Peyton Family Papers, VHS.

62. Pearson and Hendricks, *Liquor and Anti-Liquor*, pp. 85, 91–96.

63. Ibid., pp. 91–96; "The Presidential Election," *Journal of the American Temperance Union* 4 (November 1840): 168.

64. "The Old Dominion Coming," *Journal of the American Temperance Union* 6 (March 1842): 44; *Religious Herald* (Richmond), August 25, 1842; *Watchman of the South* (Richmond), August 11, 1842. Total membership in the Washingtonian-era total-abstinence societies probably surpassed total membership in the VTS-era associations. Pearson and Hendricks, *Liquor and Anti-Liquor*, pp. 92–94.

65. "Female Influence," *Journal of the American Temperance Union* 5 (May 1841): 74; "Female Temperance Benevolent Societies," ibid. 6 (February 1842): 28; *National Temperance Songster* (Norfolk, Va.: n.p., 1846), pp. 34–35. On women and the Washingtonian movement in the North, see Ruth M. Alexander, " 'We Are Engaged as a Band of Sisters': Class and Domesticity in the Washingtonian Temperance Movement, 1840–1850," *Journal of American History* 75 (December 1988): 763–85.

66. Pearson and Hendricks, *Liquor and Anti-Liquor*, pp. 97–102.

67. In 1843, a national mutual benefit society, the Daughters of Temperance, was founded to assist the work of the Sons of Temperance; only one chapter of the national organization was established in Virginia — the "Sisters of Temperance," in Richmond. Minor, "The Temperance Reformation in Virginia," pp. 426–38; Pearson and Hendricks, *Liquor and Anti-Liquor*, pp. 62, 98. On women's admission as "visitors," see Lebsock, *Free Women of Petersburg*, p. 229; Minutes of Mt. Crawford Division No. 19 of the Sons of Temperance, 1848–1856, pp. 444, 458, 464, 467, UVA. On other Daughters of Temperance organizations in the South, see Guion Griffis Johnson, *Ante-bellum North Carolina: A Social History* (Chapel Hill: University of North Carolina Press, 1937), pp. 171–72.

68. Pearson and Hendricks, *Liquor and Anti-Liquor*, pp. 93–94; Taylor speech as quoted in White, *Total Abstinence*; Julia Cabell, *An Odd Volume*, p. 268; S. J. C. Whittlesey, *Heart-Drops from Memory's Urn* (New York: A. S. Barnes, 1852), pp. 267–68; on Terhune, see Mary Kelley, *Private Woman, Public Stage: Literary Domesticity in Nineteenth-Century America* (New York: Oxford University Press, 1984), pp. 131–32.

69. Anna Maria Weisiger Diary, September 8, 1842, October 10 and December 22, 1844, LV; James Howard Gore, *My Mother's Story: Despise Not the Day of Small Things* (Philadelphia: Judson Press, 1923), pp. 23, 43–44.

70. Pearson and Hendricks, *Liquor and Anti-Liquor*, pp. 148–51. *Proceedings of the Temperance Mass Convention Held in Winchester, Virginia, July 1st and 2nd 1852: With an Argument on the Legal Prohibition of the Sale of Intoxicating Liquors, by Rev. C. W. Andrews* (Winchester, Va.: Republican Office, 1852), pp. 13–17.

71. For an example of a petition signed by men and women, see Legislative Petitions, Wythe and Giles Counties, June 3, 1852, LV. For women's own petitions, see Legislative Petitions, Cabell County, February 19, 1849, LV; Legislative Petitions, Wythe County, c. 1852, LV; *Supplement to the Enquirer, Whig, Examiner, Times, Republican and Republican Advocate*, June 23, 1851. A total of 15,000 Virginia men signed temperance petitions in 1853; the total number of female signatories is not known. Pearson and Hendricks, *Liquor and Anti-Liquor*, pp. 97–99, 122–25, 133.

72. On Northern women and temperance, see, for example, Jed Dannen-

baum, "The Origins of Temperance Activism and Militancy among American Women," *Journal of Social History* 15 (December 1981): 235–52, and Ian Tyrrell, "Women and Temperance in Antebellum America, 1830–1860," *Civil War History* 28 (June 1982): 128–49.

73. John Hartwell Cocke as quoted in Anne Firor Scott, *The Southern Lady: From Pedestal to Politics, 1830–1930* (Chicago: University of Chicago Press, 1970), p. 20.

74. *Daily Richmond Enquirer*, August 23, 1853; *The South* (Richmond), June 2, 1857; Pearson and Hendricks, *Liquor and Anti-Liquor*, pp. 135–43.

75. Pearson and Hendricks, *Liquor and Anti-Liquor*, pp. 143–49; Sara Agnes (Rice) Pryor, *My Day: Reminiscences of a Long Life* (New York: Macmillan, 1909), p. 124.

76. *Daily Dispatch* (Richmond), September 10, 1856; *Virginia Republican* (Martinsburg), August 16, 1856.

77. E. P. Elam, "Scene in Richmond," *Family Christian Album* 4 (April 1855): 118–19; "A Word about Temperance," *Family Christian Album* 6 (June 1855): 181; *Kaleidoscope* (Petersburg), January 24, 1855, February 21, May 2, and July 18, 1855. Hicks's story is told in greater detail in Chapter 4, below.

78. *Richmond Enquirer* (semiweekly), February 2, 1858; *Virginia Free Press* (Charlestown), December 9, 1858; *Minutes of the Grand Division of the Sons of Temperance of Virginia* (Richmond: MacFarlane and Fergusson, 1860), pp. 8, 18; Mark Edward Lender and James Kirby Martin, *Drinking in America: A History* (New York: Free Press, 1982), pp. 80–85.

CHAPTER TWO

1. Chapter title from "Report of the Board of Managers of the Fredericksburg and Falmouth Female Auxiliary Colonization Society" (broadside appended to letter), Mary Blackford to Ralph Gurley, May 1832, American Colonization Society (ACS) Papers, LC; Virginia Cary, *Letters on Female Character, Addressed to a Young Lady, on the Death of Her Mother*, 2d ed. (Richmond, Va.: A. Works, 1830), p. 202.

2. Cary, *Letters on Female Character*, pp. 203–9.

3. Ibid., p. 202. Cary's comments on slavery seem to have sparked no public criticism or debate; on the contrary, Virginians hailed the sobriety and rationality of her book. See, for example, *Southern Religious Telegraph* (Richmond), March 20, 1830, and *Southern Churchman* (Richmond), February 27, 1835.

4. Those whose work supports the covert abolitionist interpretation include Anne Firor Scott, *The Southern Lady: From Pedestal to Politics, 1830–1930* (Chicago: University of Chicago Press, 1970), pp. 46–61, and C. Vann Woodward, ed., *Mary Chesnut's Civil War* (New Haven, Conn.: Yale University Press, 1981), pp. xlvi–liii. Suzanne Lebsock finds that women were a "subversive influence" on the slave system, not because of their opposition to slavery in the abstract but because of their "personalism"; Suzanne Lebsock, *The Free Women of Petersburg: Status and Culture in a Southern Town, 1784–1860* (New York: W. W. Norton, 1984), pp. 137–38. Critics of the covert abolitionist thesis include Jean Friedman, *The Enclosed Garden: Women and Community in the Evangeli-*

cal South, 1830–1900 (Chapel Hill: University of North Carolina Press, 1985), pp. 88–91, and Elizabeth Fox-Genovese, *Within the Plantation Household: Black and White Women of the Old South* (Chapel Hill: University of North Carolina Press, 1988), pp. 334–71. For a potent critique of Fox-Genovese, see Suzanne Lebsock, "Complicity and Contention: Women in the Plantation South," *Georgia Historical Quarterly* 74 (Spring 1990): 59–83.

5. Douglas Egerton, " 'Its Origin Is Not a Little Curious': A New Look at the American Colonization Society," *Journal of the Early Republic* 5 (Winter 1985): 463–67. On the political goals of the organization, see "Colonization Society," *African Repository and Colonial Journal* 1 (August 1825): 161–62; "Colonization Society," ibid. 1 (December 1825): 291. On the religious goals, see Jehudi Ashmun, "Traits of the African Character," *African Repository* 1 (April 1825): 58; and *Seventh Annual Report of the American Society for Colonizing the Free People of Colour of the United States* (Washington, D.C.: James C. Dunn, 1824), p. 7.

6. Alison Goodyear Freehling, *Drift Toward Dissolution: The Virginia Slavery Debate of 1831–1832* (Baton Rouge: Louisiana State University Press, 1988), pp. 118–21; Louis Weeks III, "John Holt Rice and the American Colonization Society," *Journal of Presbyterian History* 46 (March 1968): 26–41. For colonization publicity in the religious press, see, for example, *Christian Sentinel* (Richmond), July 13, 1832; *Southern Churchman* (Richmond), April 15, 1836; and *Religious Herald* (Richmond), December 12, 1839. On black missionaries, see William A. Poe, "Lott Cary: Man of Purchased Freedom," *Church History* 39 (March 1970): 50–56; and John Saillant, ed., "Circular Addressed to the Colored Brethren and Friends in America: An Unpublished Essay by Lott Cary, Sent from Liberia to Virginia, 1827," *Virginia Magazine of History and Biography* 104 (Autumn 1996): 481–504.

7. Henry Clay, *An Address Delivered to the Colonization Society of Kentucky* (Lexington, Ky.: American Colonization Society, 1829), p. 18; Peachy Grattan, "An Address in Behalf of the Colonization Society," *African Repository* 1 (August 1825): 178.

8. On individual bequests to the ACS, see "Annual Meetings of Auxiliary Societies," *African Repository* 1 (January 1826): 343; "Intelligence," ibid. 2 (September 1826): 220; "Contributions," ibid. 2 (December 1826): 324. On the Essex and Charlottesville societies, "Notices," ibid. 1 (December 1825): 320; "Fair at Charlottesville," ibid. 6 (May 1830): 87–88. On Northern antislavery fairs, see, for example, Lori D. Ginzberg, *Women and the Work of Benevolence: Morality, Politics, and Class in the Nineteenth-Century United States* (New Haven, Conn.: Yale University Press), pp. 45–47.

9. Donald Mathews, *Religion in the Old South* (Chicago: University of Chicago Press, 1977), pp. 111–24.

10. Mary Virginia Terhune [Marion Harland], *Marion Harland's Autobiography* (New York: Harper and Brothers, 1910), pp. 99–101.

11. Louisa Cocke Diary, January 27, 1825, UVA; Louis Gimelli, "Louisa Maxwell Holmes Cocke: An Evangelical Plantation Mistress in the Antebellum South," *Journal of the Early Republic* 9 (Spring 1989): 59–64; "Contributions," *African Repository* 3 (July 1827): 159; Bell I. Wiley, ed., *Slaves No More: Let-*

ters from Liberia, 1833–1869 (Lexington: University of Kentucky Press, 1980), p. 35. The Cocke/Skipwith correspondence is documented and analyzed in Randall M. Miller, ed., *"Dear Master": Letters of a Slave Family* (Ithaca, N.Y.: Cornell University Press, 1978).

12. Charles Andrews, *Memoir of Mrs. Ann R. Page* (New York: Protestant Episcopal Society for the Promotion of Evangelical Knowledge, 1856), pp. 24–27, 36, 45–46; Ann R. Page to Mary Lee (Fitzhugh) Custis, n.d., Mary Lee (Fitzhugh) Custis Papers, VHS; Wiley, *Slaves No More*, p. 100.

13. L. Minor Blackford, *Mine Eyes Have Seen the Glory: The Story of a Virginia Lady, Mary Berkeley Minor Blackford, 1802–1896, Who Taught Her Sons to Hate Slavery and to Love the Union* (Cambridge: Harvard University Press, 1954), p. 20; on Launcelot Blackford, see Mrs. E. F. Hening, *History of the African Mission of the Protestant Episcopal Church in the United States* (New York: Stanford and Swords, 1850), p. 123; William Blackford to Ralph Gurley, October 21, 1829, ACS Papers, LC; Wiley, *Slaves No More*, p. 15; Peter Kent Opper, "The Mind of the White Participant in the African Colonization Movement, 1816–1840" (Ph.D. diss., University of North Carolina, Chapel Hill, 1972), p. 269.

14. "Female Liberality," *African Repository* 6 (May 1830): 87–88; Mary Blackford to Ralph Gurley, May 12, 1829, ACS Papers, LC.

15. Alison Goodyear Freehling, *Drift Toward Dissolution*, pp. 119–21; P. J. Staudenraus, *The African Colonization Movement, 1816–1865* (New York: Columbia University Press, 1961), pp. 173–78.

16. Marie Tyler-McGraw, "Southern Benevolence: Woman, Piety and Anger in Virginia's Colonization Movement" (unpublished typescript lent to the author), p. 3; Ann R. Page to Ralph Gurley, April 30, 1831, ACS Papers, LC; Mary Blackford to Ralph Gurley, September 1, 1829, and April 12, 1830, ACS Papers, LC.

17. Carl Degler, *The Other South: Southern Dissenters in the Nineteenth Century* (Boston: Northeastern University Press, 1982), p. 13; William W. Freehling, *The Road to Disunion: Secessionists at Bay, 1776–1854* (New York: Oxford University Press, 1990), pp. 178–82; Ira Berlin, *Slaves Without Masters: The Free Negro in the Antebellum South* (New York: New Press, 1974), p. 188; Martha Jefferson Randolph to Joseph Coolidge Jr., October 27, 1831, Edgehill-Randolph Papers, UVA.

18. John Floyd as quoted in Alison Goodyear Freehling, *Drift Toward Dissolution*, p. 83.

19. Ibid., pp. 121–25.

20. "Intelligence," *African Repository* 7 (December 1831): 310–12.

21. Mary Blackford, "The Memorial of the Female Citizens of Fredericksburg," c. 1831–32, Blackford Family Papers, UNC.

22. Ibid.; Suzanne Lebsock, *"A Share of Honour": Virginia Women, 1600–1945* (Richmond: Virginia Women's Cultural History Project, 1984), p. 77.

23. Legislative Petitions, Augusta County, January 19, 1832, LV; Tom Blair, "The Southern Dilemma: The Augusta-Rockingham Area as a Mirror to Virginia's Struggle over Slavery in the 1830s," *Augusta Historical Bulletin* 21 (Fall 1985): 73–78. Female relatives of Conrad Speece, John McCue, Samuel Gilkeson,

and William Kinney, all Augusta auxiliary officers, were among the signatories of the petition. "Augusta Colonization Society," *African Repository* 7 (June 1831): 124; John Vogt and T. William Kethley Jr., *Augusta County Marriages, 1748–1850* (Athens, Ga.: Iberian Publishing Company, 1986).

24. Augusta Petition, January 19, 1832, LV.

25. Ibid.

26. Ibid.

27. Ibid.

28. *Richmond Enquirer* (semiweekly), January 26, 1832; Leigh claimed that 343 women signed the Augusta memorial. The original petition contains 215 names; perhaps additional copies of it were circulated and signed by women. Philip Slaughter, *A Virginian History of African Colonization* (Richmond: Macfarlane and Fergusson, 1855), p. 61.

29. Louisa Cocke Diary, January 18, 1832, UVA; Alison Goodyear Freehling, *Drift Toward Dissolution*, pp. 180–85.

30. Alison Goodyear Freehling, *Drift Toward Dissolution*, p. xiv; Mary Eliza Rives to Judith Rives, April 2, 1832, William Cabell Rives Papers, LC.

31. Susan Terrell to Ralph Gurley, July 24, 1832, ACS Papers, LC; "Extracts from Correspondence," *African Repository* 8 (July 1832): 150; "Contributions," ibid. 8 (January 1833): 350. Susan Terrell's husband, James Hunter Terrell, manumitted all of his slaves in his 1856 will. In 1857, 83 were sent to Liberia. Mary Rawlings, *The Albemarle of Other Days* (Charlotte: The Michie Co., 1925), p. 135.

32. "Report of the Board of Managers of the Fredericksburg and Falmouth Female Auxiliary Colonization Society" (broadside appended to letter), Mary Blackford to Ralph Gurley, May 1832, ACS Papers, LC; *Christian Sentinel* (Richmond), June 22, 1832; Patricia Hickin, "Antislavery in Virginia, 1832–1860" (Ph.D. diss., University of Virginia, 1968), pp. 268–70.

33. Blackford made sporadic entries in this journal from 1832 to 1866; my citations include dates, where possible, and page numbers of the typescript of the journal. Mary Blackford, preface to "Notes Illustrative of the Wrongs of Slavery" (unpublished typescript of journal), p. 1, and September 2, 1832, pp. 3–4, Blackford Family Papers, UVA.

34. Ibid., September 2, 1832, p. 3, 1833, p. 6, and February 20, 1836, p. 16.

35. Ibid., February 20, 1836, p. 15, and September 2, 1832, pp. 4–5.

36. Mary Blackford to Ralph Gurley, June 19, 1834, ACS Papers, LC; Mary Blackford, "Notes," 1833, pp. 6–8, February 20, 1836, p. 16, and 1856, pp. 17–20.

37. Mary Blackford, "Notes," February 29, 1833, p. 10; Bethany Veney, *The Narrative of Bethany Veney: A Slave Woman* (Worchester, Mass.: Press of Geo. H. Ellis, 1889), p. 19.

38. Mary Blackford, "Notes," 1866, p. 20; Mary Blackford to Ralph Gurley, October 12, 1832, ACS Papers, LC; Austin Steward as quoted in Maurice Duke, ed., *Don't Carry Me Back! Narratives by Former Virginia Slaves* (Richmond, Va.: Dietz Press, 1995), pp. 37–38; L. Minor Blackford, *Mine Eyes*, pp. 48, 73.

39. Mary Blackford, "Notes," February 22, 1833, p. 11; Marie Tyler-McGraw, "Richmond Free Blacks and African Colonization, 1816–1832," *Journal of Ameri-*

can Studies 21 (1987): 209; David M. Streifford, "The American Colonization Society: An Application of Republican Ideology to Early Antebellum Reform," *Journal of Southern History* 45 (February 1979): 213–14.

40. Tyler-McGraw, "Richmond Free Blacks," pp. 210, 221–22. See also Berlin, *Slaves Without Masters*, pp. 201–4, and Brenda E. Stevenson, *Life in Black and White: Family and Community in the Slave South* (New York: Oxford University Press, 1996), pp. 282–85.

41. Sara Evans, *Born For Liberty: A History of Women in America* (New York: Free Press, 1989), pp. 75–79. Angelina E. Grimké, *Appeal to the Christian Women of the South* (New York: American Anti-Slavery Society, 1836), pp. 16–26; *Appeal to the Women of the Nominally Free States* (New York: W. S. Dorr, 1837); and *Letters to Catharine E. Beecher in Reply to an Essay on Slavery and Abolitionism* (1838; reprint, New York: Arno Press, 1969), pp. 35–40. Catharine Beecher, who thought colonization a noble scheme, published a response to Grimké's appeal to Northern women in 1837. Beecher urged Northern women not to join abolition societies. Abolitionists, she argued, were intent on the coercion of the South. They stirred up "angry passions" that threatened the Union. Woman's role, by contrast, was "to assume the office of a mediator, and an advocate of peace," to promote "rational, Christian discussion" of slavery. Catharine E. Beecher, *An Essay on Slavery and Abolitionism, With Reference to the Duty of American Females* (Philadelphia: H. Perkins, 1837), pp. 6, 23–25, 101, 128.

42. Thomas Dew, *Review of the Debate in the Virginia Legislature of 1831 and 1832* (Richmond, Va.: T. W. White, 1832), pp. 35–37.

43. Staudenraus, *African Colonization Movement*, pp. 182–87; *Christian Sentinel* (Richmond), September 6 and November 15, 1833.

44. Staudenraus, *African Colonization Movement*, pp. 182–87; *Seventh Annual Report of the Board of Managers of the Colonization Society of Virginia* (Richmond, Va.: Office of the Southern Churchman, 1838), p. 24.

45. "Remarks of the Hon. James Garland, of Virginia," *African Repository* 14 (February 1838): 44; "Virginia Colonization Society," ibid. 14 (April 1838): 119.

46. Mary Blackford to Ralph Gurley, June 19, 1834, ACS Papers, LC; "Report of the Board of Managers," *African Repository* 10 (October 1834): 252–53; "Third Annual Report of the Ladies' Society of Fredericksburg and Falmouth, for the Promotion of Female Education in Africa," ibid. 13 (October 1837): 311–13; Opper, "Mind of the White Participant," pp. 276–77.

47. On the Richmond society, see "Intelligence," *African Repository* 10 (December 1834): 314–15; "School for Orphans in Liberia," ibid. 11 (August 1835): 247. On others, "Intelligence," ibid. 9 (July 1833): 149; "Intelligence," ibid. 10 (July 1834): 149; "Latest from Liberia," ibid. 11 (November 1835): 340.

48. *Watchman of the South* (Richmond), January 25, 1838; "Schools," *African Repository* 14 (September 1838): 272–73. On Liberian benevolence, "Ladies' Benevolent Society," *African Repository* 16 (May 1840): 140–41; "The Ladies' Benevolent Society of Monrovia," ibid. 17 (October 1841): 312; Tom W. Shick, *Behold the Promised Land: A History of Afro-American Settler Society in Nineteenth-Century Liberia* (Baltimore, Md.: Johns Hopkins University Press, 1980), pp.

53–56. For the quoted assessment of educational efforts, see "Education in Liberia," *African Repository* 26 (September 1850): 257–59.

49. "Intelligence," *African Repository* 9 (November 1833): 280–81; Susan Terrell to Joseph Gales, January 30, 1836, ACS Papers, LC; Blair, "The Southern Dilemma," pp. 73–78.

50. "Female Colonization Society of Virginia," *African Repository* 16 (August 1840): 248–49.

51. *Twenty-eighth Annual Report of the American Society for Colonizing the Free People of Colour of the United States* (Washington, D.C.: James C. Dunn, 1845), p. 9; Mitchell Snay, *Gospel of Disunion: Religion and Separatism in the Antebellum South* (New York: Cambridge University Press, 1993), p. 34. For coverage of colonization in religious papers, see, for example, the *Religious Herald* (Richmond), December 5, 1844, July 2, 1846.

52. See receipts in the *African Repository*, 1845–1850.

53. Legislative Petitions, Norfolk City, March 23, 1852, LV; Staudenraus, *The African Colonization Movement*, p. 237; Marie Tyler-McGraw, "The American Colonization Society in Virginia, 1816–1832" (Ph.D. diss., George Washington University, 1980), pp. 218–20; Hickin, "Antislavery in Virginia," pp. 322–25, 331, 339–40; Berlin, *Slaves Without Masters*, pp. 360–63.

54. Virginia Colonization Society Treasurer's Accounts, 1850–59, VHS; *Virginia Colonization Society, 1st Report Since Its Reorganization* (Richmond, Va.: Macfarlane and Fergusson, 1851). The notion that female colonizationists went "underground" was suggested to me by Marie Tyler-McGraw in a conversation during the summer of 1992. The available records do not suggest that women who participated in auxiliaries were absorbed into male-run societies, but neither do they rule out that possibility.

55. For the Burke-Lee correspondence, see "Letters of the Robert E. Lee Negroes," in Wiley, *Slaves No More*, pp. 189–214. On Van Lew, see David D. Ryan, ed., *A Yankee Spy in Richmond: The Civil War Diary of "Crazy Bet" Van Lew* (Mechanicsburg, Pa.: Stackpole Books, 1996), pp. 6–7; Elizabeth Van Lew to William McLain, April 24, 1857, and December 2, 1858, ACS Papers, LC; and Mary Brown to William McLain, October 28, 1858, ACS Papers, LC.

56. Mary Blackford to William McLain, June 27, 1845, ACS Papers, LC; "Correspondence," *African Repository* 22 (October 1846): 297–98; Helen Grinnan to Mary Blackford, March 12, 1849, Blackford Family Papers, UNC.

57. Caspar Morris, *Memoir of Miss Margaret Mercer* (Philadelphia: Lindsay and Blakiston, 1848), pp. 94–95, 122, 133; Tyler-McGraw, "Southern Benevolence," pp. 1–4, 11.

58. Terhune [Harland], *Marion Harland's Autobiography*, pp. 100–101; Hickin, "Antislavery in Virginia," pp. 333–38; Anne Rice to Ralph Gurley, July 7, 1856, Anne Rice to Ralph Gurley, April 19, 1857, Anne Rice to William McLain, May 2, 1857, and Anne Rice to Ralph Gurley, April 28, 1859, ACS Papers, LC.

59. L. Minor Blackford, *Mine Eyes*, p. 61; Mary Blackford to William McLain, May 17, 1844, ACS Papers, LC.

60. Abram Blackford to Mary B. Blackford, September 9, 1844, and Febru-

ary 14, 1846, and Abram Blackford to Susan Wheeler, September 10, 1844, in Wiley, *Slaves No More*, pp. 21–25. See also Wiley's introduction, pp. 8–9. Randall Miller, *"Dear Master,"* pp. 42–43.

61. Staudenraus, *The African Colonization Movement*, pp. 182–87; Mary Blackford to William McLain, June 27, 1845, ACS Papers, LC.

62. Mary Blackford to Lucy Minor, March 22 and June 19, 1853, Blackford Family Papers, UNC; L. Minor Blackford, *Mine Eyes*, pp. 98–104; Mary Blackford to Ralph Gurley, August 10, 1841, ACS Papers, LC.

63. Mary Blackford to William McLain, August 8, 1856, and Mary Blackford to Ralph Gurley, August 23, 1856, ACS Papers, LC. Blackford's analysis of the secession crisis is returned to in Chapter 5.

64. Andrews, *Memoir of Mrs. Ann R. Page*, pp. 38, 53.

65. Morris, *Memoir of Miss Margaret Mercer*, pp. 104, 110–13.

66. *The South* (Richmond), October 13 and 22, 1857; Betty L. Mitchell, *Edmund Ruffin: A Biography* (Bloomington: Indiana University Press, 1981), pp. 108–9.

67. Legislative Petitions, Spotsylvania County, December 9, 1850, LV.

68. Alexander H. Sands, "Intellectual Culture of Woman," *Southern Literary Messenger* 28 (May 1859): 330–31.

69. Fitzhugh, *Sociology for the South*, pp. 119, 239; Albert Taylor Bledsoe, *An Essay on Slavery and Liberty* (Philadelphia: J. B. Lippincott, 1856), p. 224. Thornton Stringfellow directed his influential defense of slavery not only to men but to women: "Every man and women in the United States should not only be willing, but desirous to know, what is the matter-of-fact evidence on this all-absorbing question." Thornton Stringfellow, *Scriptural and Statistical Views in Favor of Slavery* (Richmond, Va.: J. W. Randolph, 1856), p. 110.

CHAPTER THREE

1. Chapter title from *Richmond Whig*, May 2, 1844. Joel H. Silbey, *The American Political Nation, 1838–1893* (Stanford, Calif.: Stanford University Press, 1991), pp. 270, 308–9. See also Ronald P. Formisano, *The Transformation of Political Culture: Massachusetts Parties, 1790s–1840s* (New York: Oxford University Press, 1983), pp. 262–67; Harry L. Watson, *Liberty and Power: The Politics of Jacksonian America* (New York: Hill and Wang, 1990), pp. 221–22; and Lawrence Frederick Kohl, *The Politics of Individualism: Parties and the American Character in the Jacksonian Era* (New York: Oxford University Press, 1989), pp. 72–74.

2. Robert Gray Gunderson, *The Log-Cabin Campaign* (Lexington: University Press of Kentucky, 1957), pp. 4, 7–8, 135–39; Mary P. Ryan, *Women in Public: Between Banners and Ballots, 1825–1880* (Baltimore, Md.: Johns Hopkins University Press, 1990), pp. 135–38; Jayne Crumpler DeFiore, "COME, and Bring the Ladies: Tennessee Women and the Politics of Opportunity during the Presidential Campaigns of 1840 and 1844," *Tennessee Historical Quarterly* 51 (Winter 1992): 197–98; Robert J. Dinkin, *Before Equal Suffrage: Women in Partisan Politics from Colonial Times to 1920* (Westport, Conn.: Greenwood Press, 1995), pp. 30–39. See also Paula C. Baker, "The Domestication of Politics: Women and American Political Society, 1780–1920," *American Historical Review* 89 (June

1984): 627–32, and Michael E. McGerr, "Political Style and Women's Power, 1830–1930," *Journal of American History* 77 (December 1990): 866–67. The following studies of individual women offer evidence that female partisanship was intense and sustained: Janet L. Coryell, *Neither Heroine Nor Fool: Anna Ella Carroll of Maryland* (Kent, Ohio: Kent State University Press, 1990), and her "The Woman Politico: Women and Partisan Politics in Mid-Nineteenth-Century America" (paper presented at the Southern Historical Association Annual Meeting, November 1995); Kathleen C. Berkeley, "Partisan Politics Makes Strange Bedfellows: The Political Career of Anna Elizabeth Dickinson, 1842–1932" (paper presented at the Southern Historical Association Annual Meeting, November 1995); and Christopher J. Olsen, " 'Molly Pitcher' of the Mississippi Whigs: The Editorial Career of Mrs. Harriet J. Prewett," *Journal of Mississippi History* 58 (Fall 1996): 237–54.

3. Eugene Genovese, "Toward a Kinder and Gentler America: The Southern Lady in the Greening of the Politics of the Old South," in *In Joy and in Sorrow: Women, Family, and Marriage in the Victorian South, 1830–1900*, ed. Carol Bleser (New York: Oxford University Press, 1991), pp. 129–33; William Cabell Rives to Judith Rives, June 26, 1836, Judith Rives to William Cabell Rives, September 22 and 30, 1837, William Cabell Rives Papers, LC. For a general overview of women's partisanship in the 1820s and 1830s, see Dinkin, *Before Equal Suffrage*, pp. 19–27.

4. James McDowell to Susan McDowell, January 14, 1834; Susan McDowell to James McDowell, February 21, 1832; and February 25, 1834, James McDowell Papers, UNC.

5. Helen MacLeod to Martin Donald MacLeod, September 4, 1826, MacLeod Family Papers, VHS; Anne Royall, *Mrs. Royall's Southern Tour: Or Second Series of the Black Book* (Washington, D.C.: Published for the Author, 1830), pp. 34–39.

6. *Staunton Spectator*, October 20, 1836. In an article spanning the colonial, Revolutionary, and early Republican periods, Cynthia A. Kierner argues that, by and large, Southern women were relegated to the margins of public life. The presence of women in the audience at patriotic orations and other civic rituals was rarely acknowledged by male speakers; the predominant image of women was as passive and dependent. Cynthia A. Kierner, "Genteel Balls and Republican Parades: Gender and Early Southern Civic Rituals, 1677–1826," *Virginia Magazine of History and Biography* 104 (Spring 1996): 184–210.

7. *Staunton Spectator*, September 1, 1836.

8. Lucy Kenney, *Description of a Visit to Washington* (Washington, D.C.: n.p., 1835), pp. 3–12; Lucy Kenney, *A Pamphlet, Showing How Easily the Wand of a Magician May Be Broken, and That, if Amos Kendall Can Manage the United States Mail Well, a Female of the United States Can Manage Him Better* (Washington, D.C.: n.p., 1838), pp. 2–5, 15. On Southern opposition to Van Buren, see William J. Cooper Jr., *The South and the Politics of Slavery, 1828–1856* (Baton Rouge: Louisiana State University Press, 1978), pp. 74–75.

9. Lucy Kenney, *A Letter Addressed to Martin Van Buren, President of the United States, In Answer to the Late Attack upon the Navy, By the Official Organ of the Government* (Washington, D.C.: n.p., 1838); E. B. Runnells, *A Reply to a Letter Addressed to Mr. Van Buren, President of the United States; Purporting to*

Be Written by Miss Lucy Kenny, The Whig Missionary (Washington, D.C.: n.p., 1840), pp. 4–6.

10. William W. Freehling, *The Road to Disunion: Secessionists at Bay, 1776–1854* (New York: Oxford University Press, 1990), pp. 295–99, 345, 359–63; Richard Patrick McCormick, *The Second American Party System: Party Formation in the Jacksonian Era* (Chapel Hill: University of North Carolina Press, 1966), pp. 186–98.

11. *Staunton Spectator*, September 10, 1840; *Political Arena* (Fredericksburg), March 24 and September 22, 1840.

12. Silbey, *American Political Nation*, p. 54; *Staunton Spectator*, September 10, 1840; *Daily National Intelligencer* (Washington, D.C.), September 21, 1840.

13. *Yeoman* (Richmond), October 15, 1840; James McDowell to Susan McDowell, May 24, 1827, James McDowell Family Papers, UNC; William Cabell Rives to Judith Rives, September 7, 1834, William Cabell Rives Papers, LC.

14. *Yeoman* (Richmond), October 15, 1840; *Political Arena* (Fredericksburg), September 1, 1840.

15. Lucy Kenney, *The Strongest of All Government Is That Which Is Most Free: An Address to the People of the United States* (N.p.: n.p., 1840), pp. 1, 6, 11; Lucy Kenney, *A History of the Present Cabinet* (Washington, D.C.: n.p., 1840), p. 6. Anne Royall, whom we met in Chapter 1, is another literary woman who forsook Van Buren and the Democrats in favor of Harrison and the Whigs. Having settled in Washington, D.C., after years of itinerancy, Royall founded her own newspaper, *Paul Pry*, in 1831. Her mission as the newspaper's editor was to "expose all and every species of political evil." Though she claimed to back neither party, she generally supported the policies of President Jackson. Like Kenney, Royall thought Van Buren an unworthy successor to Jackson. In the wake of the election of 1836, she dissolved *Paul Pry* and established a new newspaper, the *Huntress*; as its editor, she endorsed Harrison in 1840, hoping he could battle the corruption that had crippled the Democratic administration. *Paul Pry* (Washington, D.C.), April 9, May 7, and November 5, 1836; *Huntress*, November 25, 1837, April 28, 1838, and October 17, 1840; Bessie Roland James, *Anne Royall's U.S.A.* (New Brunswick, N.J.: Rutgers University Press, 1972), pp. 206–7, 312–16, 345–53.

16. Judith Rives to Frank Rives, February 29, 1840, William Cabell Rives Papers, LC; Sarah (Pendleton) Dandridge to Martha Taliaferro Hunter, April 18, 1840, Hunter Family Papers, VHS; Jane Gay Roberts Diary, October 1840, Robb-Bernard Family Papers, WM.

17. Lucy Lee Pleasants, ed., *Old Virginia Days and Ways: Reminiscences of Mrs. Sally McCarty Pleasants* (Menasha, Wis.: George Banta Publishing Company, 1916), pp. 6–8; Sara Agnes (Rice) Pryor, *My Day: Reminiscences of a Long Life* (New York: Macmillan, 1904), p. 47; Frances Ann Bernard Capps Diary, September 10, 1840, VHS.

18. Edith P. Mayo, "Campaign Appeals to Women," in *American Material Culture: The Shape of Things around Us*, ed. Edith P. Mayo (Bowling Green, Ohio: Bowling Green State University Popular Press, 1984), pp. 128–32, 143;

Celestia Shakes, as quoted in T. Michael Miller, " 'If Elected . . .' — An Overview of How Alexandrians Voted in Presidential Elections from 1789–1984," *Fireside Sentinel* 10 (October 1988): 100.

19. Mary Pendleton (Cooke) Steger to Sarah Harriet Apphia Hunter, September 13, 1840, Hunter Family Papers, VHS.

20. Mary T. Tardy, ed., *The Living Female Writers of the South* (Philadelphia: Claxton, Remsen and Haffelfinger, 1872), pp. 409–10.

21. *Richmond Whig*, October 9, 1840.

22. Ibid.; *Daily National Intelligencer* (Washington, D.C.), October 9, 1840.

23. *Daily National Intelligencer* (Washington, D.C.), October 10, 1840; *Richmond Whig*, October 9, 1840. Anne Royall's newspaper, the *Huntress*, excerpted Webster's speech; Royall editorialized that the speech "accords fully with our ideas respecting female education." *Huntress*, December 12, 1840.

24. Linda K. Kerber, *Women of the Republic: Intellect and Ideology in Revolutionary America* (New York: W. W. Norton, 1980); Nancy F. Cott, *The Bonds of Womanhood: "Woman's Sphere" in New England, 1780–1835* (New Haven, Conn.: Yale University Press, 1977), pp. 66–70; Baker, "The Domestication of Politics," pp. 629–31.

25. Margaret Randolph to Caryanne Randolph, October 15, 1840, Edgehill-Randolph Papers, UVA; Margaret E. Loyall to Frances Lewis, October 30, 1840, Conway Whittle Family Papers, WM.

26. *Crisis* (Richmond), September 16, 1840; *Richmond Enquirer* (semi-weekly), October 15, 1840; *Warrenton Jeffersonian*, September 19, 1840.

27. Two recent studies suggest that Whig womanhood had its roots in Federalist and Adamsite gender ideologies. Rosemarie Zagarri has found that Federalists were more inclined than Democratic-Republicans to acknowledge publicly women's civic contributions as republican mothers. Supporters of John Quincy Adams, according to Norma Basch, espoused "proto-Whig" ideas about women and politics. They offered women a "few rays of autonomy" by arguing that household and polity were intimately linked, and that the moral standards that governed the former should govern the latter; Jacksonians, by contrast, upheld the notion of a sharp demarcation between the public and private spheres. Rosemarie Zagarri, "Gender and the First Party System," in *Federalists Reconsidered*, eds. Doron Ben-Atar and Barbara Oberg (Williamsburg, Va.: Institute of Early American History and Culture, forthcoming); Norma Basch, "Marriage, Morals, and Politics in the Election of 1828," *Journal of American History* 80 (December 1993): 890–918.

28. Mary P. Ryan, *Women in Public*, p. 136; William R. Taylor, *Cavalier and Yankee: The Old South and American National Character* (New York: G. Braziller, 1957), pp. 115–40; Watson, *Liberty and Power*, pp. 219–21; Kohl, *Politics of Individualism*, pp. 72–73, 108.

29. Joe L. Kincheloe Jr., "Transcending Role Restrictions: Women at Camp Meetings and Political Rallies," *Tennessee Historical Quarterly* 40 (Summer 1981): 159; Formisano, *Transformation of Political Culture*, pp. 262–64; Richard J. Carwadine, *Evangelicals and Politics in Antebellum America* (New Haven, Conn.:

Yale University Press, 1993), pp. 33–34, 53–55, 65. DeFiore's article on Tennessee women seconds Kincheloe's interpretation. DeFiore, "COME, and Bring the Ladies," pp. 198–200.

30. Daniel Walker Howe, *The Political Culture of the American Whigs* (Chicago: University of Chicago Press, 1979), pp. 36, 158; Kohl, *Politics of Individualism*, pp. 72–74; Robert V. Remini, *Henry Clay: Statesman for the Union* (New York: W. W. Norton, 1991), pp. 179, 664; Charles Lowery, *James Barbour: A Jeffersonian Republican* (University, Ala.: University of Alabama Press, 1984), p. 229.

31. Lori D. Ginzberg, *Women and the Work of Benevolence: Morality, Politics, and Class in the Nineteenth-Century United States* (New Haven, Conn.: Yale University Press, 1990); Suzanne Lebsock, *The Free Women of Petersburg: Status and Culture in a Southern Town, 1784–1860* (New York: W. W. Norton, 1984), pp. 195–236. Jean Gould Hales, in her pioneering article on women and the antebellum nativist movement, also posits a connection between women's benevolence and their partisanship: with the precedent of their involvement in reform societies, she argues, "women could respond to nativist appeals without fear of compromising their femininity or arousing public disapproval." Jean Gould Hales, "'CO-LABORERS IN THE CAUSE': Women in the Ante-bellum Nativist Movement," *Civil War History* 25 (June 1979): 127.

32. Kincheloe, "Transcending Role Restrictions," p. 165; Baker, "Domestication of Politics," pp. 630–31.

33. Silbey, *American Political Nation*, pp. 112–17; Kohl, *Politics of Individualism*, p. 89; Sydney Nathans, *Daniel Webster and Jacksonian Democracy* (Baltimore, Md.: Johns Hopkins University Press, 1973), pp. 127–31; William W. Freehling, *Road to Disunion*, p. 361.

34. Gunderson, *Log-Cabin Campaign*, pp. 125, 144, 183; Carwadine, *Evangelicals and Politics*, p. 61.

35. William W. Freehling, *Road to Disunion*, pp. 411–36.

36. For an example of a woman attending a political debate, see Frances Capps Diary, December 15, 1843, VHS.

37. *Richmond Whig*, August 16, April 26, May 2, and September 6, 1844; *Lynchburg Virginian*, August 5, 1844.

38. *Lynchburg Virginian*, November 25, 1844.

39. *Richmond Whig*, September 3, 1844.

40. Ibid.

41. Mary Virginia Terhune [Marion Harland], *Marion Harland's Autobiography: The Story of a Long Life* (New York: Harper and Brothers, 1910), pp. 121, 127–29; Missouri Riddick to Nathaniel Riddick, August 5, 1844, Riddick Family Papers, LV; Norfleet Fillmore, *Suffolk in Virginia, c. 1795–1840: A Record of Lots, Lives, and Likenesses* (Richmond, Va.: Whittet and Shepperson, 1974), pp. 97, 104.

42. *Daily Globe* (Washington, D.C.), September 26, 1844; *Daily Richmond Enquirer*, October 7, 1844.

43. *Richmond Whig*, September 6, 1844; *Daily Globe* (Washington, D.C.), November 1, 1844; Serena Catherine (Pendleton) Dandridge to Mary Evelina (Dandridge) Hunter, December 11, [1844], Hunter Family Papers, VHS.

44. Barbour's November 17 letter and other documents that describe the formation of the Clay Association were printed as part of the coverage of the Clay statue's inauguration in the *Richmond Daily Whig*, April 12, 1860.

45. See Lucy Barbour to James Barbour Jr., c. 1817 and January 3, 1827, and James Barbour to Lucy Barbour, November 3, 1827, Barbour Family Papers, UVA; Lucy Barbour's obituary, *Richmond Daily Whig*, December 3, 1860; Lowery, *James Barbour*, pp. 9–16, 39–40, 52–53, 178–79, 196.

46. *Richmond Daily Whig*, April 12, 1860; *Daily Richmond Enquirer*, November 29 and December 2, 1844.

47. *Richmond Whig*, December 13, 1844.

48. *Richmond Daily Whig*, April 12, 1860; Virginia Association of Ladies for Erecting a Statue to Henry Clay, Subscription List, c. 1845–46, VHS. Some subscribers can be identified as men; some signed only their initials. On out-of-state contributions, see *Daily National Intelligencer* (Washington, D.C.), November 18, 1845; *Staunton Spectator*, February 6, 1845; and *Richmond Daily Whig*, March 17 and 18, 1845.

49. I compared the subscription lists of the association to the names of benevolent women in the following sources: *Constitution and By-laws of the Female Humane Association of the City of Richmond* (Richmond, Va.: Shepherd and Colin, 1843), p. 1; Legislative Petitions, Lynchburg, January 2, 1846, LV; *Lynchburg Virginian*, December 22, 1844; *African Repository* 16 (August 1840): 248–49; Mount Vernon Association, broadside dated June 1855, APCL.

50. *Lynchburg Republican*, December 22, 1844; *Lynchburg Virginian*, December 26 and January 2, 1844.

51. *Lexington Gazette*, January 9, 1845.

52. *Staunton Spectator*, June 5, 1845.

53. *Richmond Whig*, December 13, 1844; Mrs. N. K. Trout to Eliza Riddle, December 12, 1845, and Mrs. King to Joshua Fry, June 9, 1845, Watson Family Papers, VHS.

54. *Richmond Daily Whig*, February 12, 1845; Sarah J. Wright, "The Doswells of Bullfield," *Hanover Historical Society Bulletin* 13 (November 1975): 2–4; Sarah S. B. French to Henry Clay, February 27, 1845, in *The Papers of Henry Clay*, vol. 10, ed. Melba Porter Hay (Lexington, Ky.: University Press of Kentucky, 1991), p. 203; Jane Baxley to Eliza Riddle, [n.d.], Watson Family Papers, VHS.

55. John Herbert Claiborne, *Seventy-Five Years in Old Virginia* (New York: Neale Publishing Company, 1904), p. 131; Wilfred Binkley, *American Political Parties: Their Natural History* (New York: Alfred A. Knopf, 1965), p. 152; Thomas Brown, *Politics and Statesmanship: Essays on the American Whig Party* (New York: Columbia University Press, 1985), pp. 154–69.

56. Autobiography of Judith Rives, VHS; Terhune [Harland], *Marion Harland's Autobiography*, p. 122.

57. Carwadine, *Evangelicals and Politics*, pp. 72–75; Remini, *Henry Clay*, pp. 539, 544, 578, 613, 633–43, 650–58; Howe, *Political Culture of the American Whigs*, p. 138; *Richmond Daily Whig*, March 15, 1845.

58. Ellen Mordecai to Peter Mordecai, March 3, 1845, Mordecai Family Papers, UNC.

59. *Richmond Daily Whig*, April 12, 1860; W. Harrison Daniel, "Richmond's Memorial to Henry Clay: The Whig Women of Virginia and the Clay Statue," *Richmond Quarterly* 8 (Spring 1986): 40; Elizabeth R. Varon, " 'The Ladies Are Whigs': Lucy Barbour, Henry Clay, and Nineteenth-Century Virginia Politics," *Virginia Cavalcade* 42 (Autumn 1992): 72–83. The city stretched the celebration out over the next few days, with a banquet honoring Clay at which ex-President John Tyler spoke. Newspaper reports featured reprints of the host of letters that famous Americans, such as President James Buchanan and General Winfield Scott, had sent to the directors of the Clay Association, praising its work. *Richmond Daily Whig*, April 12, 13, 16, 17, and 18, 1860.

60. Sarah Hale, Whiggish editor of *Godey's Lady's Book*, summed up the doctrine of indirect influence perfectly when she stated, "This is the way women should vote, namely, by influencing rightly the votes of men." Sarah Hale, "How American Women Should Vote," *Godey's Lady's Book* 44 (April 1852): 293.

61. On the "age of sectionalism," see, for example, Henry T. Shanks, *The Secession Movement in Virginia, 1847–1861* (Richmond, Va.: Garrett and Massie, 1934); William J. Cooper, Jr., *Liberty and Slavery: Southern Politics to 1860* (New York: Knopf, 1983); Avery Craven, *The Growth of Southern Nationalism, 1848–1861* (Baton Rouge: Louisiana State University Press, 1953); and David Potter, *The Impending Crisis, 1848–1861* (New York: Harper and Row, 1976). The following analysis employs John McCardell's distinction between Southern sectionalists and Southern nationalists. Sectionalists sought to preserve Southern rights within the Union; nationalists believed that the South had to achieve independence from the North to preserve its rights. John McCardell, *The Idea of a Southern Nation: Southern Nationalists and Southern Nationalism, 1830–1860* (New York: W. W. Norton, 1979).

62. William W. Freehling, *Road to Disunion*, pp. 436–37; *Alexandria Gazette*, September 16, 1848; *Richmond Whig*, September 12, 1848.

63. *Alexandria Gazette*, July 31, 1848; *Daily Richmond Enquirer*, August 23 and October 26 and 31, 1848.

64. *Daily Richmond Enquirer*, October 2, 1848; *Richmond Whig*, October 13, 1848.

65. Cooper, *Liberty and Slavery*, pp. 215–22; Shanks, *Secession Movement*, pp. 21–23; David Goldfield, "The Triumph of Politics over Society: Virginia, 1851–1861" (Ph.D. diss., University of Maryland, College Park, 1970), pp. 120–21; *Richmond Whig*, September 17 and 27, 1852.

66. *Richmond Whig*, October 5, 1852; *Washingtonian* (Leesburg), October 1, 1852.

67. *American Beacon* (Norfolk), September 25 and October 25, 1852; *Daily Wheeling Intelligencer*, September 21, 1852.

68. *Daily Richmond Enquirer*, October 23, 1852.

69. *Daily Southern Argus* (Norfolk), September 23, 1852.

70. Pryor, *My Day*, p. 101.

71. Philip Morrison Rice, "The Know-Nothing Party in Virginia, 1854–1856," *Virginia Magazine of History and Biography* 55 (January 1947): 61–75; Goldfield, "The Triumph of Politics Over Society," p. 110.

72. Hales, "'CO-LABORERS IN THE CAUSE,'" pp. 132–35; *Richmond Daily Whig*, September 2 and 30, 1856. See also Coryell, *Neither Heroine Nor Fool*.

73. *Richmond Enquirer* (semiweekly), September 9, 1856; *Richmond Examiner*, October 24, 1856.

74. Peggie Nottingham Diary, October 6, 1856, VHS; *Richmond Enquirer* (semiweekly), October 21, 1856.

75. Martha Buxton Porter Brent, "Reminiscences," LV; Sarah Virginia Weight Hinton Diary, November 4, 1856, WM.

76. A Virginian, *The Life and Death of Sam, In Virginia* (Richmond, Va.: A. Morris, 1856).

77. Ibid., pp. 211–14.

78. Ibid., pp. 254–60, 307.

79. Richard G. Lowe, "The Republican Party in Antebellum Virginia, 1856–1860," *Virginia Magazine of History and Biography* 81 (July 1973): 259–72.

80. Patricia Hickin, "Antislavery in Virginia, 1832–1860" (Ph.D. diss., University of Virginia, 1968), pp. 711–12; Pamela Herr and Mary Lee Spence, eds., *The Letters of Jessie Benton Frémont* (Urbana: University of Illinois Press, 1993), p. xxiii; *Daily Dispatch* (Richmond), September 23, 1856. The Republican practice of according candidates' wives prominence in campaigns carried over into the postbellum period; Democrats generally did not favor such an approach. Rebecca Edwards, "Gender and American Political Parties, 1880–1900" (Ph.D. diss., University of Virginia, 1995), pp. 18–71.

81. Suzanne Lebsock, *Free Women of Petersburg*, pp. 231–32, 243.

82. *Daily Dispatch* (Richmond), September 16, 1852; *Daily Southern Argus* (Norfolk), September 20, 1852; *Alexandria Gazette*, October 20, 1852.

83. Southern nationalism and proslavery ideology have been the subjects of countless scholarly studies. See especially Shanks, *Secession Movement*, pp. 64–77; McCardell, *Idea of a Southern Nation*, pp. 69–91; Craven, *Growth of Southern Nationalism*, pp. 264–70, 290–91; and Drew Gilpin Faust, *The Ideology of Slavery: Proslavery Thought in the Antebellum South* (Baton Rouge: Louisiana State University Press, 1981).

CHAPTER FOUR

1. Chapter title from Beverly R. Wellford Jr., "Address Delivered before the Ladies' Mount Vernon Association, July 4, 1855," *Southern Literary Messenger* 21 (September 1855): 563–66.

2. Lucy Kenney, *A Refutation of the Principles of Abolition: By a Lady of Fredericksburg* (Washington, D.C.: n.p., 1830), pp. 2, 4, 7. Virginia women's literary output was meager in the 1820s and 1830s. A dozen or so women contributed poems and stories to the *Southern Literary Messenger*, and a few published full-length works of prose. Most of these fell into the category of stock Victorian romances or morality plays, oftentimes written under pseudonyms. See, for example, A. M. Lorraine, *Donald Adair* (Richmond, Va.: Peter Cottom, 1828), and Mary Mosby, *Pocahontas* (Philadelphia: H. Hooker, 1840). On the whole, until the late 1840s, Virginia's female writers eschewed the theme of regional distinctiveness and the subject of slavery.

3. John McCardell, *The Idea of a Southern Nation: Southern Nationalists and Southern Nationalism, 1830–1860* (New York: W. W. Norton, 1979), pp. 144–47, 152–54, 166–74; Henry T. Shanks, *The Secession Movement in Virginia, 1847–1861* (Richmond, Va.: Garnett and Massie, 1934), pp. 78–79.

4. Francis Pendleton Gaines, *The Southern Plantation: A Study in the Development and Accuracy of a Tradition* (New York: Columbia University Press, 1924), pp. 19–21; Ritchie Devon Watson Jr., *The Cavalier in Virginia Fiction* (Baton Rouge: Louisiana State University Press, 1985), pp. 76–77, 111; Elizabeth Moss, *Domestic Novelists in the Old South: Defenders of Southern Culture* (Baton Rouge: Louisiana State University Press, 1992), pp. 33–35; William R. Taylor, *Cavalier and Yankee: The Old South and American National Character* (New York: G. Braziller, 1957), pp. 167–68.

5. Nathaniel Beverley Tucker, *The Partisan Leader* (1836; reprint, New York: Alfred Knopf, 1933), pp. 50–51.

6. Moss's study focuses on the five most popular and influential Southern domestic novelists (Caroline Gilman, Caroline Lee Hentz, Maria McIntosh, Mary Virginia Terhune, and Augusta Evans). Only the Virginian among them — Terhune — will receive extended treatment in this chapter. Moss, *Domestic Novelists*, pp. 20, 35.

7. Nina Baym, *Woman's Fiction: A Guide to Literature by and about Women in America, 1820–1870* (Urbana: University of Illinois Press, 1993), pp. xxviii–xxxi. On sectional biases in *Northwood*, see Taylor, *Cavalier and Yankee*, pp. 132–35; on *Lovell's Folly*, see Moss, *Domestic Novelists*, pp. 78–82.

8. F***** [Martha Hunter], "Sketches of Southern Life," *Southern Literary Messenger* 14 (August 1848): 470–75; ibid. (October 1848): 630–35; ibid. (December 1848): 744–50; E. Lee Shepard, "The Hunter Family of Fonthill," *An Occasional Bulletin: The Virginia Historical Society* 59 (December 1987): 5–6; unsigned review of *The Clifford Family*, by Martha Hunter, *Southern Literary Messenger* 18 (September 1852): 576.

9. Hunter, "Sketches," pp. 470–73.

10. Ibid., pp. 473–75.

11. Ibid., pp. 633–35, 744–50.

12. Ann Douglas, "The Art of Controversy," introduction to Harriet Beecher Stowe, *Uncle Tom's Cabin: Or Life among the Lowly* (New York: Penguin, 1986), pp. 7–34.

13. See, for example, Thomas F. Gossett, *Uncle Tom's Cabin and American Culture* (Dallas: Southern Methodist University Press, 1985), and Stephen Alexander Hirsch, *Uncle Tom's Companions: The Literary and Popular Reaction to Uncle Tom's Cabin* (Ann Arbor, Mich.: University Microfilms Intl., 1982); [John R. Thompson], review of *Uncle Tom's Cabin*, by Harriet Beecher Stowe, *Southern Literary Messenger* 18 (October 1852): 630–31.

14. McCardell, *Idea of a Southern Nation*, pp. 144–47, 152–54, 166–74; Shanks, *Secession Movement*, pp. 78–79; W. R. A., "The Duty of Southern Authors," *Southern Literary Messenger* 23 (October 1856): 246–47.

15. Those five works were Mary Henderson Eastman, *Aunt Phillis's Cabin: Or, Southern Life as It Is* (Philadelphia: Lippincott, Grambo and Company, 1852);

Martha Haines Butt, *Antifanaticism: A Tale of the South* (Philadelphia: Lippincott, Grambo and Company, 1853); Mary E. Herndon, *Louise Elton: Or, Things Seen and Heard* (Philadelphia: Lippincott, Grambo and Company, 1853); Maria McIntosh, *The Lofty and the Lowly: Or, Good in All and None All-Good* (New York: D. Appleton, 1853); Caroline Lee Hentz, *The Planter's Northern Bride* (Philadelphia: A. Hart, 1854). For background, see McCardell, *Idea of a Southern Nation*, p. 166; Minrose C. Gwin, *Black and White Women of the Old South: The Peculiar Sisterhood in American Literature* (Knoxville: University of Tennessee Press, 1985), pp. 36–39; Rena Neumann Coen, "Mary Henderson Eastman: A Biographical Essay," preface to *Dahcotah: Or, Life and Legends of the Sioux around Fort Snelling* (1849; reprint, Afton, Minn.: Afton Historical Society Press, 1995), pp. ix–xxix.

16. Eastman, *Aunt Phillis's Cabin*, pp. 107–8, 112, 137.

17. Ibid., pp. 16–22. Moss argues that such ideological flexibility on the issue of slavery characterized the works of Hentz, Gilman, and McIntosh, as well — they, too, were willing to consider both positive good and necessary evil justifications for slavery. Moss, *Domestic Novelists*, p. 116.

18. Eastman, *Aunt Phillis's Cabin*, pp. 50–51.

19. Stowe, *Uncle Tom's Cabin*, p. 626; L. Minor Blackford, *Mine Eyes Have Seen the Glory: The Story of a Virginia Lady, Mary Berkeley Minor Blackford, 1802–1896, Who Taught Her Sons to Hate Slavery and to Love the Union* (Cambridge: Harvard University Press, 1954), p. 97. A number of other anti-Tom novels endorsed colonization, such as Sarah Hale's *Liberia; or Mr. Peyton's Experiments* (New York: Harper and Brothers, 1853) and John W. Page's *Uncle Robin in His Cabin in Virginia* (Richmond: J. W. Randolph, 1853). These works present slaveholders and slavery in a much more favorable light than Stowe's. Significantly, *The Southern Quarterly Review*, in its review of *Aunt Phillis's Cabin*, did not criticize Eastman for advocating colonization, while it did criticize Sarah Hale — a Northerner — for supporting colonization in *Liberia*. Both colonization and abolition, the review of *Liberia* asserted, go "upon the erroneous assumption that slavery, in the Southern States, is wrong and evil to the African." Unsigned review of *Aunt Phillis's Cabin*, by Mary Henderson Eastman, *Southern Quarterly Review* 7 (April 1853): 523; unsigned review of *Liberia*, by Sarah Hale, *Southern Quarterly Review* 9 (April 1854): 542.

20. Eastman, *Aunt Phillis's Cabin*, pp. 44, 64–68.

21. Ibid., pp. 207, 237, 279.

22. Gwin, *Black and White Women of the Old South*, p. 36. The publisher's description is on the back jacket of Martha Haines Butt's *Antifanaticism*.

23. *Daily National Intelligencer* (Washington, D.C.), October 6, 1856; unsigned review of *Aunt Phillis's Cabin*, by Eastman, *De Bow's Review* 14 (January 1853): 87; unsigned review of *Aunt Phillis's Cabin*, by Eastman, *Southern Quarterly Review* 7 (April 1853): 523. Hentz's *The Planter's Northern Bride* and McIntosh's *The Lofty and the Lowly*, two of the most conciliatory and most popular anti-Tom novels, nonetheless contain more criticism of the North than *Aunt Phillis's Cabin*. Moss, *Domestic Novelists*, pp. 94–95, 112–20; Hirsch, *Uncle Tom's Companions*, pp. 77–86.

24. Butt, *Antifanaticism*, pp. vi, 266.

25. Ibid., pp. 16–23, 26–35, 55–56, 100, 110–14.

26. Butt, *Antifanaticism*, pp. 17, 27, 38–39, 116, 152–56, 260–65.

27. Butt, *Antifanaticism*, pp. 89–94, 266–68; unsigned review of *Antifanaticism*, *Southern Quarterly Review* 8 (October 1853): 543.

28. Julia Gardiner Tyler, "To the Duchess of Sutherland and Ladies of England," *Southern Literary Messenger* 19 (February 1853): 120–26; Robert Seager II, *And Tyler Too: A Biography of John & Julia Gardiner Tyler* (New York: McGraw-Hill, 1963), pp. 402–5.

29. Julia Tyler, "To the Duchess," pp. 120–21.

30. Ibid., pp. 122–26.

31. Seager, *And Tyler Too*, p. 405; Evelyn L. Pugh, "Women and Slavery: Julia Gardiner Tyler and the Duchess of Sutherland," *Virginia Magazine of History and Biography* 88 (April 1980): 194.

32. Coen, "Mary Henderson Eastman"; Mary Tardy, *The Living Female Writers of the South* (Philadelphia: Claxton, Remsen and Haffelfinger, 1872), p. 10; Pugh, "Women and Slavery," p. 202.

33. Moss argues that the first generation of Southern domestic novelists (Hentz, Gilman, and McIntosh), who were born at the turn of the nineteenth century, were initially optimistic about sectional reconciliation but grew more pessimistic in the 1850s. She further asserts that the second generation of novelists (Terhune and Augusta Evans), born in the 1830s and raised in an era of ever increasing sectional tension, were pessimistic from the start—they "found it difficult if not impossible to envision the sort of national unity their literary forebears so fondly recalled." Moss, *Domestic Novelists*, pp. 137–67.

34. Mary Kelley, *Private Woman, Public Stage: Literary Domesticity in Nineteenth-Century America* (New York: Oxford University Press, 1984), pp. 130–32; Mary Virginia Terhune [Marion Harland], *Marion Harland's Autobiography: The Story of a Long Life* (New York: Harper and Brothers, 1910), p. 98; Mary Jo Jackson Bratton, " 'Marion Harland': A Literary Woman of the Old Dominion," *Virginia Cavalcade* 35 (Winter 1986): 136–38.

35. Kelley, *Private Woman, Public Stage*, p. 17; Moss, *Domestic Novelists*, pp. 49–51; unsigned reviews of *Alone*, by Mary Virginia Terhune, *Southern Literary Messenger* 20 (June 1854): 381; ibid. (December 1854): 726–32; unsigned review of *Moss-side*, by Marion Harland, ibid. 25 (October 1857): 319–20; unsigned review of *The Hidden Path*, by Marion Harland, ibid. 21 (October 1855): 637; unsigned review of *Nemesis*, by Marion Harland, ibid. 31 (November 1860): 398.

36. Terhune [Harland], *The Hidden Path* (New York: J. C. Derby, 1855). For a detailed analysis of Terhune's other three novels, see Moss, *Domestic Novelists*, pp. 39–51, 145–52, 203–6.

37. Terhune [Harland], *Hidden Path*, pp. 315–18. For an insightful analysis of the character of Isabel, see Kelley, *Private Woman, Public Stage*, pp. 328–30.

38. Terhune [Harland], *Hidden Path*, 247–49.

39. Ibid., pp. 13, 331–33; Terhune [Harland], *Marion Harland's Autobiography*, pp. 191–95, 325.

40. While I agree with Moss that Terhune was pessimistic about the pros-

pects for sectional reconciliation, I disagree with her notion that Terhune was less firmly committed to the Union than Hentz, Gilman, and McIntosh, the first generation of domestic novelists, had been. To make her interpretation stick, Moss discounts Terhune's many protestations of love for the Union and argues that Terhune's Unionism during the secession crisis and Civil War represents a capitulation to her Northern husband. Moss, *Domestic Novelists*, pp. 196, 215. Terhune's Unionism is discussed in the next chapter.

41. Anna Cora Ritchie as quoted in Julia Deane Freeman, *Women of the South Distinguished in Literature* (New York: Derby and Jackson, 1861), p. 197; Willie Willson to Eliza A. Willson, January 16, 1858, and Eliza A. Willson to Willie Willson, January 27, 1858, Willson Family Papers, YU.

42. L. Moody Simms Jr., "Margaret Junkin Preston: Southern Poet," *Southern Studies* 19 (Summer 1980): 94–95; Mary Price Coulling, *Margaret Junkin Preston: A Biography* (Winston-Salem, N.C.: John F. Blair, 1993).

43. [Margaret Junkin], *Silverwood: A Book of Memories* (New York: Derby and Jackson, 1856), pp. 174–78.

44. Junkin, *Silverwood*, pp. 45, 52–56, 302–4, 319; Baym, *Woman's Fiction*, p. 241; unsigned review of *Silverwood*, by [Margaret Junkin], *Southern Literary Messenger* 24 (January 1857): 76.

45. John H. Moore, "Judith Rives of Castle Hill," *Virginia Cavalcade* 13 (Spring 1964): 30–35; Judith Page Walker Rives, *Home and the World* (New York: D. Appleton, 1857), pp. 13, 26–27, 36, 84.

46. Lizzie Petit, *Light and Darkness, or the Shadow of Fate: A Story of Fashionable Life* (New York: D. Appleton, 1855), and her *Household Mysteries; A Romance of Southern Life* (New York: D. Appleton, 1856), p. 14; unsigned review of *Light and Darkness*, by Lizzie Petit, *Southern Literary Messenger* 21 (October 1855): 639; unsigned review of *Household Mysteries*, by Lizzie Petit, *Southern Literary Messenger* 23 (September 1856): 239–40.

47. Barbara H. Browder, "Our Remarkable Kinswoman" (unpublished typescript, 1988), LV, pp. 3–4, 6–7, 10–16, 17–20.

48. *Kaleidoscope* (Petersburg), January 24, 1855, April 4, 1855, and April 11, 1855 (*American Beacon* quote).

49. *Kaleidoscope*, February 14, 1855.

50. Ibid., February 7, 1855.

51. Ibid., August 22, 1855, and December 5, 1855.

52. Ibid., March 14, 1855; Browder, "Our Remarkable Kinswoman," pp. 25–26, 28.

53. Elizabeth Fox-Genovese, *Within the Plantation Household: Black and White Women of the Old South* (Chapel Hill: University of North Carolina Press, 1988), pp. 244–47, 281–88.

54. *Kaleidoscope*, March 14, 1855; September 5, 1855; February 14, 1855.

55. Ibid., March 28, 1855.

56. *Kaleidoscope*, November 7, 1855; Browder, "Our Remarkable Kinswoman," pp. 26–28, 35–41.

57. The impact of literary women is testified to by an 1856 story in the *Southern Literary Messenger* in which Frank, the husband of a literary woman, defends

his wife by arguing that only a well-educated woman can raise her children with "a noble structure of wisdom and virtue, that shall defy all the after attacks of fanaticism, infidelity, and ultraism." F.G.R.D., "The Literary Wife," *Southern Literary Messenger* 23 (December 1856): 401–8.

58. Prior to 1858, the Mount Vernon Association was also sometimes called the Ladies' Mount Vernon Association and the Mount Vernon Ladies' Association; in 1858, the organization officially changed its name to the Mount Vernon Ladies' Association of the Union, in order, according to Johnson, "to eliminate any possibility of the taint of sectionalism." The abbreviation MVA is used below to refer to all of the various incarnations of the association. Gerald W. Johnson, *Mount Vernon: The Story of a Shrine* (Mount Vernon, Va.: Mount Vernon Ladies' Association, 1991), pp. 6, 14–15, 24. The dilapidated state of Mount Vernon had drawn the notice of Virginia women before Cunningham's appeal. In September 1852, the *Southern Literary Messenger* printed a poem, "An Appeal for Mount Vernon," by Margaret Junkin. The poem bade Americans to rescue Mount Vernon "from the rust of slow decay," but did not propose any concrete plan for doing so. *Southern Literary Messenger* 18 (September 1852): 574.

59. Susan Pellet, "Reports of the Earliest Meetings of the Mount Vernon Association from the Journal of Mrs. Susan Pellet, the First Secretary," in *Charters, Constitutions and By-Laws of the Mount Vernon Ladies' Association of the Union* (Washington, D.C.: Gibson Brothers, 1890), pp. 3–5.

60. Pellet, "Reports," pp. 3–5; *Virginia Gazette* (Williamsburg), August 3, 1854.

61. John Augustine Washington to John H. Gilmer, July 26, 1854, APCL. George Washington was John Augustine Washington's father's great-uncle. Johnson, *Mount Vernon*, p. 19.

62. [Ann Pamela Cunningham], "The Southern Matron's Letter to Virginia, Addressed to Mr. Gilmer, Corresponding Secretary of the Mt. Vernon Association," *Southern Literary Messenger* 21 (May 1855): 322–25.

63. Ibid.

64. John Gilmer to Ann Pamela Cunningham, June 21, 1854, APCL; Pellet, "Reports," pp. 8–13.

65. *Richmond Enquirer* (semiweekly), October 29, 1855.

66. Beverly R. Wellford Jr., "Address Delivered before the Ladies' Mount Vernon Association, July 4, 1855," *Southern Literary Messenger* 21 (September 1855): 563–66.

67. McCardell, *Idea of a Southern Nation*, pp. 91–92, 103, 126–33; Shanks, *Secession Movement*, pp. 82–84; Charles W. Turner, *Virginia's Green Revolution (Essays on the Nineteenth Century Virginia Agricultural Reform and Fairs)* (Waynesboro, Va.: The Humphries Press, 1986), pp. 12–16, 28–35, 68–73; *Daily Dispatch* (Richmond), November 2, 1854; *Daily Richmond Enquirer*, November 9, 1858.

68. *Daily Richmond Enquirer*, November 7, 1853; *Virginia Gazette* (Williamsburg), December 1, 1853.

69. *Richmond Whig*, November 7, 1855.

70. Anna Cora Mowatt Ritchie to Ann Pamela Cunningham, June 18, 1855; Anna Cora Mowatt Ritchie to Ann Pamela Cunningham, February 29, 1856; Anna Cora Mowatt Ritchie to Ann Pamela Cunningham, March 17, 1856, APCL.

71. Anna Cora Mowatt Ritchie to Ann Pamela Cunningham, March 17, 1856; Julia Mayo Cabell to Ann Pamela Cunningham, April 18, 1856, APCL.

72. John R. Thompson, "Patriotism. A Poem," *Southern Literary Messenger* 22 (May 1856): 343; *Daily Richmond Enquirer*, May 22, 1856; Johnson, *Mount Vernon*, pp. 17, 21–22; Paul Revere Frothingham, *Edward Everett: Orator and Statesman* (Boston: Houghton Mifflin, 1925), pp. 378–87; Sherbrooke Rogers, *Sarah Josepha Hale: A New England Pioneer, 1788–1879* (Grantham, N.H.: Tompson and Rutter, 1985), pp. 88–95. Everett's aid was not without controversy. Cunningham thought that Everett's advocacy was taking the Mount Vernon cause "out of woman's hands," while Ritchie argued that male support made the project more practical, and gave to women "a far higher position than they could otherwise hold." Anna Cora Mowatt Ritchie to Ann Pamela Cunningham, May 28, 1856, APCL.

73. John Augustine Washington to William Foushee Ritchie, January 2, 1857; Julia Mayo Cabell to Ann Pamela Cunningham, April 18, 1856, APCL; *Richmond Whig*, July 13, 1857; Susan Pellet, "Report of the Mount Vernon Association," *Southern Literary Messenger* 25 (August 1857): 147–49.

74. Susan Pellet to Ann Pamela Cunningham, December 8, 1857, APCL.

75. Craig Simpson, *A Good Southerner: The Life of Henry A. Wise of Virginia* (Chapel Hill: University of North Carolina Press, 1985), pp. 118, 138, 158–60; James LaVerne Anderson, "Robert Mercer Taliaferro Hunter," *Virginia Cavalcade* 2 (Autumn 1968): 9–13.

76. Susan Pellet to Ann Pamela Cunningham, December 18, 1857, APCL; *The South* (Richmond), January 26, February 1 and 11, 1858.

77. *The South* (Richmond), February 12, 1858; Edmund Ruffin, *The Diary of Edmund Ruffin* (Baton Rouge: Louisiana State University Press, 1972), pp. 159–60.

78. Susan Pellet to John Augustine Washington, February 9, 1858, APCL; Andrew H. H. Dawson, *An Oration on the Origin, Purposes and Claims of the Ladies' Mt. Vernon Association* (Savannah, Ga.: E. J. Purse, 1858), pp. 44–45; *Daily Richmond Enquirer*, February 25, 1858.

79. Ann Pamela Cunningham to John Augustine Washington, February 14 and 18, 1858, APCL; *Daily Richmond Enquirer*, March 23, 1858.

80. Ann Pamela Cunningham to Samuel Ruggles, April 1, 1858, APCL.

81. Eliza Semmes to Ann Pamela Cunningham, May 15, 1858; C. A. Hopkinson to Ann Pamela Cunningham, December 19, 1858; Ann Pamela Cunningham to Edward Everett, c. 1859, APCL.

82. Rev. C. W. Howard as quoted in "Editor's Table," *Southern Literary Messenger* 27 (September 1858): 231–32.

83. Susan Pellet to Abba Little, November 3, 1858; Edward Everett to Ann Pamela Cunningham, December 29, 1859, APCL; Johnson, *Mount Vernon*, p. 31.

84. Johnson, *Mount Vernon*, pp. 37–42, 48–52.

85. Terhune [Harland], *Marion Harland's Autobiography*, p. 290; "Chronicles of the Life of Lucy Parke Chamberlayne" (unpublished typescript), Bagby Family Papers, VHS, p. 80.

CHAPTER FIVE

1. Chapter title from *Daily Dispatch* (Richmond), April 19, 1861; John Goode, *Recollections of a Lifetime* (New York: Neale Publishing Company, 1906), p. 67.

2. According to Drew Faust's definition, Confederate womanhood was a prescriptive ideal, which emerged, as soon as the war began, in Confederate newspapers, sermons, magazines, poems, speeches, fiction, and legislative resolutions honoring women. It sought to outline appropriate behavior for women: they were to be exemplars of passive patriotism, of sacrifice. Southern propaganda defined as purposeful and important a range of women's activities: exhorting men to enlist, cheering them at the front with letters, providing them with supplies such as socks and shirts, waiting for word from the scenes of battle, and giving up conveniences and luxuries such as fine clothing. See Drew Gilpin Faust, *Mothers of Invention: Women of the Slaveholding South in the American Civil War* (Chapel Hill: University of North Carolina Press, 1996), pp. 16–29, and her earlier article, "Altars of Sacrifice: Confederate Women and the Narratives of War," *Journal of American History* 76 (March 1990): 1200–228; see also George C. Rable, *Civil Wars: Women and the Crisis of Southern Nationalism* (Urbana: University of Illinois Press, 1989), pp. 31–49, and Catherine Clinton, *Tara Revisited: Women, War, and the Plantation Legend* (New York: Abbeville Press, 1995), pp. 57–66.

3. Faust, *Mothers of Invention*, pp. 134–37, 231–47.

4. Henry T. Shanks, *The Secession Movement in Virginia, 1847–1861* (Richmond, Va.: Garrett and Massie, 1934), pp. 86–87.

5. John S. Wise, *The End of an Era* (New York: Houghton, Mifflin, 1900), pp. 118, 135; Craig Simpson, *A Good Southerner: The Life of Henry A. Wise of Virginia* (Chapel Hill: University of North Carolina Press, 1985), p. 205; Shanks, *Secession Movement*, pp. 86–87, 101.

6. Rable, *Civil Wars*, p. 42.

7. Willie Willson to Eliza A. Willson, November 2, 1859, William F. Willson to Eliza A. Willson, December 2, 1859, and January 17, 1860, Eliza A. Willson to Willie Willson, October 29, 1860, Willson Family Papers, Ulrich Bonnell Phillips Papers, YU.

8. Amanda Virginia Edmonds, *Journal of Amanda Virginia Edmonds: Lass of the Mosby Confederacy, 1859–1867*, ed. Nancy Chappelear Baird (Stephens City, Va.: Commercial Press, 1984), pp. 31–35; Julia Gardiner Tyler to Juliana McLachlan Gardiner, November 28, 1859, and December 8, 1859, Tyler Family Papers, WM.

9. David Ryan, ed., *A Yankee Spy in Richmond: The Civil War Diary of "Crazy Bet" Van Lew* (Mechanicsburg, Pa.: Stackpole Books, 1996), pp. 4–5, 27–28.

10. *Correspondence between Lydia Maria Child, and Gov. Wise and Mrs. Mason, of Virginia* (New York: American Anti-Slavery Society, 1860), pp. 5–13.

11. *Correspondence*, p. 13; *New York Tribune*, November 12, 1859; *Richmond*

Daily Enquirer, November 5, 1859; *Alexandria Gazette*, November 17, 1859.

12. *Correspondence*, pp. 15–28.

13. Wendy Hammond Venet, " 'Cry Aloud and Spare Not': Northern Anti-slavery Women and John Brown's Raid," in *His Soul Goes Marching On: Responses to John Brown and the Harpers Ferry Raid*, ed. Paul Finkelman (Charlottesville: University Press of Virginia, 1995), pp. 107–9.

14. *Daily Dispatch* (Richmond), November 26, 1859.

15. *Richmond Whig*, December 16, 1859.

16. *Alexandria Gazette*, December 5, 1859; *Richmond Whig*, December 16, 1859; *Daily Dispatch* (Richmond), December 23, 1859.

17. *Richmond Whig*, December 16 and January 3, 1859; *Daily Dispatch* (Richmond), November 30, 1859.

18. *Daily Dispatch* (Richmond), December 16, 1859; *Alexandria Gazette*, December 20, 1859; William Asbury Christian, *Lynchburg and Its People* (Lynchburg, Va.: J. P. Bell, 1900), p. 182.

19. *Daily Dispatch* (Richmond), December 23, 1859.

20. Shanks, *Secession Movement*, pp. 104–12.

21. *Richmond Daily Whig*, August 25, 1860; *Alexandria Gazette*, September 12 and 28, 1860; *Staunton Spectator*, November 6, 1860.

22. *Alexandria Gazettte*, October 25, 1860; *Richmond Daily Whig*, July 28, 1860; *Lynchburg Virginian*, September 5, 1860.

23. *Alexandria Gazette*, November 1, 1860.

24. *Richmond Daily Whig*, August 16 and October 6, 1860; Mary Virginia Terhune [Marion Harland], *Marion Harland's Autobiography: The Story of a Long Life* (Harper and Brothers, 1910), p. 361; Elizabeth Lindsay Lomax, *Leaves from an Old Washington Diary, 1854–1863* (New York: E. P. Dutton, 1943), p. 122.

25. Lucy Wood to Waddy B. Butler, October 12, 1860, Letters and Diary of a Civil War Bride, Lomax Family Papers, VHS; Terhune [Harland], *Marion Harland's Autobiography*, pp. 360–61.

26. Eliza A. Willson to Willie Willson, October 29, 1860; Eliza A. Willson to Frank Willson, November 2, 1860, Willson Family Papers, YU.

27. *Lynchburg Virginian*, October 30, 1860; *Wellsburg Herald*, October 26, 1860.

28. Margaret Muse Pennybacker, "War Memorial," p. 2, LV; Martha Buxton Porter Brent, "Reminiscences," pp. 36–37, LV.

29. Shanks, *Secession Movement*, pp. 112–14.

30. *Daily Richmond Enquirer*, September 18 and 27, October 15 and 30, and November 3, 1860; *Winchester Virginian*, October 25, 1860.

31. Daniel W. Crofts, *Reluctant Confederates: Upper South Unionists in the Secession Crisis* (Chapel Hill: University of North Carolina Press, 1989), p. 86; *Wheeling Daily Intelligencer*, September 4, 5, and 6, 1860.

32. According to Shanks, Virginians voted the "regular party ticket" in 1860. Most traditionally Democratic counties went for Breckenridge, while most Whig counties went for Bell; Douglas was strong only in a handful of counties. Shanks, *Secession Movement*, pp. 117–31.

33. Ibid., pp. 132–55. Even within the category of "Unionist" there were great

differences of opinion. A majority of the Unionist delegates were conditional Unionists (they would support secession if the North waged war on the South); a minority were unconditional Unionists, who would remain faithful to the North in the event of secession. Crofts, *Reluctant Confederates*, pp. 104–6.

34. Otis K. Rice, *West Virginia: A History* (Lexington: University Press of Kentucky, 1985), pp. 111–23; Richard Orr Curry, *A House Divided: A Study of Statehood Politics and the Copperhead Movement in West Virginia* (Pittsburgh: University of Pittsburgh Press, 1964), pp. 27–30; S. T. Wiley, *History of Preston County (West Virginia)* (Kingwood, W.Va.: The Journal Printing House, 1882), pp. 125–27.

35. Judith Rives to William Rives, January 14, 1861, William Cabell Rives Papers, LC; Mary Louisa Dabney Carrington to Elizabeth Lewis (Dabney) Saunders, January 31, 1861, Saunders Family Papers, VHS.

36. Eliza A. Willson to Willie Willson, November 27, 1860, Willson Family Papers, YU; Eliza A. Willson to Willie Willson, December 29, 1860, Houston Papers, UVA.

37. Lucy Wood to Waddy B. Butler, January 21, 1861, Lucy (Wood) Butler Letters and Diary, Lomax Family Papers, VHS.

38. Betsy M. Fleet and John D. P. Fuller, eds., *Green Mount: A Virginia Plantation Family during the Civil War* (Charlottesville: University Press of Virginia, 1977), pp. 40, 42, 84; L. Minor Blackford, *Mine Eyes Have Seen the Glory: The Story of a Virginia Lady, Mary Berkeley Minor Blackford, 1802–1896, Who Taught Her Sons to Hate Slavery and to Love the Union* (Cambridge: Harvard University Press, 1954), pp. 148–49.

39. Shanks, *Secession Movement*, pp. 121–31.

40. A number of historians have argued that young men were, on the whole, somewhat more inclined to support secession than older ones. See, for example, J. Mills Thornton, *Politics and Power in a Slave Society: Alabama, 1800–1860* (Baton Rouge: Louisiana State University Press, 1977), p. 338; William Barney, *The Secessionist Impulse: Alabama and Mississippi in 1860* (Princeton, N.J.: Princeton University Press, 1974), pp. 295–96.

41. Louisa H. A. Minor Diary, January 27, 1861, UVA; Mary Evelyn Hill to Isabel (Belle) Howard Elliot, January 29, 1861, Isabel (Belle) Howard Elliot Papers, LV.

42. Elizabeth Randolph Preston Allan, *A March Past: Reminiscences of Elizabeth Randolph Preston Allan* (Richmond, Va.: Dietz Press, 1938), pp. 110–11.

43. Kate Virginia Cox Logan, *My Confederate Girlhood: The Memoirs of Kate Virginia Cox Logan*, ed. Lily Logan Morrill (Richmond, Va.: Garrett and Massie, 1932), pp. 1–2, 25.

44. *Daily Richmond Enquirer*, November 29, 1860.

45. Sallie A. (Brock) Putnam, *Richmond during the War: Four Years of Personal Observation by a Richmond Lady* (New York: G. W. Carlton, 1867), pp. 17, 22.

46. For a similar appraisal of women's part in the convention, see Charles Osborne's recent biography of Jubal Early, who was a convention delegate and

later a Confederate general. Charles Osborne, *Jubal: The Life and Times of Jubal A. Early, CSA* (Chapel Hill: University of North Carolina Press, 1992), pp. 34–35.

47. Shanks, *Secession Movement*, pp. 158–74.

48. George H. Reese, ed., *Proceedings of the Virginia State Convention of 1861 in Four Volumes* (Richmond: Virginia State Library, 1965), 1:3, 13, 26–27.

49. Judith Rives to William Rives Jr., April 7, 1861, William Cabell Rives Papers, LC; David Ryan, *A Yankee Spy*, p. 29; "Chronicles of the Life of Lucy Parke Chamberlayne" (unpublished typescript), p. 123, VHS; Diary of Mrs. William B. (Sally Lyons) Taliaferro, March 21 and 28, 1861, LV; Lucy Wood to Waddy B. Butler, February 11, 1861, Lomax Family Papers, VHS; Ellen Mordecai to Ellen Mordecai [her niece], March 23, 1861, Mordecai Family Papers, UNC; Osborne, *Jubal*, pp. 38–40.

50. Nina Silber, *The Romance of Reunion: Northerners and the South, 1865–1900* (Chapel Hill: University of North Carolina Press, 1993).

51. Reese, *Proceedings*, 1:138, 205, 234.

52. Ibid., 1:56, 90, 116, 199; Shanks, *Secession Movement*, pp. 172–73.

53. Shanks, *Secession Movement*, pp. 174–76.

54. Mary P. Coulling, *The Lee Girls* (Winston-Salem, N.C.: John F. Blair, 1987), p. 80; Samuella (Hart) Curd Diary, February 18 and 19, and March 10, 1861, VHS; Angelina Selden Edrington Diary, March 3, 1861, Edrington Family Papers, VHS; Judith Carter (Lewis) McGuire to Mary Anna (McGuire) Claiborne, March 3, 1861, Claiborne Family Papers, VHS.

55. Shanks, *Secession Movement*, pp. 182–83.

56. *Daily Dispatch* (Richmond), March 14, 1861; Reese, *Proceedings*, 2:186, 259.

57. Reese, *Proceedings*, 2:246, 757; *Richmond Whig*, March 25, 1861; *Alexandria Gazette*, March 27, 1861; *Daily Richmond Enquirer*, March 25, 1861.

58. Shanks, *Secession Movement*, p. 183; *Daily Richmond Enquirer*, March 15 and 26, 1861.

59. Louisa H. A. Minor Diary, March 23, 1861, UVA; *Daily Dispatch* (Richmond), March 11, 1861; *Staunton Vindicator*, April 5, 1861.

60. *Daily Dispatch* (Richmond), March 15, 1861; *Democratic Mirror* (Leesburg), April 3, 1861.

61. *Staunton Vindicator*, April 5, 1861; *Daily Dispatch* (Richmond), March 8 and 30, 1861.

62. Reese, *Proceedings*, 2:353.

63. Ellen Mordecai to Ellen Mordecai [her niece], March 23, 1861, Mordecai Family Papers, UNC.

64. Terhune and her husband moved to New York in 1859 but returned to Richmond briefly in the spring of 1861. Elizabeth Moss, *Domestic Novelists in the Old South: Defenders of Southern Culture* (Baton Rouge: Louisiana State University Press, 1992), p. 200; Terhune [Harland], *Marion Harland's Autobiography*, p. 306. Judith Rives to William Rives Jr., April 7, 1861, William Cabell Rives Papers, LC.

65. Shanks, *Secession Movement*, pp. 194–95.

66. Goode, *Recollections of a Lifetime*, p. 53; Shanks, *Secession Movement*, p. 199.

67. Cloe Tyler (Whittle) Greene Diary, April 15, 1861, WM; Cornelia McDonald, *A Diary with Reminiscences of the War and Refugee Life in the Shenandoah Valley, 1860–1865*, annotated by Hunter M. McDonald (Nashville, Tenn.: Cullom and Ghertner, 1934), p. 14; Sara Agnes (Rice) Pryor, *Reminiscences of Peace and War* (New York: Macmillan, 1904), p. 124; Allan, *A March Past*, p. 115.

68. Terhune [Harland], *Marion Harland's Autobiography*, pp. 372–73; Samuella (Hart) Curd Diary, April 13, 1861, VHS.

69. After April 17, Virginia forces quickly seized control of the Federal arsenal at Harpers Ferry and of Gosport navy yard, the premier naval base in the country. Robert E. Lee accepted command of the Virginia forces on April 23. James M. McPherson, *Battle Cry of Freedom: The Civil War Era* (New York: Oxford University Press, 1988), p. 280; Shanks, *Secession Movement*, pp. 203–5.

70. *Daily Dispatch* (Richmond), April 19, 1861.

71. *Richmond Daily Whig*, April 22 and May 6, 1861; Crofts, *Reluctant Confederates*, p. 316; *Daily Richmond Enquirer*, April 25, 1861.

72. On relief work see, for example, *Lynchburg Virginian*, May 16, 1861; *Staunton Spectator*, May 7, 1861. For quote, see *Daily Dispatch* (Richmond), April 23, 1861.

73. *Alexandria Gazette*, May 4, 1861; Henry W. R. Jackson, *The Southern Women of the Second American Revolution* (Atlanta: Intelligencer Steam-Power Press, 1863) p. 24; Lucy (Wood) Butler Letters and Diary, Lomax Family Papers, May 24, 1861, VHS.

74. Faust, *Mothers of Invention*.

75. After the Virginia convention passed the secession ordinance on April 17, the leader of the northwestern Unionists, John Carlile, left Richmond under a cloud of threats and returned to his home in Clarksburg. When safely back in northwest Virginia, Carlile and other Unionist leaders convened a series of Unionist mass meetings, leading up to the First Wheeling Convention (May 13–15, 1861). That convention provided for the election of delegates to a second convention in June; the June Wheeling Convention passed an ordinance for the reorganization of the state government and elected Francis H. Pierpont as the governor of the Reorganized Government of Virginia. The restored government established its headquarters in Alexandria and began to lobby for support and recognition from the federal government. That campaign culminated in December 1862 in Lincoln's signing of the West Virginia statehood bill. Rice, *West Virginia*, pp. 111–23, 150–60; Anna Pierpont Siviter, *Recollections of War and Peace, 1861–1868*, ed. Charles Henry Ambler (New York: G. P. Putnam's Sons, 1938), p. xxviii; Byron Farwell, *Stonewall: A Biography of General Thomas J. Jackson* (New York: W. W. Norton, 1992), p. 424.

76. Terhune [Harland], *Marion Harland's Autobiography*, pp. 372–73.

77. Van Lew, "Occasional Journal," [1861], Elizabeth Van Lew Papers, LV; David Ryan, *A Yankee Spy*.

78. Lee's decision-making process is detailed in his letters to his cousin and

confidante Markie Williams and to his sister Ann Marshall. While Williams herself reluctantly accepted secession, Marshall, who lived in Baltimore with her Unionist husband, never abandoned her own Unionist principles. In his April 20, 1861, letter to Ann, Robert E. Lee told her apologetically of his resignation from the U.S. army. "I know you will blame me; but you must think as kindly of me as you can, and believe that I have endeavored to do what I thought right." Avery Craven, ed. *"To Markie": The Letters of Robert E. Lee to Martha Custis Williams* (Cambridge: Harvard University Press, 1933), pp. 56–60; Robert W. Winston, *Robert E. Lee: A Biography* (New York: William Morrow, 1934), pp. 91–92.

79. Judith W. McGuire, *Diary of a Southern Refugee during the War* (New York: E. J. Hale and Son, 1867), pp. 12, 16.

80. Sidney Sophia Gore Journal, May 23, 1861, as quoted in James Howard Gore, *My Mother's Story: Despise Not the Day of Small Things* (Philadelphia: Judson Press, 1923), pp. 41, 72–75.

81. Fleet and Fuller, *Green Mount*, pp. 53–56, 84; L. Minor Blackford, *Mine Eyes*, p. 171.

82. Emma Mordecai to Nell (Ellen) Mordecai, April 21, 1861, and Emma Mordecai to Nell Mordecai, April 25, 1861, Mordecai Family Papers, UNC. Ellen (who is quoted above) and Caroline were the daughters of Jacob Mordecai and his first wife, Judith Myers; Emma was the daughter of Jacob's second wife, Rebecca Myers. On the Mordecai family, see the reminiscences of Jacob's granddaughter: Ellen Mordecai, *Gleanings from Long Ago* (Raleigh, N.C.: The Raleigh Historic Properties Commission and the Mordecai Square Historical Society, 1974), pp. 43–48, 129–30.

83. Diary of Mrs. William B. (Sally Lyons) Taliaferro, April 17 and May 10, 1861, LV; McDonald, *A Diary with Reminiscences of the War*, p. 13; Edmonds, *Journal of Amanda Edmonds*, pp. 47–49.

EPILOGUE

1. George C. Rable, *Civil Wars: Women and the Crisis of Southern Nationalism* (Urbana: University of Illinois Press, 1989), pp. 151–53; Drew Gilpin Faust, *Mothers of Invention: Women of the Slaveholding South in the American Civil War* (Chapel Hill: University of North Carolina Press, 1996), pp. 20, 231–32.

2. Cloe Tyler (Whittle) Greene Diary, April 15, 1861, WM.

3. Lucy Breckenridge, *Lucy Breckenridge of Grove Hill: The Journal of a Virginia Girl, 1862–1864*, ed. Mary D. Robertson (Kent, Ohio: Kent State University Press, 1979), p. 132; Caroline Kean (Hill) Davis Diary, February 14, 1865, VHS.

4. Rable, *Civil Wars*, pp. 151–53; Faust, *Mothers of Invention*, p. 232.

5. Rable, *Civil Wars*; Faust, *Mothers of Invention*, esp. pp. 244–47.

6. Anne Firor Scott, *The Southern Lady: From Pedestal to Politics, 1830–1930* (Chicago: University of Chicago Press, 1970), pp. 82–102; Rable, *Civil Wars*, pp. 265–88; Suzanne Lebsock, *The Free Women of Petersburg: Status and Culture in a Southern Town, 1784–1860* (New York: W. W. Norton, 1984), pp. 247–49, and her *"A Share of Honour": Virginia Women, 1600–1945* (Richmond: Virginia State Library, 1987), pp. 88, 93, 96, 101; Faust, *Mothers of Invention*, pp. 248–54.

7. On postwar benevolence in Virginia, see, for example, Virginia D. Cox, *Memorial Foundation for Children, Formerly Memorial Home for Girls, Formerly Female Humane Association, 1805–1865* (Richmond, Va.: Fifth Avenue and Front Street, 1965); W. Asbury Christian, *Richmond: Her Past and Present* (Richmond, Va.: L. H. Jenkins, 1912), p. 355; and Steven Elliot Tripp, *Yankee Town, Southern City: Race and Class Relations in Civil War Lynchburg* (New York: New York University Press, 1997), pp. 213, 216. On evangelical societies, Lebsock, *"A Share of Honour,"* p. 98; Scott, *The Southern Lady*, pp. 136–41; Jean Friedman, *The Enclosed Garden: Women and Community in the Evangelical South, 1830–1900* (Chapel Hill: University of North Carolina Press, 1985), pp. 114–18; and Joan Jacobs Brumberg, "Zenanas and Girlless Villages: The Ethnology of American Evangelical Women, 1870–1910," *Journal of American History* 69 (September 1982): 350–53. On temperance, see C. C. Pearson and J. Edwin Hendricks, *Liquor and Anti-Liquor in Virginia, 1619–1919* (Durham, N.C.: Duke University Press, 1967), pp. 159, 199; *Daily Dispatch* (Richmond), October 24, 1873; *Staunton Spectator*, October 14, 1873; Marie Tyler-McGraw, *At the Falls: Richmond, Virginia, and Its People* (Chapel Hill: University of North Carolina Press, 1994), p. 231.

8. Joel Chandler Harris, "The Women of the South," *Southern Historical Society Papers* 18 (January–December 1890): 277–81. On connections between antebellum and postwar benevolence elsewhere in the South, see, for example, LeeAnn Whites, *The Civil War as a Crisis in Gender: Augusta, Georgia, 1860–1890* (Athens: University of Georgia Press, 1995), and Marsha Wedell, *Elite Women and the Reform Impulse in Memphis, 1875–1915* (Knoxville: University of Tennessee Press, 1991).

9. On Confederate memorial societies and the UDC, see Whites, *The Civil War as a Crisis in Gender*, pp. 160–198; Gaines M. Foster, *Ghosts of the Confederacy: Defeat, the Lost Cause, and the Emergence of the New South, 1865 to 1913* (New York: Oxford University Press, 1987); and Angie Parrott, "'Love Makes Memory Eternal': The United Daughters of the Confederacy in Richmond, Virginia, 1897–1920," in Edward L. Ayers and John C. Willis, eds., *The Edge of the South: Life in Nineteenth-Century Virginia* (Charlottesville: University Press of Virginia, 1991), pp. 219–38.

10. On wartime literature, see Faust, *Mothers of Invention*, pp. 168–78. For examples of novels of sectional reconciliation, see the books discussed in Jane Turner Censer, "Reimagining the North-South Reunion: Southern Women Novelists and the Intersectional Romance, 1876–1900" (unpublished manuscript lent to the author). On the theme of sectional reconciliation in Northern literature, see Nina Silber, *The Romance of Reunion: Northerners and the South, 1865–1900* (Chapel Hill: University of North Carolina Press, 1993).

11. Elsa Barkley Brown, "Uncle Ned's Children: Negotiating Community and Freedom in Postemancipation Richmond, Virginia" (Ph.D. diss., Kent State University, 1994), pp. 310–13, 322, 345–47, 358–61, 388–92, 410–11. Glenda Gilmore's study of North Carolina offers additional evidence of black women's Republican partisanship and supports Brown's contention that blacks saw the ballot as collectively owned. Glenda Gilmore, *Gender and Jim Crow: Women and the Politics of White Supremacy in North Carolina, 1896–1920* (Chapel Hill:

University of North Carolina Press, 1996), pp. 18, 102–7. On black women's participation in Republican party politics, see also Myrta Lockett Avary, *Dixie after the War: An Exposition of Social Conditions Existing in the South, During the Twelve Years Succeeding the Fall of Richmond* (New York: Doubleday, Page and Company, 1906), pp. 231–32; Peter Rachleff, *Black Labor in the South: Richmond, Virginia, 1865–1890* (Philadelphia: Temple University Press, 1984), pp. 31–32; and Robert J. Dinkin, *Before Equal Suffrage: Women in Partisan Politics from Colonial Times to 1920* (Westport, Conn.: Greenwood Press, 1995), pp. 79–80.

12. David Ryan, ed., *A Yankee Spy in Richmond: The Civil War Diary of "Crazy Bet" Van Lew* (Mechanicsburg, Pa.: Stackpole Books, 1996), pp. 19–21, 113–34; *Richmond Enquirer and Examiner*, March 23, 1869; Elizabeth Van Lew, "To Northern Democrats: An Appeal Which Should Not Go Unheard" (newspaper clipping), October 27, 1876, Van Lew Papers, LV.

13. Elizabeth Van Lew to Mr. Rogers, April 10, 1877, Elizabeth Van Lew, handwritten response to newspaper article "Men and Monopolists," c. 1885, and Elizabeth Van Lew to John K. Childress, November 28, 1892, Elizabeth Van Lew Papers, LV.

14. Susan B. Anthony et al., *History of Woman Suffrage: Volume 3, 1876–1885* (New York: Arno Press, 1969), pp. 823–24; Anthony et al., *History of Woman Suffrage: Volume 4, 1883–1900* (New York: Arno Press, 1969), pp. 964–65; Sandra Gioia Treadway, "A Most Brilliant Woman: Anna Whitehead Bodeker and the First Woman Suffrage Association in Virginia," *Virginia Cavalcade* 43 (Spring 1994): 166–77; Orra Langhorne, *Southern Sketches from Virginia, 1881–1901*, ed. Charles Wynne (Charlottesville: University Press of Virginia, 1964), pp. xvi–xviii. For an overview of the suffrage movement in the South, see Marjorie Spruill Wheeler, *New Women of the New South: The Leaders of the Woman Suffrage Movement in the Southern States* (New York: Oxford University Press, 1993).

15. Treadway, "A Most Brilliant Woman," p. 177; *Richmond Whig*, October 22, 1872, and October 17, 1873; *Daily Richmond Enquirer*, October 3, 1872.

16. *Richmond Whig*, November 14, 1873; *Daily Dispatch* (Richmond), October 7, 1876; *Staunton Spectator*, October 24, 1876. On Democratic women's support for white supremacy in North Carolina, see Gilmore, *Gender and Jim Crow*, pp. 96–99. On the differences between the Republicans' and Democrats' gender ideologies in the 1880s and 1890s, see Dinkin, *Before Equal Suffrage*, pp. 93–98, and Rebecca Edwards, "Gender and American Political Parties, 1880–1900" (Ph.D. diss., University of Virginia, 1995). For examples of Democratic coverage of women's partisanship in the 1880s and 1890s, see *Richmond Dispatch*, October 8, 12, and 14, 1880, October 5, 7, and 8, 1884, October 9 and 25, 1892, and October 18, 1896.

17. Scott argues persuasively that Southern women's postwar organizing was on a "different order of magnitude" than their prewar efforts. Scott, *The Southern Lady*, pp. 137–63.

18. *Daily Dispatch* (Richmond), May 19, 1869; Robert Lewis Dabney, "Women's Rights Women," *The Southern Magazine* 8 (February 1871): 330–31; *Richmond Whig*, March 1, 1870. Elna C. Green's book explores the paradoxes of

Southern antisuffragism, noting that female "antis" were as a group dedicated supporters of the Democratic party, politically active on behalf of conservative causes such as the United Daughters of the Confederacy, and members of families that had been prominent in antebellum politics. Elna C. Green, *Southern Strategies: Southern Women and the Woman Suffrage Question* (Chapel Hill: University of North Carolina Press, 1997).

19. *Richmond Whig*, May 23, 1871.

Index

Abolitionism/abolitionists, 1, 3, 8,
9, 27, 42–43, 44, 55–59, 66, 68, 70,
75, 95–96, 158, 189–90 (nn. 52, 53),
196 (n. 41); portrayals of in
Southern literature, 103, 110, 111,
112, 113
Abram (slave), 46, 64–65
Accomac County, 89
Adams, John Quincy, 46, 84, 201
(n. 27)
Africa, 42, 43, 44, 45, 58, 60, 63, 113.
See also Liberia
African colonization movement,
27, 32, 196 (n. 41); support for in
proslavery literature, 109–10, 113,
116, 118. *See also* American Colo-
nization Society; Virginia Colo-
nization Society
African Repository, 6, 44, 49, 60, 61,
62
Agricultural reform movement, 6,
142
Alabama, 143, 148, 172
Albemarle County, 5, 33, 61, 62, 73,
77, 91, 117, 119, 157, 171, 195 (n. 31)
Alexandria, Va., 20–21, 73, 76, 78, 89,
94–95, 141, 143, 145, 167, 183 (n. 3),
216 (n. 75)
Alexandria Gazette, 94, 101, 141, 143,
145, 165
Allan, Elizabeth Randolph Preston,
152, 162
Alleghany County, 148
Always Ready Club of Fairfax, 94
Amelia County, 114
American Anti-Slavery Society, 142
American Beacon (Norfolk), 120
American Bible Society, 23, 24, 82,
186–87 (n. 34)
American Colonization Society, 3, 6,

82; founding principles of, 43;
black support for, 43, 65; female
auxiliaries to, 44, 46, 53, 60–62;
black opposition to, 56–57, 62, 65;
abolitionist criticism of, 56–58;
decline in popularity of, 62–66.
See also Gender roles: and colo-
nization movement
American Education Society, 23, 186
(n. 34)
American Home Missionary Soci-
ety, 23, 187 (n. 34)
American ("Know-Nothing") Party,
3, 38, 97–99, 144
American Sunday School Union, 23,
25, 28, 187 (n. 34)
American System, 75, 84. *See also*
Clay, Henry
American Temperance Society, 30
American Temperance Union, 33, 37
American Tract Society, 23, 24, 25,
82
Anderson (slave), 45, 64
Andrews, Charles, 67
Anthony, Susan B., 37
Anti-mission movement, 24–27
Antisuffragism, 9, 93, 176–77, 219–20
(n. 18)
Arnold, Laura Ann Jackson, 165
Ashmun, Jehudi, 67
Augusta County, 31, 61, 174; anti-
slavery petition from, 50–51, 194
(n. 23), 195 (n. 28)

Back Creek Valley, Va., 36
Bain, Miss, 96–97
Baldwin, John, 158, 159
Baltimore, Md., 34, 217 (n. 78)
Baptist Female Missionary Society
(Richmond), 24

Baptists, 24, 25, 26, 30, 32–33, 36, 54, 62

Barbour, James, 75, 79, 82, 83, 88

Barbour, Lucy, 5, 88, 89, 93, 124, 143, 174

Barboursville, Va., 88

Basch, Norma, 201 (n. 27)

Baxley, Jane, 91

Beckly, Alfred, 39

Bedford County, 159

Beecham, Mrs., 28

Beecher, Catharine, 8, 196 (n. 41)

Bell, John, 144

Benevolence: definition of, 2–3; historiography on, 182–83 (n. 2). *See also* Evangelical benevolence; Female charities

"Benevolent femininity": concept of, 13, 21–22, 83, 184 (n. 9)

Bennett, Martha Haines (Butt). *See* Butt, Martha Haines

Berlin, Ira, 184 (n. 14)

Betsy (slave), 55

Blackford, Mary Berkeley Minor, 5, 29; Fredericksburg colonization auxiliary, 45–47, 53, 60, 65; anti-slavery petition by, 49–51; "Notes Illustrative of the Wrongs of Slavery," 53–56, 195 (n. 33); emigration of Abram, 64–65; opinion of *Uncle Tom's Cabin*, 110; and secession crisis, 151–52, 154, 167

Blackford, William, 46, 56, 65

Blacks: legal status of, 2, 7, 15, 27–29, 54, 173, 184 (n. 14); exclusion from white voluntary associations, 7, 15–16, 35, 185 (n. 17); mutual aid societies of, 7, 16, 173; resistance to slavery, 7, 27–28, 47–48, 54–55; education of, 27–30, 188–89 (n. 45); and temperance movement, 32, 190 (n. 58); and colonization movement, 43, 56–57, 62–65; political activism during Reconstruction, 173, 218 (n. 11); petitioning by, 184 (n. 14). *See also*

Racism; Slavery; Slaves; Slave Women

Blanchford, Mr., 28

Bledsoe, Alfred Taylor, 69

"Bleeding Kansas," 138, 148

Bodeker, Anna Whitehead, 174

Boston, Mass., 89, 186–87 (n. 34)

Botetourt County, 26

Botts, John Minor, 98

Bowser, Mary Elizabeth, 166

Boycott movement (1859–60), 6, 142–44

Breckenridge, John, 144, 146–49

Breckenridge, Lucy, 169

Brend, Eliza, 89

Brent, Martha Buxton Porter, 99, 147

Brown, Antoinette, 120

Brown, Elsa Barkley, 7, 173

Brown, James Leftwich, 10

Brown, Mary, 63

Brown, Thomas, 92

Bruce, George, 158

Brunswick County, 119

Buchanan, James, 99, 204 (n. 59)

Buckingham County, 85

Buckingham Female Collegiate Institute, 10

Burke, William and Rosabella, 63

Butler, Waddy, 146, 151

Butt, Martha Haines: *Antifanaticism: A Tale of the South*, 111–12, 114, 116, 120, 121, 142, 172; and postwar suffrage movement, 174

Cabell, Julia Mayo, 35, 89, 125, 127, 129, 130; *An Odd Volume of Facts and Fictions*, 17, 21

Cabell County, 36

California, 95, 134

Campbell, Alexander, 25, 33

Campbell County, 31, 145

Capps, Frances Ann, 77

Carlile, John, 216 (n. 75)

Carrington, Eliza, 15, 16, 185 (n. 16)

98–99, 219 (n. 16); election of
1856, 98–100; and Mount Vernon
Association, 125, 129, 130–32; elec-
tion of 1860, 144, 147–49; during
Reconstruction, 173–76; and anti-
suffrage movement, 219–20 (n. 18)
Democratic-Republican Party, 201
(n. 27)
Denominational schisms, 30, 62
Dew, Thomas R., 69, 104, 172; "Dis-
sertation on the Characteristic
Differences Between the Sexes,"
14; *Review of the Debate in the
Virginia Legislature of 1831 and
1832*, 58
Dinkin, Robert J., 71
Doggett, David, 21, 25
Domestic novel: genre of, 104–5,
108–19 passim
Domesticity: ideology of. *See* "Sepa-
rate spheres": doctrine of
Doswell, Susan, 91
Douglas, Stephen, 144, 147
Douglass, Margaret, 29–30
Duchess of Sutherland, 113, 114

Early, Mary, 10
Early Republic, era of: gender roles,
199 (n. 6), 201 (n. 27)
Eastman, Mary H.: *Aunt Phillis's
Cabin: Or, Southern Life As It Is*,
108–11, 114, 116, 120, 142, 172, 207
(n. 19)
Edmonds, Amanda Virginia, 140,
168
Edmunds, John, 128
Edrington, Angelina Selden, 157
Education: of white females, 6,
11–12, 18–20, 186 (n. 29); of blacks,
27–30, 59–61, 188–89 (n. 45)
Elam, Mrs. E. P., 22, 38–39
"Elizabeth" (temperance correspon-
dent), 31
Ellis, Catherine, 61
England, 113
Episcopalians, 24, 26, 45

Essex County, 6, 44, 77, 87, 105, 160
Evangelical benevolence: Bible,
tract, and Sunday school organizations, 8, 10–11, 23–31, 33, 34, 43,
53, 58; opposition to, in South,
26–27
Evangelical religion, 82–83
"Evangelical womanhood": concept
of, 44, 47
Evans, Augusta, 172, 208 (n. 33)
Everett, Edward, 125, 129–30, 131,
144, 146, 211 (n. 72)

Fairfax County, 87, 94
Family Christian Album, 22, 38
Fauquier County, 94, 140, 168
Faust, Drew Gilpin, 137, 171, 212
(n. 2)
Federalist Party, 201 (n. 27)
Federal Relations Committee, 157
Female Bible Society of Richmond
and Manchester, 24
Female Cent Society of Eastern
Shore Parish, Princess Anne
County, 24
Female charities: founding of, 11;
incorporation of by legislature,
12; coverage of in press, 12–13;
exclusion of blacks by, 15–16;
fundraising, 16–21. *See also* Gen-
der roles: and female charities
Female Charity School (Fredericks-
burg), 11, 12, 18
Female Colonization Society of Vir-
ginia, 61–62, 89
Female Humane Association (Rich-
mond), 12, 13, 15, 16, 22, 171
Female Liberian Society of Essex
County, 44
Female Orphan Asylum of Norfolk,
17, 22, 24, 185 (n. 17)
Feminism. *See* Woman's rights
movement/Feminism
Fillmore, Millard, 97
"Fire-eaters." *See* Secessionists;
Southern nationalism

First African Baptist Church of
Richmond, 7, 16
First Presbyterian Church of Richmond, 89
Fitzhugh, George, 4, 37, 69, 104;
Sociology for the South, 1
Fleet, Maria Louisa Wacker, 167
Floyd, John, 48, 129
Fluvanna County, 14, 27, 31, 61; antislavery petition from, 48–49
Formisano, Ronald P., 82
Fort Sumter, S.C., 138, 161, 162
Fox-Genovese, Elizabeth, 42, 122,
182–83 (n. 2)
Frazier, Julia, 28
Frederick County, 27, 45
Fredericksburg: colonization movement in, 5, 45–46, 49, 53–56, 60,
62–63; female charities in, 11,
12, 18–20, 184 (n. 5); evangelical
benevolence in, 28–29; temperance movement in, 34; female
partisanship in, 74–75. *See also*
Blackford, Mary Berkeley Minor;
Kenney, Lucy
Fredericksburg and Falmouth
Female Auxiliary to the American
Colonization Society, 46, 53, 60, 65
Fredericksburg Female Orphan Asylum, 18–20
Fredericksburg Total Abstinence
Society, 34
Free blacks, 2, 15–16, 28, 29, 43, 48,
57, 62–65
Freehling, Alison Goodyear, 52
Freehling, William W., 75
Freeman, Douglas Southall, 138
Frelinghuysen, Theodore, 82
Frémont, Jessie Benton, 100
Frémont, John, 100
French, Sarah, 91

Gage, Matilda Joslyn, 174
Garland, James, 59
Garnett, James M.: *Lectures on
Female Education*, 13

Garnett, Mary, 13
Garnett, Muscoe, 98, 149
Garrison, William Lloyd, 48, 59;
Thoughts on African Colonization,
56
Gender roles: and female charities,
13–14, 21–22; and evangelical
benevolence, 25; and temperance
movement, 31–32; and colonization movement, 44, 47–51, 58–59,
66–70; image of women as political partisans, 69, 80, 99–100,
143–44, 154, 159–60, 164; image of
women as political mediators,
85–86, 92, 105, 108, 110–11, 123–24,
126, 127, 129, 132, 134–36, 145, 146,
147, 156–59, 164–65
General Assembly of Virginia,
36–37, 62, 68, 74, 149; and female
charities, 7, 11–12, 18–20; and legal
status of blacks, 7, 15, 27–28, 184
(n. 14); and debates over slavery,
43, 48, 52; and Mount Vernon
Association, 129, 130–32. *See also*
Petitioning: by white women
Gentleman's Benevolent Society
(Richmond), 22
Georgia, 89, 105, 133, 153, 156
Gilman, Caroline, 105, 207 (n. 17),
208 (n. 33), 209 (n. 40)
Gilmer, John H., 125–26
Gilmore, Glenda, 218 (n. 11), 219
(n. 16)
Ginzberg, Lori D., 184 (n. 9)
Gloucester County, 164
Godey's Lady's Book, 8, 35, 114, 119,
130, 204 (n. 60)
Goggin, W. L., 156
Goochland County, 14, 61, 85
Goode, John, 137, 162
Gore, Sidney Sophia, 36, 167
Gradual emancipation: doctrine of,
45, 47, 49, 53, 56–57, 63–64, 69
Grand United Order of Tents (Norfolk), 7
Grant, Ulysses S., 173, 174

Ladies Benevolent Society of Monrovia, 60
Ladies' Lee Monument Association (Va.), 172
Ladies Society for Promoting Female Education in the Colony of Liberia (Richmond), 60
Ladies' Society of Fredericksburg and Falmouth, for the Promotion of Female Education in Africa, 60
Langfitt, O., 129, 130
Langhorne, Orra, 174
Laurel Grove Temperance Society, 31
Lawrenceville, Va., 120
Lebsock, Suzanne, 16, 22, 101, 170, 182–83 (n. 2), 192 (n. 4)
Lee, Ludwell, 63
Lee, Mary Custis, 63, 157
Lee, Robert E., 63, 138, 157, 166, 216–17 (n. 78)
Leesburg, Va., 77, 160
Legal system. See Blacks: legal status of; General Assembly of Virginia
Leigh, Benjamin Watkins, 52, 195 (n. 28)
Letcher, John, 127
Lexington, Va., 24, 31, 35, 90, 117, 152–53
Lexington Gazette, 90
Lexington Union Temperance Society, 31
Lewis, Edward and Helen, 57
Liberator (Boston), 48, 56, 189–90 (n. 53)
Liberia, 3, 27, 43, 45, 46, 56–65 passim
Life and Death of Sam, in Virginia (Anonymous), 99–100
Lincoln, Abraham, 138, 146, 147, 148, 149, 150, 216 (n. 75)
Lippincott, Grambo and Company, 110
Literacy, 6–7
Literary Fund, 18–20
Logan, Kate Virginia Cox, 153
Lomax, Catherine, 19, 21, 46

Lomax, Elizabeth Lindsay, 146
Lomax, John Tayloe, 19
Louisa County, 53, 163
Louisa County Temperance Society, 31
Loveland, Anne, 27
Lovingston, Va., 24
Lowell Mill girls, 158
Lower South, 8, 42, 149, 151, 182 (n. 14). See also names of individual Southern states
Loyall, Margaret E., 81
Lynchburg, Va., 10, 17, 58, 65, 85, 89, 90, 145, 171, 174
Lynchburg Dorcas Society, 10, 17, 171
Lynchburg Republican, 90
Lynchburg Virginian, 85, 90, 145
Lyons, James, 79

McCardell, John, 204 (n. 61)
McClelland, Mary Greenway, 172
McCord, Louisa, 122–23
McCue, John, 50, 52
McDonald, Cornelia, 162, 168
McDowell, James, 73, 76
McDowell, Susan, 73, 76
McFarland, William, 125
McGuire, Judith Carter (Lewis), 157
McGuire, Judith W., 167
McIntosh, Maria, 105, 207 (nn. 17, 23), 208 (n. 33), 209 (n. 40)
McLain, William, 63, 64, 65
MacLeod, Helen, 73
McPherson, James M., 163
Madison, Dolley, 46
Madison, James, 43, 46
Madison County, 143
Magruder, Julia, 172
Manassas/Bull Run, battle of, 165, 168
Manchester, Va., 24, 25, 60, 61
Marshall, Ann, 216–17 (n. 78)
Marshall, John, 11, 43
Martinsville, Va., 148
Maryland, 8, 26, 60, 63
Mason, James M., 127, 139, 140

Reconstruction: and gender roles, 156, 171–77
Relief associations (Civil War), 164–65
Religious Herald (Richmond), 25
Remini, Robert V., 92
"Republican motherhood": concept of, 11, 80
Republican Party, 3, 100, 102, 133, 139, 140, 144, 147, 148; during Reconstruction, 173–75; in Gilded Age, 205 (n. 80)
Retreat for the Sick (Richmond), 171
Revolutionary era, 11, 50, 66, 80, 110, 126–28, 134, 164
Rice, Ann, 45, 64, 69
Rice, John Holt, 13, 25, 27, 45, 172
Richmond, Va.: female charities in, 12, 13, 15, 16–18, 22, 183 (n. 3); evangelical benevolence in, 24–25; temperance movement in, 32, 34, 191 (n. 67); colonization movement in, 43, 60; female partisanship, 77–79, 89, 93, 145–46, 173–75; and Mount Vernon Association, 124–35 passim; secession crisis in, 142–43, 154–55, 158–63, 166, 168; Reconstruction in, 171–77; postwar suffrage movement in, 174
Richmond African Missionary Society, 43
Richmond and Manchester Sunday School Union, 25
Richmond Daily Whig, 145, 146, 164
Richmond Enquirer (semiweekly), 39, 52, 81, 125, 129, 139, 141, 147, 148, 175. See also *Daily Richmond Enquirer*
Richmond Enquirer and Examiner, 173
Richmond Tract Society, 24
Richmond Whig (semiweekly), 79, 85, 86, 88, 89, 92, 96, 98, 130, 142, 143, 158, 175, 176–77
Riddick, Missouri, 87
Riddle, Eliza, 91

Rising Daughters of Liberty, 173
Ritchie, Anna Cora, 117, 128–29, 131, 132, 133, 211 (n. 72)
Ritchie, William F., 125, 129, 131, 132
Rives, Judith Page Walker, 5, 6, 73, 77, 91–92, 117–18, 127, 135, 150, 153, 155, 161; *Home and the World*, 118–19
Rives, Mary Eliza, 52
Rives, William Cabell, 6, 73, 76, 118, 150
Roanoke, Va., 95
Roberts, Jane Gay, 77
Roberts, Mary, 164
Robinson, Clara, 184 (n. 14)
Robinson, Margaret Harvie, 24
Rockbridge County, 62, 117, 139
Rockingham County, 44, 61
Rough and Ready Club of Henrico, 95
Royall, Anne Newport, 74, 200 (n. 15), 201 (n. 23); *Black Book*, 26; *Mrs. Royall's Southern Tour*, 26
Ruffin, Edmund, 32, 68–69, 128, 131, 149
Ruffner, Mrs., 98
Ruffner, William Henry, 62
Runnells, Eliza B., 75
Rural Cass and Butler Association of Alexandria, 94–95
Rutherfoord, Margaret, 32
Ryan, Mary P., 71

Salem Temperance Society, 33
Sands, Alexander H., 68
Saunders, Robert, 98
Scott, Anne Firor, 5, 170, 182–83 (n. 2), 219 (n. 17); "covert abolitionist" thesis, 42, 66–70
Scott, Winfield, 94, 101, 204 (n. 59)
Secession crisis, 4; and secession of lower South, 138, 149; and election of 1860, 144–49; and Virginia convention of 1861, 154–63
Secessionists, 149, 156–57, 164, 214 (n. 40); women as, 152–53, 155,

GENDER & AMERICAN CULTURE

We Mean to Be Counted: White Women and Politics in Antebellum Virginia,
  by Elizabeth R. Varon (1998)

Women against the Good War: Conscientious Objection and Gender on the
  American Home Front, 1941–1947,
  by Rachel Waltner Goossen (1997)

Toward an Intellectual History of Women: Essays by Linda K. Kerber (1997)

Gender and Jim Crow: Women and the Politics of White Supremacy in
  North Carolina, 1896–1920,
  by Glenda Elizabeth Gilmore (1996)

Delinquent Daughters: Protecting and Policing Adolescent Female Sexuality
  in the United States, 1885–1920,
  by Mary E. Odem (1995)

U.S. History as Women's History: New Feminist Essays,
  edited by Linda K. Kerber, Alice Kessler-Harris, and Kathryn Kish Sklar (1995)

Common Sense and a Little Fire: Women and Working-Class Politics
  in the United States, 1900–1965,
  by Annelise Orleck (1995)

How Am I to Be Heard?: Letters of Lillian Smith,
  edited by Margaret Rose Gladney (1993)

Entitled to Power: Farm Women and Technology, 1913–1963,
  by Katherine Jellison (1993)

Revising Life: Sylvia Plath's Ariel Poems,
  by Susan R. Van Dyne (1993)

Made From This Earth: American Women and Nature,
  by Vera Norwood (1993)

Unruly Women: The Politics of Social and Sexual Control in the Old South,
  by Victoria E. Bynum (1992)

The Work of Self-Representation: Lyric Poetry in Colonial New England,
  by Ivy Schweitzer (1991)

Labor and Desire: Women's Revolutionary Fiction in Depression America,
  by Paula Rabinowitz (1991)

Community of Suffering and Struggle: Women, Men, and the
  Labor Movement in Minneapolis, 1915–1945,
  by Elizabeth Faue (1991)

All That Hollywood Allows: Re-reading Gender in 1950s Melodrama,
  by Jackie Byars (1991)

Doing Literary Business: American Women Writers in the Nineteenth Century,
  by Susan Coultrap-McQuin (1990)

Ladies, Women, and Wenches: Choice and Constraint in Antebellum
  Charleston and Boston,
  by Jane H. Pease and William H. Pease (1990)

The Secret Eye: The Journal of Ella Gertrude Clanton Thomas, 1848–1889,
  *edited by Virginia Ingraham Burr, with an introduction by Nell Irvin Painter
  (1990)*

Second Stories: The Politics of Language, Form, and Gender in
  Early American Fictions,
  by Cynthia S. Jordan (1989)

Within the Plantation Household: Black and White Women of the Old South,
  by Elizabeth Fox-Genovese (1988)

The Limits of Sisterhood: The Beecher Sisters on Women's Rights and
  Woman's Sphere,
  by Jeanne Boydston, Mary Kelley, and Anne Margolis (1988)